FROM CLASS STRUGGLE TO THE POLITICS OF PLEASURE

This book arises from reading and teaching gramscian work in cultural studies, education, media studies, leisure and politics over the last twenty years. It argues that gramscian work is undoubtedly powerful and persuasive. Indeed by the 1990s one can almost say that it has become the governing orthodoxy. This book tries to read the work critically and in detail, tracing arguments across time and across different specialisms, assessing them, and trying to examine how they deal with critics and with new challenging topics. The author maintains that cultural studies contains many absences, silences and closures, and that it deploys a number of narrative techniques to remain credible.

Wide ranging and critical, the book provides an ideal critical assessment of one of the most fashionable and powerful intellectual traditions in contemporary social science. The book will appeal especially to students in cultural studies, media studies, leisure studies, education and the sociology of culture. They will find a way of critically reading gramscian work which should enable them to decide where its strengths and weaknesses lie for themselves, and make them less dependent on the gramscians' own accounts and agendas.

David Harris is Senior Lecturer in Sociology at the College of St Mark and St John, Plymouth.

FROM CLASS STRUGGLE TO THE POLITICS OF PLEASURE

The effects of gramscianism on cultural studies

David Harris

London and New York

First published in 1992
by Routledge
11 New Fetter Lane, London EC4P 4EE

Simultaneously published in the USA and Canada
by Routledge
a division of Routledge, Chapman and Hall, Inc.
29 West 35th Street, New York, NY 10001

Typeset in 10/12pt Baskerville by LaserScript, Mitcham, Surrey
Printed and bound in Great Britain by
Mackays of Chatham plc, Chatham, Kent

British Library Cataloguing in Publication Data
A catalogue record for this book is available from the British Library.

Library of Congress Cataloging in Publication Data
Harris, David, 1947–
From class struggle to the politics of pleasure: the effects of gramscianism on
cultural studies/David Harris.
p. cm.
Includes bibliographical references and index.
1. Culture. 2. Gramsci, Antonio, 1891–1937. 3. Popular culture–Political
aspects. 4. Leisure–Political aspects. I. Title.
HM7101.H288 1992
306–dc20   92-4878
CIP
ISBN 0–415–06223–3
0–415–06224–1 (pbk)

For Andy

CONTENTS

AUTHOR'S NOTE

In order to make this book more accessible to readers who might be unfamiliar with the details of the context in which the work reviewed here is located, including readers in the USA, it might be helpful to offer some background information about some of the major writers and their institutional bases. It also gives me a chance to mention some recent material which has appeared since the writing of the main part of this book.

Gramscian cultural studies in Britain has been organised around a number of groups, networks or 'colleges', both concrete and invisible. This has given it a consistency and a continuity which has been almost taken for granted by those of us who have followed the work over the years: we know that writers in particular centres or groups in particular universities will be developing particular traditions, and that their work will reflect these traditions. There are also less formal groups clustered around particular journals or particular conferences. Those journals and conferences also sponsor or commission publications of collected essays, often as student 'readers', intended for academic courses.

Given the relatively small scale of operations of academic life in Britain, the personnel concerned can also form an interlocking élite: particular individuals work together in departments or centres, edit journals, appear at conferences, get their work published in collections of conference papers, refer to each other's work, meet in the same political or academic groupings, and are very often closely involved in the design, validation or examination of academic courses in other institutions too. These days, doubtless, they communicate internationally and almost instantaneously via electronic mail. In this way, the approach to cultural studies and cultural politics I have discussed in this book – gramscianism – has simply been able to locate itself at the centre of British work, with both good and bad effects, as I try to argue in detail in what follows.

It would be fascinating but too large a task to outline all the inter-connections between centres, journals, conferences and courses over the last twenty years. Despite the relatively small size of the group concerned, it would also be impossible here to give details of each individual or work I have mentioned. Even a casual reader will soon notice that the name of Stuart Hall crops up in most of the areas, though, to take the most obvious example. I have not offered a comprehensive review even of Hall's work (which would be quite a task), but have chosen examples to illustrate critical themes.

I hope that the account which follows gives sufficient information to follow the main arguments, and I have tried to include a fairly full bibliography and to encourage readers to go on to pursue their own critical readings of it. Nevertheless, perhaps a brief and partial account of the central institutions and personnel might be required too.

THE BIRMINGHAM CENTRE FOR CONTEMPORARY CULTURAL STUDIES

The usual abbreviation for the Centre, used throughout this book, is CCCS. (Given the recent rise to public prominence of another CCCS in Britain, the Centre for Crop Circle Studies, it might be better in the future to refer to the BCCCS to denote the Birmingham Centre, however.) Founded at Birmingham University, England, in 1964 under the Directorship of Richard Hoggart, a founding father of the British new left (see p. xiii–xiv), CCCS took off in cultural studies terms after 1969, when Stuart Hall became Director.

Hall has given his own version of the struggles faced by the Centre in its early years, in the opening article in Hall *et al.* 1980, and there is a brief discussion of this account in Chapter 1. Other accounts have now appeared, since I completed the main body of this work, including an introduction by Turner (1991), and a very brief history of the growth of British cultural studies courses and academic departments in a new magazine (Institutionalisation Group 1991). As the latter account makes clear, a number of other universities also established centres, including the ones devoted to work in mass media at Leicester and Glasgow Universities, both of which make fleeting appearances in this book.

According to his own account, Hall managed to steer a very difficult route through academic rivalries with different faculties in Birmingham, and initial scepticism from funding bodies, to move his postgraduate centre into a very powerful public position. One reason for his success, he maintains, was the way work was organised at the Centre in a distinctive combination of individual research and collective endeavour: at one stage, all students were apparently expected to contribute to a general seminar on cultural studies to show how their individual projects contributed to the substantial theoretical and political debates under way, for example.

Less formally, particular groups formed around common interests and worked on collaborative publications, such as the 'specials' which are cited in the bibliography (e.g. CCCS 1981, Hall and Jefferson 1976, Women's Study Group 1978). These publications, all of which mention the assistance of a certain Claire L'Enfant at Hutchinson, became standard texts, but even before that, the work of CCCS was well-known, thanks to the decision to circulate, directly from Birmingham University, seminar papers, lectures and other working documents called the *Stencilled Papers* and a journal *Working Papers in Cultural Studies* (lists of these appear in the back of the 'specials').

As the name implies, stencilled papers were short pieces of work which were often simply reproduced on office presses, stapled together, and despatched to individual enquirers for a small fee. I have seen no figures revealing their circulation, but most academics in the various fields surveyed in this book seem to have been well aware of them and to have used them in their own work and in their courses. CCCS materials appeared centrally in the new cultural studies, media studies or communication studies courses developing in British polytechnics and colleges, as well as in more established academic subjects like history, sociology, education, and even English. The impact of this work on English courses or on debates in history has been particularly neglected in this book, but examples can be found in Hall *et al.* (1980), and Turner (1991) fills in some of the missing pieces.

This stunningly simple idea for publication and dissemination has been copied since, of course, and has much potential these days, given the new technology in desktop publishing. Its main result in the 1970s was to establish the Birmingham Centre beyond any doubt, at least to those who were in on the network, as an exciting, new, interdisciplinary, radical and democratic research grouping really at the forefront of things.

To round off the story of publication technologies, there have been two modern versions of the old annual 'specials' published recently. (CCCS alumni had routinely published other materials in the meantime, of course, as part of their normal participation in British academic life.)

Both collections aim to bring earlier specials up to date, in the fields of women's studies and education studies respectively. Franklin *et al.* (1991) contains a number of pieces exploring knowledge, culture and power, in 'official culture' as well as subcultures, and includes a useful opening chapter by Franklin outlining the uneven relationship between gramscianism and feminism (and other approaches) at the CCCS. As readers will see, this is primarily how feminist work appears in my book – as a continuing source of critique and discovery from the point of view of gramscianism. This is not an attempt to devalue feminism as an approach in its own right, of course, but a matter of emphasis. Nevertheless, had there been more time, Franklin *et al.* would have helped greatly in the construction of this book, especially in chapters on symbolic politics and media (e.g. Chapters 4 and 7).

The CCCS's Education Group II, under its third Director, Richard Johnson, also revived the tradition of 'specials' with their 1991 collection, and this is reviewed at greater length in Chapter 3.

CCCS has now re-formed as a Department of Cultural Studies at Birmingham University, under Jorge Larrain. Turner suggests this reorganisation will have contradictory effects, both to strengthen the organisational base but also to incorporate cultural studies much more firmly into orthodox undergraduate teaching systems. The new Department recently (winter 1991) announced a new journal to carry on the tradition, although this will clearly have to compete with a number of other well-established rivals, including the influential *Theory Culture and Society*.

CCCS produced a whole generation of alumni who went on to produce substantial work of their own including, in alphabetical order: Brunsdon, Burniston, Chambers, Clarke, Critcher, Ellis, Finn, Geraghty, Gilroy, Hall, Hebdige, Hobson, Jefferson, Johnson, McNeil, McRobbie, Morley, O'Shea, Schwartz, Tolson and Willis. Combinations of these writers still work together, as an examination of a number of recent texts reveals.

CCCS work deeply influenced a number of other writers, and virtually established an agenda for the next decade. Perhaps the single best-known example of this, for American readers, can be found in the work of John Fiske, now at Wisconsin. Gramscian perspectives can also be found described in American collections like those of Angus and Jhally (1989), and Giroux *et al.* (1989), and I mention these versions in the main body of the text. Grossberg has also been influential in introducing Hall's work to an American audience (Grossberg 1986), and in editing a very recent collection of essays (Grossberg 1991). Hall has been active himself in the USA recently. Several recent major conferences seem to have been held in the USA too. Hall has also been ready to acknowledge the reciprocal influence of his American experience on his own work, especially in further dethroning British concepts of social class as a privileged level and site of struggle.

John Clarke's 1991 essay also picks up the issue of relevance to the USA, and offers a detailed account of American society, class and consumerism. These analyses are of great interest in that they deliberately attempt to apply the British cultural studies tradition (i.e. gramscianism) to some detailed empirical work on another society. As a result, Clarke's book clearly reveals the strengths and the weaknesses of the whole approach, not just for US readers but for all of us, and, again, it could have found a much more central place in what follows had it not appeared when the writing was almost over.

It is impossible to do more than offer a quick summary here, but Clarke's chapters on class and consumerism are probably the best for our purposes. US social history provides a rich source of material for explaining the specific combinations (or articulations) of cultural movements and material forces. Yet, as before, this material is still being worked through a set of familiar theoretical and conceptual frameworks which have apparently largely survived any encounter with empirical complexity. Clarke offers what is more or less the gramscian version of the old 'relative autonomy' model to manage the articulations.

Even on the new terrain, Clarke finds only the old dilemmas. He wants to disarticulate social class, say, from any simple economic determinants and in so doing refers to some arguments about the new middle class, which is the first time gramscians have referred to this material, to my knowledge. Yet he also wants to rearticulate class and consumerism with class, race and gender to stave off the individualism and relativism that awaits once determinants are dissolved. The slippery ground between determinism and relativism is occupied by the familiar mechanisms – articulations, condensations, and, of course, hegemonic struggle.

In other pieces, there have been different emphases. American influence is detectable in the subtle shift of ground under way in current uses of the term 'articulation', I suggest in Chapter 2. However, McRobbie, in a recent piece (McRobbie 1991), uses (unspecified) American work as an example of the dangers of an uncritically idealist analysis of popular culture which ought to be avoided, even in the new liberation from 'serious' analysis which she sees as a major benefit of postmodernism. She does not give any examples, but her description of the approach seems to fit much of what Fiske does. Fiske, and the impeccably British Paul Willis's 1990 piece can certainly be criticised on these grounds, in my view (see Chapter 8).

THE COMMUNIST PARTY

E. P. Thompson (see p. xiii–xiv) and some other leading figures (including Doris Lessing and Christopher Hill) were still members of the Communist Party in the early 1960s but had shown themselves able and willing to engage in debates about culture and politics with interested non-members (including Hall and Williams). McIlroy (1991) suggests that Thompson's critique of Williams's *Culture and Society* in an early *New Left Review* (see p. xv–xvi), helped convert the latter to an interest in western marxism which was to lead to the emergence of Gramsci as a major figure for the new left. Various discussion groups were formed with these non-members, including the Party's Sociology Group and the so-called Communist University of London, which produced collections mentioned in the main text like Bridges and Brunt (1981) and Hunt (1977).

The British Party, like many others, has been through a series of changes lately, some of which are discussed in Samuel (1987), and has recently abolished itself and re-emerged as a new Democratic Left group. It is still strange to find it gone, and to note the sudden absence of marxist vocabulary among academics that McRobbie describes. The left, Party members and fellow-travellers, have clearly suffered an enormous failure of nerve, as a number of journalists have noted, especially since the 'momentous events' in the former Soviet Union.

The academics discussed here did try to develop a 'western' version of marxism and have distanced themselves clearly from the regimes of official communism, but never as rigorously as other groups (especially, say, 'critical theorists' or Trotskyite writers) – yet it seems they too now find it necessary simply to associate Soviet and Chinese communism with marxism after all. In some way they want to see those societies in the most vulgar bourgeois way as simply failed 'experiments in marxism'. The defunct Communist Party of Great Britain can also be confirmed as some kind of privileged bearer of marxist theory whose fortunes determine the fate of that theory. Following these standard petit bourgeois perceptions leads to the dignifying of the British Labour Party as the sole remaining bearer of socialism.

It is astonishing to find such simple articulations at the centre of recent analyses of politics in Britain even on the left. The residual humanism in gramscian approaches, identified in an early article by Coward (1977), where historical agents fight out some pre-determined struggle via parties or societies which somehow directly represent them, might be responsible.

The political future of the left is anyone's guess, of course, although Laclau at least is optimistic (see *Marxism Today* p. xiv–xv). The future academic allegiances for former gramscians now seem likely to lie in 'post-marxism', with its mixture of surface indifference ('value freedom', one might call it!) and apologetically coded deeper radical commitments, as identified so well in Geras (1987, 1988).

THE NEW LEFT

The new left in Britain seems to have been launched by a number of academics in the late 1950s, many of whom seem to have first met at the élite universities of Oxford and Cambridge. One account (McIlroy 1991) describes the early debates between Raymond Williams, Richard Hoggart, and E. P. Thompson, who each produced seminal pieces in the first generation of writings on British working-class culture (which are all detailed in McIlroy for those who do not know them).

It is hard to describe the impact of these pieces (and some critical realist films and novels of the 1960s) upon persons like myself who were, or were about to become, socially mobile via university places and scholarships. We had survived a school system that was surprisingly but unevenly meritocratic, yet which still devalued working-class culture in the ways which later generations of black and feminist activists have clarified: for mainstream British education, there simply was no working-class culture, or at best a sadly deficient one, a mere 'otherness', best forgotten and hidden under a continual attempt to police the speech, manners, diet, modes of dress, leisure pursuits and ambitions of able working-class students.

Hoggart, and for me, Thompson above all, opened our eyes to our own traditions and cultures, restored our history, raised our consciousness, and rattled the confidence of the middle classes by destroying the old myths about an inferior, passive, ignorant and deferential proletariat.

Despite the specifics of British social history, however, there are some parallels to be drawn with the emergence and dilemmas of the new left in the USA too, and Walker (1979) offers a collection of essays that has considerable significance. Briefly, the US new left also drew from radical middle-class strata and student movements, contributors like the Ehrenreichs argue, and it has struggled to find a constituency in the new times: its black activist and feminist allies have emerged as separate and autonomous organisations, while its blue-collar radical allies have become increasingly estranged by the bourgeois values still influential in much academic cultural politics, and the barely hidden class interests of its proponents. This sort of analysis can be applied to Britain too, I argue in Chapters 9 and 10, although there are some more specific determinants to consider too.

MARXISM TODAY

The British Communist Party was always small, but curiously influential among left-wing academics since the 1930s. Like many European parties, it had undergone a number of political crises following the death of Stalin, and the cycles of liberalisation and repression in eastern European satellites. Following the electoral successes of the Parties in France and Italy in the 1970s, a strong 'Eurocommunist' faction had developed (advocating, briefly, a 'popular democratic', conventionally political organisation, under Party leadership, aimed at mobilising all those interest groups and factions excluded by the new alliances between advanced capital and the modern state). In the late 1970s, the moment for electoral routes to power was lost, though, and Eurocommunism waned.

According to the account in the final edition (Jacques 1991), a member of that Eurocommunist faction (and an academic) was invited (by another academic) to edit one of the Party's journals, *Marxism Today* (*MT*). Under Martin Jacques (editor 1977–91) and an editorial board that included Hall, the magazine launched a series of much more conventionally 'popular' analyses of British politics and culture. In the process, *MT* changed beyond all recognition, from a 'serious' theoretical journal for the party faithful to a more commercial, stylish, rather trendy and lightweight 'life-style' type magazine, with articles by Tory politicians, more advertisements, and more features on style and fashion. After an 'energetic' career, the magazine closed in December 1991

One of the main projects launched by that journal – the analysis of Thatcherism – is discussed in Chapter 9, and again there are several major published collections from *MT* mentioned in the text and the bibliography (Hall and Jacques 1983, Hall 1988, Hall and Jacques 1989). The rather celebratory final edition of the magazine appeared in December 1991, and Jacques's own account of his editorship claims a fairly large circulation in the early 1980s (fourteen thousand on average).

Politically, *MT* claims to have had a considerable influence in affecting Labour Party policy too (largely, and typically, a negative one it seems – driving off the 'real socialist' challenge, according to Jacques himself). Samuel (1987) offers a good account of some of the internal bitterness, division and in-fighting that arose in the Communist Party too as a result of the new emphases in *MT*'s 'designer socialism'.

My own assessment is found in Chapter 9, and I have read nothing in the final edition of *MT* which changes it. Hall's final piece on Thatcherism still looks idealist, and it is still baffling to see a distinguished Professor of Sociology writing an account which has the effect of ending apparently on the verge of naively discovering Durkheim or J. S. Mill on the relations between the social and the individual (Hall 1991). Laclau's piece, left to the end as a 'last word', finally acknowledges the dangerous aspects of the vaunted politics of identity in the xenophobia and anti-semitism now emerging in eastern Europe, yet assures us that 'democracy' will and must triumph in the end, presumably on functionalist or social-evolutionary grounds (Laclau 1991). Beneath the triumphalism, confident Micawberism and nostalgia, there is a large echoing silence, and more than a hint of evasion and embarrassment.

NEW LEFT REVIEW

New Left Review is an influential academic journal which is still published. Its origins lay apparently in an earlier journal launched by the founding fathers cited above – the *Universities and Left Review* (based at Cambridge), founded in 1957. This journal became the *New Left Review* (*NLR*) in 1959 under the editorship of the ubiquitous Stuart Hall. It publishes quarterly.

NLR enters our story with a series of influential essays by Anderson and Nairn in the early 1960s, diagnosing the sad state of British political culture as one of imminent crisis. These essays are discussed by Johnson (in Hall *et al.* 1980) and in Chapter 9 of this work. To be very brief, British political culture lacked a native radical tradition due to its peculiar history, and, not to put too fine a point on it, the role of the academic new left, via *NLR*, was to investigate and popularise serious marxist theory found in various other (mostly European) countries. Academically, *NLR* and its associated publishing house New Left Books introduced to British academic life the works of Marx, Althusser and Gramsci, and a whole host of other major thinkers and writers in Germany, the USSR, America, and the 'third world'. Gramscianism appears in *NLR* but does not enjoy a monopoly there, as it has done in other publications. A glance at the bibliography will reveal the importance of the journal for this work.

THE OPEN UNIVERSITY

The OU began transmitting its courses in 1971 after a rapid series of still mysterious manoeuvres inside the British Labour Party and the wider apparatus of the British State (including the BBC), beginning with a speech by the then Prime Minister, Harold Wilson, in 1963. The best-known aspect of the OU is its teaching system, which operates 'at a distance', sending students correspondence packages and tapes, and also arranging local tutorials and some residential schools. It operates across the entire nation, catering for 'mature' students. Unlike any other British university, no formal entry qualifications are required for its students – hence its main claim to openness.

The OU has been a great success. At the most obvious level, it has produced over one hundred thousand new graduates in twenty years, which is substantial for Britain. Its supporters claim that many of these new students are those who have been deprived by earlier educational discrimination, especially women. Every year, press stories appear which reveal that an OU graduate has just undergone spectacular social mobility as a result of having taken the course, and there are surveys which show other benefits like increased confidence, raised ambitions, greater security and so on.

The courses produced by the OU are widely published, and are known to other colleges and university departments, partly because many academics are involved in designing or teaching those courses as consultants, part-time local tutors or examiners. OU cognoscenti tend to refer to these courses by their code numbers. The letters indicate the faculty running the course – A is Arts, D is Social Science, E is Education, M is Mathematics, S is Science, T is Technology. The numbers following the letters indicate the level of the course and its status in terms of the credit it earns.

The courses referred to in this book (listed in the bibliography under Open University) are: *Mass Communication and Society* coded *DE353* (i.e. a third level full credit course run jointly by Social Sciences and Education), various E courses including postgraduate ones with the code number 8 (*E814* for example), and a famous course *Popular Culture*, coded *U203*. The

U code indicates that the University was offering this course as a free-standing course which people could take just out of interest, on its own, as well as being able to collect a second level credit for it, should they wish to proceed to gain the six credits needed for a degree.

The best account of the emergence of the OU is mine (!) (Harris 1987). The OU must be understood as a complex combination of open and closed aspects: apparent openness to those with no formal qualifications can lead to susbsequent failure if the curriculum penalises the educationally inexperienced, for example. Although the OU attracted a number of left-wing academics in its early days (including me, in a very junior capacity), it has never really taken seriously the issue of popular education in my view, and it remains dominated by some rather dubious assumptions about 'proper' (i.e. bourgeois) education and pedagogy, which affect even those courses which try to be radical and critical.

The School of Education at the OU was the first faculty to offer such radicalism, in fact, well before Social Sciences. The OU became one of the main sources for 'new sociology of education' courses (along with the Institute of Education, London), and for subsequent marxist sociology of education courses. These are discussed in Chapter 3. Ironically, the myth of the OU as a hotbed of socialism has been fostered as much by right-wing critiques, like the Gould Report (Gould 1977), which seized upon some of the contents of these radical sociology of education courses, especially *E202*, and denounced them, rather crudely, as propagandist and 'unbalanced'. Tracing the effects of courses is far more complex than this, of course, and Gould never really closed with the issues. The attack apparently did enough damage to worry the OU managers, however.

The University's structure is less radical than it looks in several other ways too: it has been in the forefront of developing modern management techniques for course design, including an advanced eye for public relations and marketing. It has also developed a number of ways to manage any excessively critical courses. These developments make Hall's recent scorn for university academics who gave in to managerialism 'without a shot fired' (Hall 1991) rather ironic, perhaps.

The overall impact of the OU on the occupational structure is probably less liberal than many socialists think too – it is currently in the business of credentialising many semi-professions, for example, and this is a classic bourgeois closure device, of course. Weberian, rather than gramscian, theory would be needed to grasp this possibility, though.

I air some of these general possibilities when discussing specific radical OU courses, especially *U203*, produced as it was by the OU Popular Culture Group. Many members of the Group, if we include consultants especially, were CCCS alumni, and of course Hall's involvement with the OU predates his appointment there as Professor of Sociology in 1980 (he was a contributor to the earlier media course *DE353*, for example).

Bennett (1980a) gives an insightful account of some of the politics involved in establishing *U203*, and I attempt to read the course critically and to place it in its institutional context (in Chapters 7 and 8). As with much of the material here, considering the conditions of production of these courses is a crucial aspect of critique: the authors' struggle with the OU system to maintain their accounts in the face of demands for 'balance', 'effective teaching', assessable material and popularity with contradictory audiences becomes an important dimension in grasping the detailed shape and effects of the course in question.

Since the ending of *U203* in 1986, the Popular Culture Group at the OU tended to break up, although many of the personnel still work together on journals and ensuing collections of articles as in the *Formations* group publications.

Bennett now works in Australia, as do several other migrant gramscians and new left veterans, including Tulloch and Turner (and, for a while, Fiske). This has spawned a number of analyses of Australian popular culture, listed briefly in the biographical section of Turner (1991). The Australian Government is on the threshold of launching its own 'university of the air' (the Television and Open Learning Project), and one of the courses planned for 1992, very probably with Bennett's involvement, will concern Australian popular culture: it will be interesting to see what approach is adopted, and whether there are any new ideas for resisting the conventions of 'academic realism' in this 'distance education' context.

ACKNOWLEDGEMENTS

I would like to thank all those who have helped me, knowingly and unknowingly, to write this book, including family, friends, students and colleagues (past and present) at the Open University and at the College of St Mark and St John.

INTRODUCTION

It is clear that you cannot really write a book on cultural studies. Hebdige has explained why – there is an embarrassing naivety about claiming to have a single authorial voice, a secure position from which to survey the field in a masterly [*sic*] manner (Hebdige 1988). This book is written with a combination of voices or subject positions, some those of a provincial outsider, others speaking from the point of view of an insider – inside the tradition of cultural politics described here, for example, and inside an academy. I confess to them simply to enable readers to see how they have influenced my inevitably partial account of gramscianism.

One voice is the voice of a (now) middle-class, middle-aged, white, heterosexual, male provincial. One obvious consequence of this position is to feel marginal to, and to some extent marginalised by, arguments for the leading political role played by black people and women, however sympathetic one might feel in an abstract sense. I make this statement to show a serious limitation, not to make one of those playfully 'human' gestures with which famous professors introduce their work.

After a working lifetime of apology, though, I am inclined now to see the omission of this voice as a loss for the authors of these pieces not for me. Without grasping the significance of their work for provincials, the analysts are doomed to 'asymmetry', to uncritical populism when studying activities of which they approve, and blank incomprehension of those which they do not, even if this is concealed under the surface of some elegant or 'incantatory' writing. Like the black people, women, and 'normal youth' in cultural studies, or the 'earoles' in *Learning to Labour*, I find myself invisible, relegated to a 'natural' substratum, untheorised, an empty signifier, a mere 'Other' against which more glamorous identities are defined. Like those groups too, the first task in self-awareness is to criticise the consensus view, separate oneself from it, withdraw from the dominant gaze, and settle accounts, and some of this is what has inspired this book.

I want to preserve not the undoubted anti-intellectualism of provincial

1

life, but that element of provincial good sense that looks sceptically at the latest fashions before leaping on the bandwagon, and that resists metropolitan arrogance, sophistry and 'citycentrism' which suggests that there is no life, no struggle, no activities of any real political interest outside the city wall (or outside the city university wall), until someone in London 'articulates' a position. I suppose I am seeking a metropolitanism of the intellect and a provincialism of the sensibility. To calm any premature fears, I should make it clear that this book is not a 'new right' critique of gramscianism.

If there is an outsider's voice to begin with, there is some insider knowledge to share too. Academic writers and speakers are difficult to decode when you first meet them, partly because of the extraordinary language they use, but mostly because of their unusual relevance systems. It is partly, as Bourdieu has said, a matter of distancing, being able to maintain an apparently neutral, purely technical and scholarly agenda when discussing matters like culture, class, oppression, death. But as insiders, who have done it themselves also know, it is a matter of managing difficult material, making it conform to the conventions of academic work. These conventions are explored more seriously in the last chapter, but the main ones concern being able to tell a story as if it were a natural account, to maintain a position, to defend it against likely criticism, to win over and involve different audiences, to create an impression that something has been revealed or learned, while not offering too radical a challenge to familiar and existing knowledge. Any analyst of the media knows of work on the conventions of popular TV or film, but academics have them too, and they are rather similar.

I would have liked to have demonstrated the effects of these conventions in the classic manner – by flouting them in this book, but, apart from a lack of courage, I still have to try to find a non-conventional style that suits me. If Hall's Open University Units are classic realist pieces, Hebdige, Chambers or Corrigan develop a kind of high-powered 'writerly' art movie alternative. I want to work towards a more participatory home video style, but I think I know how to do this better in lectures and handouts than in books.

As with popular media, academic work aims to conceal its conventions from the audience, to let the audience experience the effects of these conventions as their 'own' genuine reactions. I want to share some of these tricks of the trade with the reader, partly to try and encourage a deeper engagement with the texts than is usual for the 'cruiser' (and for those textbook writers who organise the easy cruises). I am not concerned to debunk the writers or reduce the arguments to merely academic concerns. Doing academic work is difficult and honourable, although it is hard to say this publicly in England without risking a storm of derision. Writing critiques in an academic context does have an effect on the discourses deployed, though: there is an academic 'level' of determinacy to these texts as well as a theoretical and political level.

This aspect of being an insider affects the shape of this book too. It is a considerable problem, to know just how to write another book on popular culture, media or education. There are so many good books and articles summarising the main trends, works, prospects for the future and so on. Further, the field itself is massive, with substantial amounts of work in particular traditions, like 'screen theory' or the sociology of youth or race, or around particular authors like Lacan or Bakhtin, or on major debates like the ones on 'postmodernism'. Clearly, a selection has to be made, a story told which will provide some kind of route, however fragmented, through a colossal amount of work. There is the politics of publishing to consider too – how is my book going to be different from the others, how can I keep it to a reasonable length, and what sort of readership is it going to appeal to?

I have chosen to focus on the 'British gramscians', those writers who stitch together their stories using Gramsci's work at strategic moments. Roughly, anyone who lets Gramsci always, necessarily, have the last word, in any debate whatsoever, is a gramscian, although I have also further reserved the use of the term to mean those who use selected concepts, based on a reading of Gramsci, to develop a definite 'mobility', to be able to manipulate these concepts, define them flexibly, and make them refer to a wide range of phenomena, or use them to endlessly generate a sense of newness, relevance and beginning. Gramscians vary in terms of how they manage a return to the familiar terrain.

Within that body of work, I have selected the popular and pedagogic texts for particular attention – the ones published by CCCS, or those Open University materials associated with the famous courses on education, the media and popular culture. Making so much of Open University courses might need some explanation, unless you know that they have a tremendous influence, well beyond any effects on the thousands of students who take them, in fixing the agendas for discussion. The OU course *Popular Culture* (*U203*) had as great an influence as the Birmingham Centre, for Cubitt (1986), and it brought together a number of scattered gramscian and other pieces, including articles in *Screen* and *Screen Education* in a very convenient manner for a critic.

I chose these materials partly because they are the ones that I met (and gladly used as definitive) as a lecturer in those fields myself, and those are the ones I know students have access to. I want to reconstruct a picture of gramscian work as it might be available to students, because I am especially interested in the student audience. I have tried not to rely on obscure work – theses, for example – even though this might diminish the scholarly virtues (if any) of this book. For this reason, and to try to limit the task somehow, I have relied upon published collections of work, rather than the articles in *Marxism Today*, or the unpublished CCCS papers.

I know, in fact that students rarely do read these pieces in the way I think they should read them, and so I hope to offer a 'deeper' reading than usual of these familiar texts, and to offer a 'symptomatic' reading too, by referring to some of the background debates and argumentational twists which are often missed by the 'raider'.

Bennett and Woollacott have given us a useful model for analysis like this, only they have chosen the much more immediately gripping topic of James Bond, and so have less substantive exegetical work to do (Bennett and Woollacott 1987). I find that the popular texts of gramscianism are famous, and often can seem familiar, although they are not usually very thoroughly read, or placed in a context, especially a 'production context'. I think it particularly important to devote some time to the earlier works that are often reduced and rendered abstract in the later ones. Apart from leading to an insight into techniques for making one's cultural capital as productive as possible, tracing the developments of gramscian pieces can also help readers to break with the narrative strategies of the later works, which can sometimes stage-manage a 'discovery' that really replicates work carried out several years before. I want readers to ask why texts are written like that.

My own interests, in critical theory and in distance education, are not fully developed here, nor is any other systematic alternative to gramscianism, but, to borrow again from Bennett and Woollacott, critical resources of this kind act within a 'reading formation' for me to construct my 'intertextual' reading of the pieces I have selected. Such a reading will be partial, of course, and may not be shared by many readers. This is one reason I have tried not to close my accounts excessively.

I have grouped texts around substantive areas, to reflect some common academic divisions of labour into education courses, media courses, recreation courses and the like. This has proved unwieldy at times – 'popular culture' embraces media and recreation, for example, and books like *Policing the Crisis* discuss youth cultures, race, media and politics. On the other hand, grouping the topics like this does help demonstrate both a certain repetition and an unevenness in the works, and helps show the oddly contingent development of arguments in each of the fields: the absence of discussion of media in the early work on youth cultures or education, for example, or the general silence about educational institutions except in education.

I am aware that this range of topics probably makes the book seem too ambitious. I can only say that, because of the peculiarities of a fairly long career spent largely in a small college, I am accustomed to teaching across a range of areas that would look preposterous to a university academic. I have not always ventured into other fields willingly, but I have sometimes benefited from the results. My knowledge is that of the teacher, though, not the specialist researcher.

The reception of gramscian texts and readings in my own courses is interesting in that students often behaved completely contrary to my expectations when I taught. I expected them to be enthusiastic about the politics, or at least about the content: in cultural studies, it was their cultures I was talking about, and I felt they should be flattered, and be prepared to see me as a 'regular guy'. I thought that teaching about popular media would make me and my courses popular, once I had quietly insinuated some of the more difficult theory in behind the dazzling analyses of T-shirts or recipes. However, those closest to the activities in question found it hard to take the contributions seriously: when we read Willis's descriptions of bikers and their 'piratical' style, on one occasion, or Hebdige's account of punk as surrealism, they sniggered. I had encountered the reactions of 'normal' and suburban academic youth, who are probably less common in famous universities, and this helped me clarify my own views.

Students did often appreciate the organising capacity of gramscianism, though, especially its use as a framework to do academic assignments. A hard-pressed student last year realised with relief that 'hegemony can explain everything'. Some of the instrumental ones wrote it all down with no comment, went away and produced 'correct' assignments – and no doubt did the same in English lectures, or in Public Relations courses, with very different methodological procedures and very different notions of 'correctness'.

I think I can also detect the kind of malicious absorption that Baudrillard writes about, as all my efforts disappear into a 'black hole', along with all the other lectures and texts encountered in the course of the day. These points allude to some of the competencies brought to gramscianism which I wish to explore in further work.

Try as I might, I found it difficult to suppress a giggle myself, on occasions, and was tempted to adopt a purely instrumental approach to teaching the stuff. I cannot always avoid hearing in gramscianism the echoes of the fatuities of the *Guardian* pop music column, or *Private Eye*'s 'pseuds' corner', or the 'morale boosting' of pedagogues I have encountered talking up their well-worn lectures (or rather their 'workshops') as both educationally, politically and culturally valid and as fun, or chaplains talking about their pleasure in pop music or soap operas to show they are no Holy Joe. I have had good reasons to bless the naturalistic closures, and the organising capacities of gramscian work myself, in course design at various levels.

I hope I have hit the right style of commentary. I would like this book to be seen as lively rather than aggressive, focused on the issues rather than on the authors as persons, as critical but as appreciative. If my commentary sometimes strays into parody, carnivalesque inversions or other pleasures of the 'second degree', I hope readers/raiders will enjoy 'having a laff', but will understand my intentions: I am not interested in simply rubbishing one of the few critical traditions British academic life possesses. There might be an irony rebounding on me in this: I might appear to be too 'serious' for some gramscians, who can seem keener to abandon their heritage than I am.

Of course, I do not exempt myself or this book from any further demonstration of the same trends and possibilities in some subsequent 'third degree'. What worries me, as later chapters suggest, is that there will only ever be more and more parodies and inversions and reorderings, more playful professorial poetry and stylistic indulgencies, more incantatory, cynical or defensive writing, in cultural studies or cultural politics especially, rather than any actual first degree work.

It is not my prime concern to make any drastic new suggestions for research, but my own interests lie in critical insider research of bourgeois culture (especially of academic culture), and more open studies of proletarian or common culture, without the necessity to propagandise about it.

Here, I feel the resources of two neglected traditions – sociology and critical theory – have been abandoned far too early by gramscians. The first chapter starts with an account of how this happened.

1

THE CONTEXT: BREAKING INTO MARXISM

INTRODUCTION

The history of the development of gramscianism can be conceived as a series of debates with a number of rival disciplines and perspectives. There are other determinants too, as we shall see, but the formal and polite way of locating what I have called gramscianism, the way it often represents itself in public, is in terms of running debates with a number of 'bourgeois' social sciences, including various sociologies and sub-sociologies; community studies; certain philosophies, 'humanities' and histories; and a number of marxisms, including different readings of Gramsci and Althusser, as well as rather vaguer 'mass culture theorists' and 'orthodox marxists'. Later, the debates concerned some traditions in linguistics, structuralist and post-structuralist, 'discourse theorists' and Russian formalists; and postmodernism. This chapter considers some of the earlier debates, and Chapter 2 discusses some of the later ones.

Hall has given his own account (Hall *et al.* 1980) of some of these debates and the different 'problematics' which have coloured the work of the Birmingham Centre for Contemporary Cultural Studies (hereinafter known as CCCS), and there is some common ground between my account and his. However, Hall argues that the debates show an ongoing heterodoxy and openness in CCCS publications, but I want to suggest that beneath this pluralism lies a deeper conformity to a continuing project – the development and defence of gramscianism. I shall also argue later that although Hall's account mentions a number of contextual micropolitical factors in the development of the Centre's work, he has not theorised their effects adequately. The same arguments occur in discussing certain of the Open University courses which exhibit gramscianism, especially *Popular Culture*, or *U203*, as it is known to enthusiasts (Open University 1982).

My point about continuity is shown intially by the astonishing tendency for the figure of Gramsci to keep coming to the fore, as a leading theorist and guide, as a source of specific pieces or concepts which guide analysis, or less specifically as a kind of model of good practice, able always to 'teach a lesson', keep the faith, and see off the rivals. For me, this tendency is linked to the academic context of the production of these works: briefly, it is conventional in academic writing to conduct a debate with rivals before allowing the chosen theorist to emerge as the person most likely to synthesise the offerings, make sense of the debates, or offer some suitably pleasurable resolution and closure. This underlying narrative structure, which might be called 'academic realism', not an innocent pluralism or heterogeneity, is what lies behind the accounts of the specific twists and turns of the debates which are summarised below.

The ways of dealing with rivals have varied, from attempting critiques of, or 'breaks' with them, to admitting their force then laughing at (or possibly off) the consequences. As well as what might be called formal academic responses, there have been a number of other responses to the challenge offered by these rivals, like the partial admission of some of the points made, sometimes 'genuinely', sometimes in a spirit of 'inoculation', 'gesture' or 'apology', or the deployment of a number of rhetorical arguments, including appeals to authority, to political or emotional loyalties, to privileged inside knowledge, to common-sense, or to shared beliefs. Again, these are recognisable techniques, well-developed in the common room or seminar.

Discussion of these less formal manoeuvres is left to the substantive chapters that follow, and to the final chapter. It should suffice for now to say that the discussion of these ploys in gramscianism in no way involves comparing the texts against some 'pure' model of academic discourse, 'correct' reading, or 'science': all science involves rhetoric, and all academic argument uses ploys like these. 'Pure' science is a snark that no one is hunting any more.

There are signs of that snark hunt in the earlier and central pieces of the gramscian tradition, though, largely thanks to the influence of Althusser and his attempt to read marxism as a break from 'ideology' into 'science'. Other 'founding fathers' of sociology may well have considered their work in this way too (see Crook 1991), but marxism was seen as offering a particularly attractive version of a radical 'epistemological' break designed to found a new science, and to open up a hitherto dark and unexplored continent. The model of a radical social theory, guiding revolutionary practice from the findings of a science, reaches its best development here too. Thus the first way of conceiving of the novelty and the promise of gramscian work was as a break from bourgeois social scientific or literary appropriations of culture into marxist ones.

THE BREAK WITH 'BOURGEOIS' DISCIPLINES

I have used the term 'discipline' to cover not just a range of 'subjects', but to highlight a claim that gramscianism is not just another 'discipline' but a new interdisciplinary study, or rather a 'metadiscipline', a discipline that focuses on some sort of 'totality'. Thus behind the disputes with particular academic subjects in individual fields, like education or youth studies, lies a common claim that some context has been suppressed, some set of determinants omitted.

This claim is made clearly in intentions to 'break with or to reform a number of separations. . .between "past" and "present", between "history" and "sociology", between the empirical and the theoretical, between the study of the cultural and the study of the not-cultural-at-all' (Clarke *et al.* 1979: 9). More specifically, Critcher critiques the tradition of 'community studies' for its attempt to 'appropriate working class culture in terms of a discrete sociological variable: in this case the family' (*ibid*: 14), and, later, when praising work which shows the connection of 'community' with 'broader, national, sets of apparatuses or ideological fields' (*ibid*: 23). The sociological material, on working-class affluence and embourgeoisment, fails to explicate 'the relation between. . .changes in material life and the forms of working class consciousness and culture' (*ibid*: 15). The literary tradition, including the seminal material by Hoggart, is criticised in terms of its method, and in terms of its neglect of the material factors that shaped that '[apparently] eternal working class weltanschauung' (*ibid*: 20).

Johnson, in the same volume, illustrates the limits of 'labour history' in a similar way, pointing to unduly narrow focuses on the economic factors, leaders, or Parliamentary politics in the various approaches in the tradition (including those developed by 'Leninists'), and arguing for a 'break' in radical history too (*ibid*: 66). He goes on to flesh this out in terms of some compromise between 'culturalist' and 'structuralist' approaches (a continuing theme, as we shall see).

All the gramscian work reviewed throughout this book makes similar claims, as individual chapters will show. The 'new sociology of education' exhibits an early form of a break with the old sociology of education (seen as largely 'functionalist'), bringing to bear a rather loose coalition of symbolic interactionist, 'social phenomenological' and marxist approaches, and offering a good deal of work to establish the role of any kind of critical sociology at all in areas that were seen as the proper preserve of philosophy. The 'sociology of knowledge' was the route to restoring a social context omitted in the rather odd 'formal philosophy' of the curriculum, and the first step was to argue for the 'social construction of knowledge' by a variety of agents, from abstract individuals to rather amorphous 'powerful groups'. Again, this would break the monopoly of philosophy, but also open the possibility for a powerful new synthesis between the fields of sociology of education and sociology of knowledge, and, via Berger and Luckmann (1966), connect together the founding fathers, all of whom could be seen as offering a proto-sociology of knowledge. The struggles within this 'new' approach which led to the eventual emergence of gramscianism eased the passage of later 'breaks', and was copied in other fields.

The CCCS work on cultural studies shows an intent to perform a similar break, this time with a definite tactical 'inflection': cultural studies had to steer 'between . . . two entrenched – but in their different ways, philistine and anti-intellectual – positions [sociology and humanities]' (Hall *et al.* 1980: 22), leading to a tactic of the 'appropriation of Sociology from within' (*ibid*: 23). This tactic involved searching out and using all the alternative sociological traditions, in the same initially messy mixture of Weber, Becker and Schutz that characterised the new sociology of education.

Luckily, the New Left project to translate and publish the major works of 'western marxism' was underway, and the Centre were soon able to develop their own 'complex marxism'. As a result, the first major collection, *Resistance Through Rituals* (Hall and Jefferson 1976), is awash with confident marxist terminology, still used rather eclectically, and locates itself firmly within this 'western marxist' 'alienation problematic'.

The new marxist approach would restore the hidden relations between youth subcultures, parent culture and dominant cultures that the old work had omitted. The shift to the level of 'real' as opposed to 'phenomenal' forms would lose none of the specificity of the old analysis, however: each of the phenomenal forms could be seen as valid variants of the underlying real ones as in the (not specifically mentioned) notion of critical transcendence in marxism. Devices like the 'double articulation', the conception of style as an 'imaginary solution' to structural problems, or the concept of 'homology' were tried out as means to perform this non-reductive connection.

Although echoes of the old eclectic radical sociology crept back in with Critcher's piece on 'structures, cultures and biographies', marxism was firmly distinguished from its old radical allies (like symbolic interactionism), even if in a rather strange way (see the fuller discussion of the work on youth in Chapters 4 and 5). For the first time, ideas of 'the crisis', and the 'levels' model of the social formation were used in applying modern marxist analysis to this particular project in an attempt to demonstrate the self-sufficiency of marxism.

Here too, the emerging claims of women and black people to be included in any adequate analysis were made: bourgeois social science (and some marxisms) had omitted them, and rendered them 'invisible' or permanently outside the scope of analysis. Bringing back these groups, and recognising the structuring effects of race and gender, in conjunction with class, became an important subsequent task, and this spawned whole collections of CCCS work, and whole Open University (OU) courses of their own.

SEXISM AND RACISM IN THE OLD DISCIPLINES

Women had been judged by male and bourgeois standards in sociology and other social sciences, and factors specific to their lives had been neglected, or grasped in male terms (one of the best examples arises in the field of leisure – see Chapter 8). Women had also been neglected in 'orthodox marxist' work too, in Marx himself, and even in the work of prominent modern marxist theoreticians like Hindess and Hirst (Women's Study Group 1978, especially Chapter 3). To restore the dimensions specific to women's oppression required a synthesis of marxist economics and anthropology, and Freudian theory. This new synthesis would focus primarily on the site of oppression most commonly foregrounded in women's experience – the family and its economic, political and ideological determinants and functions.

Hall suggests that this work was decisive and affected all subsequent analysis (Hall *et al.* 1980). No longer could the Centre see class as the final determinant of culture, and most of the subsequent published collections contained chapters on women and black people. Specific work developed by former members of the Women's Study Group at CCCS was to reinstate largely female forms of leisure and resistance, in shopping, in watching television, and in fantasy. These activities were not only not trivial, but were proto-politics of a highly suitable kind in the new postmodernist age. In the latest work, this argument has swept all before it, and the women's movement has become the very model of 'new times' politics.

Black people had been studied already in ethnocentric ways, often largely as pathological (e.g. in terms of how their family lives compared to the bourgeois ideal), so the gramscians had a familiar task to accomplish. The same sorts of devices were employed to expose the limits of these traditional conceptions and explain them as 'phenomenal', unable to grasp the structuring influences of economic, political and ideological determinants on the surface characteristics of the black working class, both in the UK and in the countries of origin (for Hall *et al.* 1978). Later work (CCCS 1982) pursued the same argument via analysis of the structuring effects of the blatant racist discrimination of the police, and the effects of the education system in Britain in the 1980s.

The misunderstandings in bourgeois social science extended to failed attempts to grasp 'work-refusal', patois, black family life, the social position and non-passivity of Asian women, the political significance of Rastafarianism (as opposed to its phenomenal religious or consolatory forms – see Gilroy in CCCS 1982), and, above all, the real connections

11

between race, crime, sexuality and the inner city. Here, bourgeois sociology in particular (and popular journalism) offer an ideological 'environment-alism', or a straightforwardly racist 'moral pollution' argument respectively (Hall *et al.* 1978).

In a famous (actually fairly insignificant) section in *Policing the Crisis* (Hall *et al.* 1978), and in a lengthier account in *The Empire Strikes Back* (CCCS 1982), labelling theory and ethnography (respectively) are blamed specifically for some of these inadequacies. These approaches ignore issues of power, including the power of the police to decide when 'standing on a street corner becomes the criminal act of "attempting to steal"' (CCCS 1982: 151), and they display a rather dangerous convergence between their concepts and 'Home Office [or police] thinking', especially in terms of the enthusiasm for 'community', and the slide towards 'community policing' (see CCCS 1982: 164–73).

Once more, we need an account of ideology to fully understand how race came to be central to the 'mugging phenomenon' (later the riot phenomenon), and a (gramscian) theory of crisis to show how this in turn reveals the State's 'tilt towards coercion' (Hall *et al.* 1978: 216).

Butters, writing in anticipation of the completion of 'the mugging project', is one of the most enthusiastic supporters of the new approach in this field. He sees it offering a whole new methodology, breaking with the old dilemmas of inductivism found in ethnography, or tautologous deductivism in marxist theories of the State (in Hall and Jefferson 1976). Chapter 5 explores his argument in more detail.

BREAK OR INVERSION?

The distinctiveness of the break was not to be simply a matter of adding new elements in a broader context. The relation between those elements was to be reconsidered: old simple unities (generalisations or convergencies) were to be 'deconstructed', and new complex unities put in their place, preserving complexities among the different levels ('relative autonomy' was to be the key term here, or later 'moving equilibrium' or 'organic unity'). Empiricism was to be abandoned, including its ethnographic variants, and empirical phenomena were to be 'read', interrogated for their political, symbolic or cultural significance, a move which was to become distinctively shaped by the 'linguistic turn' discussed below.

The old sociological and orthodox marxist connections with social democratic, Labourist, or orthodox Communist Party politics were to be abandoned, too, in favour of a new activism. This emerged steadily but unevenly as the work progressed, and ranged from support for the campaign against the sentences on the Handsworth muggers, to activist organisation of black people on the 'front line', or to a commitment to the Women's Liberation Movement with its various struggles (including women-only consciousness-raising), or to work with radical community or occupational groups, or to a more diffuse activism in whatever site one found oneself – see Bennett's Unit 3 of *Mass Communication and Society* (*DE353*) (Open University 1977). The early work also displayed, notoriously, a refusal to condemn, and a tendency to 'talk up', deviant, sometimes criminal, activities from street fighting to shoplifting.

Of course, the notion of a break reflects the influence of Althusser's work, which we will consider below. Briefly, Althusser had proposed that marxism be read as offering a complete 'epistemological break' with earlier knowledges, with its own characteristic concepts and 'objects', and a whole Althusserian literature grew up attempting to refine these notions, and spot where the break had actually occurred in Marx's work. This whole exercise required a 'symptomatic' reading of Marx, which eventually led to Althusser's own problems and difficulties (see Hirst 1979).

By Althusser's criteria, though, it is in fact doubtful if the new gramscian work does reveal much in the way of a break with the old disciplines. At the level of appearances at least, Cohen has noticed that the old methods and the old sorts of data have appeared in the new work too, for example (Cohen 1987). He singles out for attention Hebdige (1979), but one can find survey data as well as ethnographic data largely untransformed in a number of gramscian pieces including the ones cited above. Some of the old themes are there too, not far beneath the surface, especially in the rediscovery in the work on youth cultures of anomie theory or other variants of 'strain' theory (Downes and Rock 1988: 260f). It is not at all clear that many of the new concepts came from a break with conventional methodology either: even the famous notion of style as a 'magical solution' is not confined to gramscian work, for example.

Of course, these earlier theories are suitably radicalised, but radicalising a theory is not the same as breaking with it. Young's comments on his own early attempts to found a critical criminology make this clear, and he uses a familiar marxist figure to perform an auto-critique – he says the early work offered only an inversion of conventional work (in Fine *et al.* 1979). In inversion, the categories of conventional work are preserved, but one inverts the conclusions to be drawn from them or reverses the arithmetic signs placed in front of them, to shift the metaphor slightly – what was once good (plus) becomes bad (minus), what was once 'society' becomes 'capitalism', what was universal becomes sectional, and so on. Gramscian work on youth cultures shows this well – what was adaptive or compensatory for bourgeois studies now becomes conservative or reactionary (like the attempt by skinheads to recreate working-class community), while what was negative and malicious becomes proto-revolutionary and admirable (notoriously in the discussions of street crime or football hooliganism). Some later gramscian work shows a number of inversions of terms in the old bourgeois sociological couplet 'individual/society' too, as we shall see.

13

There are other forms of similarity too, involving not so much inversion, perhaps, as appropriation followed by inversion. As examples, McRobbie cites a popular film that expresses a number of points about femininity that she wants to make (McRobbie and Nava 1984): Hollywood is somehow on the same track as, although facing in a different direction from, the specialist analysis of critical feminism (perhaps because it reads critical feminism – see Hebridge below). Carter in the same collection mentions a project undertaken by a number of German market researchers and advisers to construct the modern shopping mall as a public place for the new woman, and to focus on her body as a site of pleasure – Fiske rediscovers this project some twenty years later and puts a minus sign in front of it to claim it as a source of proto-resistance (Fiske 1989a). Brunsdon (in Seiter *et al.* 1989) suggests that a TV advertisement was the first to argue that video games were more interactive that just watching TV, as a sales pitch, but the same argument turns up radicalised, as evidence of semiotic warfare, in Fiske (1989a). As a final example, gramscians take over many of the same definitions of work and leisure despite their attempt to 'break' with the bourgeois disciplines in the field, according to Rojek (1985).

This theme is addressed in a dramatic way by Gilroy (in CCCS 1982) who notices that not only bourgeois sociology but even *Policing the Crisis* has been used to inform and construct a police version of mugging – it is not just gramscians who can perform an exchange of plus and minus signs in front of the same categories, it seems. In other areas, Hebdige too notices that 'advertisers read Roland Barthes. . .Hollywood reads *Screen*' (Hebdige 1988: 150).

These convergences are not well theorised in gramscianism, and this points to a missing account of the modern culture industry or surveillance apparatuses, and their capacity to fight back by incorporating critics and inverting their work. This account goes missing partly because of the early decision to reject 'mass culture theses', and to construct a caricature out of Adorno's and Horkheimer's version of it. Yet as their classic work shows (Adorno and Horkheimer 1979) the culture industry has long welcomed critique and shown itself able to use it to generate novelty: critical cultural studies in particular becomes dangerously compromised as a result. The omission of critical theory might also be one reason for an insufficiently deep and open critique of sociology in gramscianism, allowing it to return at crucial moments.

Critical analysts can also show themselves to be insufficiently critical of the forms and conventions with which they work themselves. We can often find an adherence to particular literary and academic conventions, for example, itself the product of the gramscians' strange choice of base in academies of various kinds. The cultural politics of the 'new times' is also riddled with classically 'new petit bourgeois' adverse judgements of working-class groups as we shall argue. In these respects, gramscians seem unable to break with bourgeois common-sense, let alone bourgeois science!

It is quite possible, though possibly unfair, to see the new cultural or lesiure or communication studies as being largely the results of a wave of radicalism in the 1960s that was becoming institutionalised and academicised, (not exhausted and disillusioned, necessarily, as other commentators claim). Johnson, Director of CCCS after Hall moved to the OU, himself seems to take this view, according to Tolson (in Maccabe 1986). Gramscianism shares all the limits of a generational revolt, it could be suggested, rather than appearing as an exciting new break into an unknown area. The rather stage-managed and incomplete nature of the break with bourgeois science looks more like an early rebellion, followed by a compromise in maturity. Much of the pace of later work seems to be set by an attempt to 'talk up the new' or found a research programme or school or centre, to engage in a little academic politics, to establish an agreement on discrete spheres of influence with the old disciplines and faculties. Hall's account of the establishment of the Birmingham Centre (in Hall *et al.* 1980) and Bennett's story of the establishment of his Open University course *U203* (Bennett 1980a) are revealing here, and will be discussed further below.

Finally, what is extraordinary about the break with sociology is how selective the treatment of sociology has been. Individual chapters below point to some of the strange omission of specific sociological work of the most direct relevance – on class consciousness, for example. Sociology has been discussed in a highly selective manner. Lack of expertise means I can do little more than suggest similar significant selections and omissions in the debates with history or linguistics. As a quick example, though, in sociology the CCCS and OU discussions of theoretical positions, which took so much time and energy, seem to have proceeded without a single direct reference to the major works of Anthony Giddens. With omissions like this, it is easy to give the impression that sociology is naively atheoretical, ignorant of continental theory, still content with its little empirical studies, and that gramscianism is the only sophisticated theory in town.

CRITICAL THEORY AND MASS CULTURE

There was a marxist tradition that seemed suitable as a basis for new work on culture and aesthetics – the 'Frankfurt School' (Adorno, Horkheimer and Marcuse especially), and, later, the most prolific of the modern 'critical theorists' Habermas and his associates like Apel, Wellmer and Offe. However, the gramscians have shown nothing but scorn for this tradition, and have been responsible for a whole cohort of students of cultural studies dismissing this work as Bennett does, as 'pessimistic', or 'elitist', as a blind alley, or 'a theoretical movement whose thrust is now, by and large, spent'

(Open University 1977, Unit 3: 37). With the exception of the Bennett discussions, and possibly one paper given at the CCCS which reviewed Adorno's musicology – mentioned in the OU course *Popular Culture* (*U203*) (Open University 1982, Unit 16) – there has been very little direct and detailed analysis of the key works in this tradition by the main gramscian writers. The classically generational tactic of simple dismissal of the past to the lumber room of history seems to characterise the approach here.

Bennett does review some of the debates in critical theory with more care. Even he can not resist using 'advance organisers' or 'textual shifters' (see Chapter 7) – words like 'pessimistic' or 'gloomy' – to preface the discussion, and to contrive things so that the activists have the last word. In discussing the Adorno/Brecht/Benjamin controversy, for example, summarised in Unit 25 of *U203*, he and Donald give Adorno his due as a substantial critic of the new means of mechanical reproduction of art, but do not mention any of his 'methodological' critiques of Brecht or Benjamin, and so the case against activism is never properly heard. The authors also smoothly switch from Marcuse to Adorno at one point to strengthen the thesis that all critical theory is 'gloomy': Nava, reviewed below, uses the same switch to implicate Adorno with the 'false needs' approach in Marcuse.

To borrow an argument from the 'mugging project' (and elsewhere – like Hall's critiques of broadcast news in Cohen and Young 1973), this makes Adorno's pessimism seem simply 'irrational', and opens the way for a sociologistic reading of this pessimism as the product of his dreadful experiences in Nazi Germany. To continue the borrowed argument, it seems there is never a need to address any social or biographical reasons for optimism or activism: no one in gramscianism sees Brecht's or Volosinov's politics as a 'problem'.

There is no real space to attempt to redress the balance here, and point to the concrete work on media or on propaganda which seems so contemporary in Adorno (Adorno and Horkheimer 1979, or the pieces in Arato and Gebhardt 1978, or the accounts in Held 1980). Adorno's own 'breaks' with social science, via his work on the subject–object relation, the construction of individuality, or the 'identarian' nature of social theory prefigured many of the themes which Althusser was to make famous (and which were greeted much more solemnly in that French form). Marcuse was an early theorist of 'new social movements' (Marcuse 1964), and Habermas also directs our attention to them (see Bernstein 1985) – yet from the hectoring manner in which they address us, anyone would think that gramscians alone and uniquely have 'discovered' them. Finally, in this short catalogue of unacknowledged rediscoveries, Adorno and Horkheimer looked quite cheerful about mass culture compared to the thanatoid predictions of Baudrillard on the media and their role in the death of the social (Baudrillard 1988). This unfortunate similarity seems now to have quite put Nava off Baudrillard (Nava 1991).

If one wanted to be equally dismissive after a quick reading, Gramsci easily could be seen as élitist in the personal sense – when he says for example that 'in the masses as such, philosophy can only be experienced as a faith' (Smith and Hoare 1971: 339), or 'Common sense is a chaotic aggregate of disparate conceptions and one can find there anything that one likes' (*ibid*: 422), or 'Individualism is merely brutish apoliticism' (*ibid*: 147), or a number of other unfashionable things. O'Shea and Schwartz tell us (rhetorically) that Gramsci was

> never the slightest bit interested in. . .the cinema and radio, he systematically subordinated self to politics, had nothing interesting to say on the symbolic forms of popular cultures or their elements of fantasy, wrote incomprehensibly on psychoanalysis. . .and so on: a grizzled old Bolshevik.
>
> (O'Shea and Schwartz 1987: 106)

More seriously, Gramsci's advocacy of traditional education can seem dreadfully elitist and 'unfortunate', as we shall see, and gramscians simply have had to ignore much of his work here.

The real merits of critical theory have not disappeared, despite a consistent effort to marginalise them, and many of the themes have returned, as the repressed usually does. Some of the work returns in some of the specific sections which follow below too. Again, it is necessary to deny any attempt to defend critical theory in any simple sense, or to gloss over its problems or internal developments. My point is simply that the gramscians have dealt with critical theory largely using tactics of easy dismissal and a form of generational abuse rather than by any kind of systematic discussion.

In the debates on postmodernism above all, and in the face of perhaps the most serious challenge to radical social theory (see Chapter 2), critical theory refuses to be written off. Adorno gets closer to resisting the tendencies towards foundationalism and 'privilege' than most, for example, and Habermas's work has proved a major source for debate and opposition to postmodern excesses. Terms like 'culture industry' now seem less easy to dismiss as mere personal élitism. Critical theory's aesthetics seem relevant too (see Featherstone 1991). As much gramscian work shows too, Adorno is not the only one who finds an escape from 'serious' politics and a consolation in art, although he embraced the avant-garde, while Fiske and Bennett cruise trade exhibitions, and Corrigan looks back nostalgically to punk.

Gramscian refusals to countenance critical theory, even now, when the case against (such as it was) has collapsed, looks irrational, to put it mildly.

17

Presumably, it is only the 'pessimism' which serves as the barrier. But there is much in Adorno's case against Brecht or Sartre (in Arato and Gebhardt 1978, especially Part II) that activism distorts the object of its study and dominates and trivialises it in the name of some easy link between 'theory' and 'practice'. Pessimism looks less like an uncured psychological response to political tragedy, after twelve years of conservatism in Britain, and now, indeed, it is those who want to enshrine 'struggle' as a metaphysical centre for theory or politics who look as if their personal or socially positioned preferences and experiences are intruding, as we shall suggest.

This sort of critique lies behind some of the accusations of 'asymmetry' which occur from time to time in this account. If asymmetry in analysing youth cultures is the result of dominating the object of study by some immediate (if fantasised) politics, the chapter on politics (Chapter 9) raises the opposite possibility that gramscianism is too 'theoretical' (too closely determined by its academic institutional base really) to be useful as a practical mass politics. I am not saying that critical theory is any more suitable immediately, of course, but it is certainly not so naively optimistic, nor so eager to conform to institutional politics.

Critical theory seems to remain for gramscians as a symbolic condensation of all things wrong with earlier marxism, enabling a consoling distance to be opened between it and new work. Nava begins her cautious attempt (1991) to convince 'new times' socialists of the good side of consumerism with the old tired list of the problems with the mass culture thesis, and she manoeuvres round the newer work by Held by saying that this represents merely a 'nuanced' version of her preferred account. Despite Held, let alone Rose (1978), or other modern texts, critical theory is still the same whether developed by Marcuse or Adorno, still conservative, still psychologically warped by Nazism. The whole attack can only be seen as diversionary: perhaps it will be easier for gramscians to change their minds and abandon their own grave doubts about consumerism as the new politics if they can unite against the old foe first. In politics that old foe is the equally symbolic 'traditional left', in academic contexts it is critical theory.

Finally, to get us to the next section, it is interesting to note the reactions of those marxists with whom the gramscians did want a dialogue, mostly followers of Althusser initially. Althusserians considered themselves to be already on the other side of a break, busy exploring the exciting 'dark continents' of knowledge illuminated by the lightning flash found in Marx's work. They did not seem at all keen to welcome their new colleagues, though, and objected violently to some of their baggage.

THE DEBATE WITH ALTHUSSER

In the 1960s, it was relatively easy to become a marxist, since the work of the young Marx in particular seemed to offer a convenient concept – alienation – that linked with a number of radical projects from Catholicism to existentialism, and all those who feared for the future of 'Man'. In his Introduction, Althusser said that in those pleasant days all that was necessary was to ask whose side were you on, and if it was the proletariat's, you could be a marxist (Althusser 1966). Althusser had developed a rather different reading of Marx, however, one that claimed that marxism was a science or it was nothing, and that some irrational personal decision in favour of socialism was no longer adequate.

One aspect of the critique, connected to the whole project of making a sharp distinction between 'science' and 'ideology', and thus grounding the idea of the epistemological break we were discussing above, was an insistence that the other radicalisms which had been linked to marxism were contaminated by certain errors. Historicism is defined variously, but involves the idea that the march of history itself, and the meaning of specific historical periods, can be seen against the unfolding of some essential logic or development, such as the development and ending of alienation, or the glorious law-governed march towards inevitable proletarian revolution. Idealism amd empiricism were two linked if inverted methodological errors about the source of knowledge, and the role of the knowing subject, both with implications for the claims to scientificity of bourgeois thought (see Althusser *ibid*). Crook (1991) has a good summary.

Althusserianism was resisted at first by some British radicals who wanted to deny the scientificity of the project ('science' was still a bad word for enemies of positivism), and who opposed the apparent functionalism and potential elitism of the approach. Nevertheless, Althusserianism had gained ground in Britain, and there was a flourishing group of British Althusserians who were to play a key part in the debates on marxism and on the work of the gramscians.

Indeed, Coward directly (1977), and Hirst indirectly (in Taylor *et al.* 1975) had already made critical interventions at early stages in the development of the CCCS projects. Both had argued that the very objects of interest, like crime or youth culture, had been constituted in bourgeois disciplines, and could not in fact be studied by marxism at all – there were no concepts in marxism with which to think them. As argued above, a proper break meant the abandonment of those old concepts, and the systematic use of marxist ones in order to produce marxist knowledge. Given Althusser's rejection of idealist or empiricist epistemologies mentioned above, knowledge could be generated only as an 'effect' of the deployment of the correct concepts (this interest in 'discourse theory' was to end in Hirst's critique and abandonment of Althusser too, in fact).

In the late 1970s, work was already under way to establish what the central concepts were, and how consistently they were deployed (Hindess and Hirst 1975), or to begin to produce a new materialist study of subjectivity, based on Althusser's rejection of traditional conceptions of the knowing subject, and his reading of Lacan (especially as in 'screen theory').

The response to this sort of criticism was to be prolonged and to be readdressed several times in different ways. Whatever other effects they might have had, the British Althusserians undoubtedly set an agenda, and required a response, and this is traceable very clearly in works like CCCS (1978), Hall *et al.* (1978), or Hall *et al.* (1980).

There had already been an investment in Gramsci, though. Williams had turned to Gramsci as one response to a lack of adequate theory he had felt particularly after a debate with certain Communist Party historians, especially Thompson (see McIlroy 1991), and seemed to be one of the first converts to the early projects by the *New Left Review* group to introduce continental or 'western' marxism to British radicals. Gramsci seemed to offer the sort of marxism that was congenial to British radicals for several reason, as we shall see: briefly, it was theoretically respectable, non-reductionist, and optimistically activist in its implications, once suitably symptomatically read, of course. Early and influential examples of the deployment of gramscian concepts are to be found in the analyses by Nairn and Anderson of the British crisis (largely, the strange and idiosyncratic 'corporatist' development of the British Labour Movement) in *New Left Reviews* of the 1960s, collected in the seminal *Towards Socialism* (Anderson *et al.* 1965). Anderson (1976), or R. Johnson (in Hall *et al.* 1980) contains later references to, and a discussion of, these seminal pieces.

However, Althusser and Balibar (1970) had criticised Gramsci at some length for his historicism, in the sense of seeing successive social formations and their politics as 'essentially' explicable by their historicity, their place in the unfolding scheme of development. Describing marxism as 'the philosophy of praxis' seemed to offer a particularly flawed reading of marxism, so abstract as to confuse it with other philosophies of general human action, almost the same error as Sartre had made (a real insult this!). Gramsci's reading was liable to reduce the significance of marxism to a mere ideology of the working class in a particular period of capitalist development. Gramsci's use of irredeemably bourgeois conceptions like 'civil society' had shown a failure to think with marxist concepts, as a proper marxist science should. A major associate of Althusser had continued the critique (Poulantzas 1973).

The issue came to a head explicitly, at the level of theory, in a famous collection of essays on ideology in CCCS (1978). According to Rustin (1989), the Althusserian attack prompted Hall to reread Gramsci, this time with an explicitly Althusserian agenda to address. The gramscian pieces in CCCS 1978 (and the briefer accounts in Hall *et al.* 1980) were well-researched, well-argued, and suitably open-ended contributions to what was a continuing, and still fraternal debate.

Gramsci's claims were advanced in one article by Hall, Lumley and McLennan (CCCS 1978), for example, through a particular reading of Gramsci (of course, a contested one). Faults with Gramsci's conceptions of marxism as a 'philosophy of praxis' were acknowledged – it did look like an historicist attempt to render marxism as a mere ideology for and on behalf of the working class. Althusser's and Balibar's points about the abstract and general nature of the term were not addressed so directly, however. The concept of civil society was explained, if not entirely explained away, as an early equivalent of Marx's own model in the Introduction in *Grundrisse* (Marx 1973), one that Althusserians approved of and used a good deal themselves. Another holy text for Althusserians – Marx's *Eighteenth Brumaire*. . .(Marx and Engels 1950) – was cited to show that even Marx continued to use the term 'civil society'.

Most crucially of all, the concept of hegemony was 'enlarged' and in this broader sense, made central to marxism. The political and ideological aspects or levels of a social formation were the places where the 'whole fabric of capitalist society is drawn. . .into conformity with the long term needs of Capital' (CCCS 1978: 67), and this was 'terrain which Gramsci was instrumental in opening up' (*ibid*: 66). Further, class struggle was central to the whole model:

> there is no state or moment of hegemony which is not contested. . .
> And this is so even when the site of that class struggle is apparently far removed from the terrain of the economic and the direct confrontation between the fundamental classes.
>
> (*ibid*: 68)

This politicisation of the reproduction of the social formation, especially in this enlarged sense, clearly offers a distinct advantage over Althusser and Poulantzas, it is claimed: the emphasis on class struggle already present in Gramsci pre-dates a point arrived at only recently in Althusser's self-criticism. Struggle is the activity which unifies social formations – not some abstract theoretical mechanism of social reproduction found in the Althusser and Balibar piece, and much criticised since.

The enlarged conception also offered the distinct advantage of dignifying a lot of activities as 'politics', even if they seemed remote from the classic struggles between proletariat and capitalist, or the particular dilemmas of the Communist Party. This helped clear the ground for a bit of British activism, which took place, of course, without a significant Communist Party presence or leadership (or a significant level of struggle by the British proletariat itself).

Further, Gramsci's work was 'materialist', or scientific, in one sense identified by Althusser – it offered 'to point us directly to the terrain of Lenin: the "concrete analysis of concrete situations"' (CCCS 1978: 69), or to conjunctures, 'particular moments of hegemony and of the relations of class forces which sustain one kind of "unstable equilibrium" or provoke a rupture in it' (*ibid*: 68). Lenin was still fashionable then, although he has since become associated with a workerist and male-dominated 'traditional left', of course.

This analysis 'appears to us to offer a rich promise – and to have hardly begun' (*ibid*: 69). Apart from the licence to practise activism, the appeal to those on the threshold of launching major research projects or centres is also clear. Indeed, this is an early example of a kind of permanent beginningness which seems to haunt the work: ten years or more later, gramscians are still only just beginning, as we shall see.

Gramsci is by no means entirely satisfactory as a theorist – he has certain 'lacks at the level of systematic theorisation' for example (*ibid*: 70) – but he compares well enough with Althusser and Poulantzas, and indeed they even owe him a debt. It is not, anyway, a 'straightforward matter of a theoretical choice' (*ibid*: 70), but (presumably) a tactical political matter. Here too we can see a recurrent theme – how a shift to claims of political effectiveness can rescue theories in difficulty.

The piece on Althusser in the 1977 collection does not reply exactly to the piece on Gramsci (rather typically). Had a direct reply been made, it might well have pointed out that the general politicisation, claimed as a great advance, could be seen as linked rather closely to the flawed pieces in Gramsci that had been disowned: the *Prison Notebooks* develop many points about the hidden politicisation of social life in order to deny its naturalness and explain its inherent historicity, for example, and it is not clear that one can embrace the one and regret the other simultaneously. There is also a lurking danger that the politicisation of everything will produce exactly the kind of abstract 'anthropology' or theory of human action that Althusser and Balibar feared – the era of 'Struggling Man'.

The actual chapter on Althusser by McLennan, Molina and Peters (CCCS 1978) attempts a thorough reading of the material to date, unlike most of the earlier Gramscian pieces which tended to focus almost exclusively on the *ISAs Essay* (Althusser 1971). This helps context that disputed essay, and ends with the insight that the model of the social formation in it already includes, centrally, a notion of class struggle. This had emerged, as we have seen, from Althusser's self-criticism. This clearly is at odds with the most widespread criticism of the essay '[which] is to reduce it to a static or "functionalist" account in which class struggle is almost entirely absent' (*ibid*: 97), a criticism found, indeed, all over the work we are going to review, from Young and Whitty to Johnson, to Gilroy, to Hall himself (e.g. his piece in Curran *et al.* 1977). The same section also argues that by locating ideology in definite apparatuses, Althusser too had at least 'allow[ed] the possibility of more concrete analysis of ideologies', which seems to dispose of another easy dismissal.

Most radically of all, perhaps, especially in view of the defence of

Gramsci which had preceded it, McLennan *et al.* argue that 'we can study in concrete detail as many ideologies as we like, but unless we have a clear conceptual idea of what theoretically separates ideology from other realities (and concepts) – including science . . . we will not know what it is we are studying' (*ibid*: 99). The nature and location of science as somehow outside the social system raises problems for Althusser – but does so equally for gramscians who claim that struggle is universal, and who rarely identify, or even acknowledge the influence of, their own social location.

Finally, Althusser's earlier critique of the epistemological assumptions in other radical positions remains: identifying problems in Althusser is no guarantee of the strength of gramscianism – or any other of those tendencies which

> require a fairly unproblematic or transparent generation of ideology (and politics) from an economically defined class struggle. . .[which in turn]. . .depends on a certain untheorised but necessary philosophical materialism which regards class struggle and 'practice' as both 'given'. . .and therefore as 'more real'. . .a marxist philosophy can not be wished away under essentialist slogans like 'back to practice'.
>
> (*ibid*: 103)

As the end of the McLennan article suggests, there may be an alternative to simply 'going back' to some pre-Althusserian position – to pursue the trajectory even then being sketched by Hirst, and one which was itself to lead to another looming crisis.

These criticisms seem to have been largely ignored, however, in much of the subsequent work – but they return to haunt many of the discussions and qualify many of the findings. And despite the good work of the writers reviewed above to clarify and isolate points of agreement and disagreement, much of the substantive work tends cheerfully to asset-strip both Gramsci and Althusser, as we shall see. Often, a strange hybrid is produced – Althusser's 'levels' model of the social formation, say, or the even earlier formulation of a 'structure in dominance', somehow coupled to a theory of crisis (usually suspiciously close to an historicist view of the necessary struggle between the classes), borrowing from Gramsci. It is as if the authors want to play safe and acknowledge the strengths of both writers in some liberal (and characteristically academic) way.

The one exception here is the Women's Studies Group of CCCS, who broke the consensus and explicitly worked with Althusserian problematics to grasp the specificity of the reproduction of the domestic sphere, and pursued these into debates with Lacanian and structuralist analysts, with no real mention of Gramsci. Their pursuit of this problematic took them into fresh encounters with the concrete, as we shall see. Their early decision not to partake of the attempt to gramscianise everything almost certainly

23

accounts for their continued vitality and openness as researchers and analysts: the feminists have been the much-needed outsiders and others who, like black musicians for Hebdige, continually refresh and revitalise the stale parts of the mainstream.

For many other writers, however, Gramsci's work remained as some kind of sacred touchstone. Hall *et al.* acknowledge the difficulties in reading Gramsci's *Prison Notebooks*, though: not only are there difficulties produced by the need to outwit the censors and by the need to work without access to an adequate library, but the whole political context of the discussion affects the work.

READING GRAMSCI: SOME DEBATES

Many of Gramsci's notes, including some of the famous sections on intellectuals, hegemony, civil society and the State, wars of position and manoeuvre, organic and occasional conjunctures, all of which are quoted frequently in the substantive work done by the gramscians, are chronically liable to multiple readings depending on the significance attributed to the political context of Italy in the 1920s. Should the politics be seen exclusively in the context of the specific struggles of the Italian Communist Party (PCI) to relate to rival parties, including the Comintern? Do the military analogies relate exclusively to the Italian State and the role of the military after World War One, or to internal debates about how to respond to Mussolini's Fascist squads and help the Party develop a fighting wing ready to intervene, or are they to be taken as a general metaphor for 'struggle'? Does a revolution need a military wing in the literal sense? Were the references to 'permanent revolution', 'passive revolution' or 'united front' merely short-term tactical ones with the struggles in the Russian Party in mind, or is there an embryonic general theory of power and revolution, a left-wing Machiavellianism? How important was the Party as a coordinator of political struggles in the move from the war of position to the war of manoeuvre? Was a 'war of manoeuvre' available in the west at all, and if not, what should a Party do?

None of these questions can be settled by a simple reference to Gramsci's 'own' notebooks. In these circumstances, it is hardly surprising that there are many alternative readings of Gramsci's notes, other than the ones developed by the CCCS. Some of these will be summarised during the specific discussions of education or the State, principally to remind readers of the argument developed here that Gramsci's work is not coterminous with gramscianism, that writers in the CCCS or the OU Popular Culture Group have offered a symptomatic reading of Gramsci, and an inevitably partial one. Perhaps the first step is to point to some possible ambiguities in Gramsci's central concepts.

One context for the discussion of Gramsci's work lay in the attempt by the post-war PCI to appropriate his writings as a justification and strengthening of their own programme of popular democratic 'Euro-communism'. As Forgacs (1989), and a number of other commentators (e.g. Jessop 1982), make clear, this led to an attempt to emphasise Gramsci's orthodoxy, to stress certain of his alignments with Lenin (especially in the policy of 'united front'), and his endorsement of the central role of the Party. This is accompanied with a corresponding downplaying of the sections in the *Notebooks* which seem to review Gramsci's 'non-orthodox' activities, like his work in establishing factory councils as the organ of proletarian hegemony, even after the Russian Party had rejected their near-equivalent soviets as the basis of Bolshevik rule.

A tremendous scholarly, largely historical, effort has ensued to attempt to settle the issues of the two different sorts of politics in Gramsci, to explain the need to embrace one and reduce the other, or to explain their coexistence in the *Notebooks*, as a matter of tactical interventions in the continuing internal struggles of the PCI in Gramsci's day. Smith and Hoare (1971), in the lengthy Introduction to the first English edition of the selections from the *Notebooks*, discuss some of these options.

One particularly influential discussion, because it was written by one of the founders of the New Left who was once a prominent Gramsci enthusiast, is to be found in Anderson (1976). The piece is difficult to summarise or criticise since it is so weighty and complex and scholarly. Briefly, it explores the context for many of Gramsci's discussions in the ongoing debates inside the Second and Third Internationals, and suggests that we read many of the famous passages as referring to those debates: the abstract and general quality of many of Gramsci's remarks should be seen as necessarily imposed by the need to evade censorship.

As one example, the famous remarks about the 'war of position' as the only serious option is read by Anderson as being primarily directed against the adventurist 'revolutionary offensives' undertaken by the German Party in the late 1920s that had led to widespread disillusionment and to a serious rebuke from Lenin and Trotsky: this open insurrectionary strategy was the premature 'war of manoeuvre' which Gramsci was rejecting, claims Anderson. Gramsci's advocacy of the united front in prison (having rejected it as a strategy while leading the Party) is meant as an echo of this rebuke to the German adventurists against similar tendencies beginning to assert themselves in Italy. Here too, it is necessary to remind the adventurists that the bourgeois state is different from the Russian one, even though, according to Anderson, Gramsci himself never really adequately theorised the difference, let alone got around to a theory suitable for a specific strategy for Britain in the 1990s.

If these points were never meant to be seen as general policies, there *is* a definite trend in Gramsci to develop a more general account of hegemony, says Anderson. Gramsci sometimes uses the term in a way long familiar to the Russian 'social democrats' to mean the leading role to be played by the proletariat in its necessary alliances with the peasantry. The proletariat was never meant to exercise hegemony over the bourgeoisie in this model, though: it was to establish itself after a military victory as a straightforward dictatorship.

This original conception was developed by Gramsci into a more general account of bourgeois rule and leadership, argued Anderson, partly as a deliberate attempt to extend Marxist theory, and partly because of the need to use 'floating referents' in prison, like the term 'dominant class', without making it clear whether this means bourgeoisie or proletariat. In any event, Gramsci never properly theorised the site or specific mechanisms of bourgeois hegemony, and failed to ground a proper revolutionary strategy as a result.

The doubts, the 'antinomies' and 'aporia', are evident in the different models of the State and civil society. Again, to be brief, Anderson identifies three models of the relation in Gramsci.

First, in the 'east/west' model, the State and civil society are separate, but related to each other as concentric rings in a complex fortification. Beneath the obviously different arrangements of these rings (in the west, the State was a mere outer ring), the main difference lies in the fact that in the west, civil society is a 'very complex structure' and 'resistant to the catastrophic incursions of the immediate economic elements (crisis, depressions etc)' (Smith and Hoare 1971: 235), while 'in Russia, the state was everything' (*ibid*: 238). This model implies that in the west, the main struggle will be in civil society, a view that will lead, according to Anderson, to a dangerous reformism: there are parallels with reformists in both Britain and in the Germany of the Second International period who were arguing that the state itself is neutral, so to speak, and that the secret of bourgeois rule lay in the cultural and ideological power exercised over the proletariat in civil society to make it conservative or corporatist. This view places too much emphasis upon the cultural level, though.

Second, there is the 'balance' model, where state and civil society combine to preserve capitalist rule. Here, Gramsci suggests that the state does play an active part in hegemony in the west. The state is 'educative', for example, not only in terms of an education system, but through the use of law (an argument deployed in Hall and Jefferson 1976), but largely, there is a 'dual perspective', with the State handling coercion, and civil society managing consent. Anderson suggests that this is too neat and abstract a division of labour, missing the crucial issue that the State does both consent and coercion.

Third, in the 'enlarged State model', the State includes political and civil society (perhaps as in 'But since in actual reality, civil society and the State are one and the same, it must be made clear that laissez-faire too is a form of State regulation' Smith and Hoare 1971: 160). This is the reading that leads to Althusser and Balibar, and the *ISAs Essay*. Anderson argues that this model generalises between different forms of states (especially between bourgeois and fascist ones) in an 'ultra-left' purism, and again blurs the strategic issues for any party concerned to build struggle in the relative autonomy of civil society in order to overthrow the 'normal' bourgeois state.

To cut a long analysis short, Anderson argues that none of these models really establishes the correct relation – that in bourgeois society, the normal state of affairs involves 'domination by culture but determination by coercion' (Anderson 1976: 42). Any strategy devoted to the overthrow of the coercive aspects of the State alone is prone to adventurism or ultra-leftism. On the other hand, cultural politics alone will not defeat the State, and indeed runs the risk of a dangerous pacification and incorporation of the proletariat: only through their experience of the expansion of *proletarian* democratic (and cultural) forms, not immediately available just from 'struggles' in bourgeois civil society, can the proletariat desire to come to power (unless we are to assume that revolution is somehow 'in the air', that the time is somehow ripe irrespective of the actual conditions – a mistake made by the German adventurists in the 1920s for Anderson, and occasionally detectable, perhaps, in the 'new times' writings in the 1980s).

Anderson ends his article as a revolutionary militant and activist, with a recommendation that a proper revolutionary politics be prepared to take on both cultural domination and the coercive powers of the State by military means. These conclusions are far from the gentler academic gramscianism of cultural politics, of course, and a good deal of political and theoretical rethinking was to follow Anderson's discussion. In the process, many of the strengths and weaknesses in Gramsci's work identified in this article were to change sides, so to speak.

'ENRICHING' AND 'ELABORATING' GRAMSCI

There are a number of sources for what Forgacs (1989) calls 'enriched Gramscianism', but the writings of Mouffe and Laclau are identified as crucial by him, and acknowledged as influential by gramscians themselves (see Hall 1985, Donald and Hall 1986, or Gilroy in CCCS 1982). The enrichment, briefly, comes from reading Gramsci as a theorist of hegemonic discourse, reinterpreting the work on the formation of hegemonic blocs to refer to the ways in which a dominant group is able to actually incorporate some popular opinions and aspects of the common-sense of the subordinate groups into a specific hegemonic discourse of its own.

The main example is, obviously, the analysis of 'Thatcherism' as an attempt at just such a unificatory discourse, and the specific work, from

Policing the Crisis onwards, shows the attempt made by Thatcherism to disconnect elements of common-sense from earlier political discourses and reintegrate them, or 'condense' them, into a new ideology. Laclau's work explains how ideologies can be 'articulated' both internally and by being joined on to 'class subjectivities' (see, for example, the piece in Donald and Hall 1986, or Hall's Unit 28 of *U203*) to produce a new 'common-sense' including perceptions of national identity (especially 'Englishness'), 'respectability', a tradition of self-help and so on.

'Articulation' is used to analyse British liberalism and Italian Fascism (Hall's and Mercer's chapters in Donald and Hall 1986). More specifically, the concept of 'articulation' is seen as a crucial step in the understanding of media effects and some aspects of popular culture (so says Fiske 1989a). Some of the later work expresses the view that the Left can do the same trick, forge a new 'popular-democratic' discourse linking the traditional 'class-based' concerns with new trans-class issues of peace, civil liberty and women's rights, as we shall see.

In American work, the term 'articulation' is particularly ambiguous, however, in its relation to gramscianism on the one hand, and 'discourse theory' on the other (see Chapter 2). When analysts like Grossberg (Giroux *et al.* 1989), or Kipnis (Maccabe 1986) use the term, they probably mean to suggest a greater distance from Gramsci than does Hall (see Grossberg 1986). It is hard to tell, though, since the relation to Gramsci is carried largely by a kind of 'hall of fame' approach, where Gramsci is merely a founding father of radical work.

Finally, 'elaborated' gramscianism arises from an attempt to incorporate some of the work of Foucault on power as an effect of certain discourses or 'disciplinary technologies'. A certain ambivalence greeted Foucault's work in gramscian circles (see Hall's footnote 97 in his opening piece in Hall *et al.* 1980: 286, and his interview with Grossberg 1986). Initially it seemed possible to stave off (or ignore at least) the anti-marxist implications and see disciplinary technologies as merely elaborating, or extending and diversifying, the network of power in the hegemonic project to normalise the pro-capitalist person. One particular application of this idea is considered in Chapter 8 in the work of Hargreaves on sport as a disciplinary technology. Whether such elaborations amplify and rescue gramscianism, or simply quietly replace it in practice while retaining a polite deference to former colleagues, will be discussed there too. The argument closely resembles the eventual settlement with feminism: the effort to achieve some theoretical integration gives way to a more tactful political alliance of like-minded critics, a coalition of different approaches united only by their opposition to the status quo.

CONCLUSION

Whatever the abstract theoretical or political merits and shortcomings of these debates, and of gramscianism's position in them, (discussed in more detail in subsequent chapters), it is useful to remember that these modifications and extensions take place in a definite context of academic struggle. I want to suggest that these debates are best understood not as a long-term coherent policy to reread and rethink gramscian concepts in the light of new developments, but as a more localised and tactical adaptation to specific pressures and controversies developed rather unevenly in different academic fields. Still more extensive renovations of gramscianism were to follow, as the next chapter reveals.

2

FLOATING SIGNIFIERS

INTRODUCTION

The enrichment by discourse theory discussed in the previous chapter helps the gramscians unlock the secret of Thatcherism, to their own satisfaction at least, but it also marks a phase in a longer relation with emerging trends in structuralist and then post-structuralist linguistics. There was a need to open dialogues with these traditions for good academic reasons, one might suggest, as well as some micropolitical ones, no doubt, since earlier work on youth cultures had run into difficulties in specifiying the actual mechanisms of the transmission of identities and ideologies. Some borrowed concepts like 'homology' or 'convergences' or 'coding and decoding' had been pressed into service to explain the relations between lived experiences and the details of actual meaning systems or ideologies, but these were limited and in danger of looking banal, circular, or 'asymmetric' in the words of an early critique (Murdock and McCron in Hall and Jefferson 1976). It was one thing to be able to trace back cultures, curricula or media messages to the alleged deeper interests of those who constructed them, but this strategy failed to develop any predictive or 'progressive' impetus, and looked rather deterministic in linguistic terms.

This critique remains to haunt the work, I shall suggest, but it is possible to see a recognition of the difficulty as leading to an interest in structural linguistics, which apparently did concern itself with the *generation* of meanings from a given set of structural possibilities. The search for a 'proper theory of signification' as it might be termed, looked as if it might well lead to a fully rounded account of ideology. However, the search would have unintended and ironic consequences, as we shall see.

DEBATES WITH DISCOURSE THEORIES

Again, the details of some aspects of the story will be considered in the specific chapters which follow, but an outline of some of the issues seems appropriate here. One struggle with one version of discourse theory has been mentioned already in the debate with the 'screen theorists'. Hall says that the Media Group at CCCS were determined to close with the issues raised by 'screen theory' and did so during 1977–8 (Hall's introduction to Hall *et al.* 1980). 'Screen theory', it will be recalled, was emerging as a major rival to cultural studies. The CCCS work tried to reuse a version of the argument that had been pressed into service against idealism and against some sociological work, especially symbolic interactionism. Briefly, the discourse theorists were accused of linguistic reductionism, and the systematic exclusion of powerplays. Their attempts to depict universal linguistic forms merely 'naturalised' particular types of linguistic behaviour which bore hidden within them the effects of 'struggle'. However, just as with the debates with Althusser, much of this sort of argument avoided what might be called the 'epistemological' thrust of discourse theory – the radical challenge posed to attempts to find some non-discursive 'reality' rooted in a 'given' (class) struggle, to rehearse the terms used in the McLennan *et al.* quote in Chapter 1.

Hindess and Hirst, for example, had already gone on from their Althusserian phases to develop a version of discourse theory that was to establish a very broad range of critical targets. Moving from the Althusserian insistence that knowledge was produced not from a correct relation between subject and object, discourse theory of this kind proposed that all self-styled 'sciences' be ruthlessly dissected to establish whether or not the central concepts were being deployed consistently and according to their own version of logical rigour. No existing sciences stood up to this rigorous examination, in fact, neither bourgeois nor marxist versions. All used concepts either 'incoherently' or 'dogmatically', and, in a critique which was to act as the 'trojan horse' (Crook 1991) for postmodernist scepticism, Hindess and Hirst argued that the very structure of many of these sciences was suspect, involving a dubious 'foundational' claim for privileged concepts, and relying on a fundamentally religious metaphor, whereby social life has a surface and a depth, at the very heart of their claims to scientificity.

One particular encounter with gramscianism is revealing. In a symposium on social class (Hunt 1977), Hirst raised doubts about the very concept of 'relative autonomy' claiming to find in it a classic example of incoherence, and pointing out how easily the term lent itself to evasiveness. How could a level be both autonomous and yet still determined, even in the last instance? Hall's reply insists on the need to explore the notion and counterposes a supposed empirical complexity to Hirst's insistence on logical rigour, but Hirst's general question was never really answered – how could we interrogate empirical complexity except through a coherent discourse about it?

The same example featured in a debate between Geras and Laclau and Mouffe, with a similarly inconclusive confusion of the grounds of argument: Geras claimed at one stage that he had given an empirical example of relative autonomy (Geras 1988), but Laclau and Mouffe (1987) were raising questions about how the terms 'autonomy' and 'determination' were being defined in the debate, partly to make the point that empirical examples require some attention to linguistic practices, even if it is only to matters of definition.

It should be clear by now that, once again, gramscians were applying to join a club that was not sure it really wanted them, that they had tried to solve one crisis in their work, only to find themselves on the verge of another. It was no longer easy to be a linguistic theorist, or to just 'bolt on' linguistics to 'enrich' a basically marxist project.

Hebdige's work (1979) tells a similar story but with a slightly different linguistic skirmish (discussed in more detail in Chapter 4 below). Barthes' work had looked once as if it were assimilable with marxism, and it had also seemed to fit with the existing 'literary' methods of the founders of cultural studies at the Birmingham Centre. However, Barthes' work developed away from marxism, with a shift towards a concern in linguistic theory with the signifier and not the signified, with the 'floating' or 'slipping' signifier, that is (briefly) the realisation that meaning was produced by signifiers relating to other signifiers and not to some fixed 'object' or social practice.

One consequence of this trend was to dethrone the notion of one specific 'centred' reading of cultural events or styles, including the reading that saw culture as a matter of ideology, as being fixed, however subtly and relatively autonomously, by some past class struggle. With the new flexibility in 'reading' the text, the search for (linguistic) pleasure rather than ideological enlightenment comes to the fore as a political force too, with consequences which will become clear. These developments seemed to undermine the old concepts of ideology, the 'real' and the 'phenomenal' levels and so on, although later gramscians managed to try to incorporate some of the implications into a new politics of pleasure. Nevertheless, linguistics proved to be an energetic tiger to have to try to hold by the tail.

POST-MARXISM

The incipient slide from marxism can be detected in a number of other areas too, most disappointingly of all, perhaps, in the defection of Laclau and Mouffe to a 'post-marxist' version of discourse theory that looked remarkably like the British versions that had caused so much trouble already. Now, discourses constituted the being of all objects, or, in a phrase that must have sounded mockingly familiar to those veteran British readers familiar with the 'social phenomenology' that had once had to be seen off as 'idealist', all around us was 'socially constructed' (Laclau and Mouffe 1987). This process of construction could be grasped as a material process, as with 'screen theory' earlier, this time coupled with a claim to have transcended the old stale dichotomies between materialism and idealism.

The whole of marxism had to be reassessed in terms of this insight – and, largely, rejected. Marxism seemed to work with an inadequate theoretical apparatus, a causal, positivist one, or an essentialist/dualist one with social life being seen as an 'expressive totality', 'sutured' by some underlying defining central process. Marxist politics failed to grasp the emergence of new pluralist political discourses developed far away from the conditions of social polarisation and revolution, which Marx had seen as a necessary basis of politics.

Gramsci was still the marxist who had come the closest to realising the need to develop a suitable version, but, in the end, even he had to have his thought completed. Nevertheless, what were once faults in the gramscian opus for Althusserians are now signs of acceptability for the post-marxists, especially the realisation that social practices were hegemonic and articulatory. This kind of materialism openly embraces the 'radical historicity of being' instead of having to apologise for it as in the old bad days of 'marxist science'.

Now, the whole ground of politics depended on the existence of a suitable discourse to turn a mere subordination into an active antagonism (a sense of difference into a sense of oppression, to borrow a phrase from feminism). Political action depended upon embracing the plurality of discourses introduced by the destabilisng tendencies of capitalism and choosing a suitable organising discourse to mobilise collective opposition. But choice could not be guided by some non-discursive 'foundational' facts or inevitabilities: '[there are] no intrinsically anti-capitalist struggles, although a [any?] set of struggles. . .could become anti-capitalist' (Laclau and Mouffe 1987: 104).

Politically at least, the post-marxist project looks very much like some recent work in leisure studies, which also operates with a plurality of dispersed 'subject positions', and is inclined to see any form of struggle or antagonism as politically significant. Here though, this kind of struggle is permanent, thanks to an inbuilt and inevitable (dysfunctional one might say) lack of control over consumption and the pleasure of the body (for example, see Fiske 1989b). For Laclau and Mouffe, any basis for struggle is even more abstract and lies in the necessary 'partial opaqueness of the social' (Laclau and Mouffe 1987: 106).

Naturally, not all marxists were able to agree that marxism had been outdated, and Hall argued, rather briefly and simply, that Laclau and

Mouffe had gone too far (in Hall 1985, and in Grossberg 1986). Geras wrote two articles that were highly critical of post-marxism which might help us reconstruct a fuller gramscian retort, however. The issues of marxist scholarship and the different readings of the likes of Lenin or Luxemburg need not detain us here, but Geras was able to offer three arguments of significance for the future development of gramscianism as it edged towards post-marxism.

First, post-marxism diffuses and dilutes 'politics' to mean almost any antagonism, of the kind which arise wherever there are rival discourses: arguments between neighbours on the one hand, or, equally, the politics of 'slavery, apartheid, concentration camps' on the other (Geras 1987: 77). Geras says that Laclau and Mouffe are forced to smuggle in other criteria to deny this trivialising tendency, to borrow the language of marxism, of all things, specifically to commend 'progressive' rather than 'insignificant' politics and so on. We shall see Fiske using a similar strategy, and 'enriched gramscianism' displaying a similar ambiguity.

Second, a (linked) theoretical void lies at the heart of discourse theory, seen best in its attempt to reject all kinds of essentialism. For one thing, discourse theory is itself essentialist (a similar point is made by Crook about Hindess and Hirst – Crook 1991), since it claims that discourse constitutes all being.

Third, the heart of the gramscian enrichment, the notion of 'articulation', is also incoherent for Geras: briefly, the issue is whether the connections between the elements in an articulatory practice are merely contingent or somehow necessary. The former option allows elements to have some being outside of the discursive practice that articulates them, while the latter assumes the meaning of the articulated elements is already given by their relationship, and this, apart from being essentialist, makes the articulating practice redundant (Geras 1987: 67–71). A version of this objection can also be levelled against gramscian accounts of Thatcherism, which can seem to oscillate betwen 'organic' and 'arbitrary' accounts of the nature of Thatcherite discourse, and is unsure whether the connections between, say, 'Englishness' and 'conservatism' are established inside or outside of a Thatcherite discourse (the confusion is demonstrated best, perhaps in the closing sections of *Policing the Crisis,* as we shall see).

Geras suggests that these voids are camouflaged by a number of devices, some of which will look familiar in the detailed accounts of gramscian argument which follow. Smuggling in concepts that have allegedly been criticised, from disciplines that are supposed to be abandoned, has been mentioned (see the section in Chapter 1 on the debate with sociology, for example). Geras also refers to a tendency to use exaggerated or overgeneralised accounts of arguments so that all general concepts in the discipline to be critiqued must be essentialist. Similarly grotesque 'straw men' holding hopelessly naive positions can also be found in gramscianism's hall of infamy, especially, perhaps, when addressing 'critical theory'.

There is a version of 'asymmetry' in Laclau's and Mouffe's attempt to work backwards from where they want to be, to read past theories as 'weak anticipations. . .[of a]. . .currently fashionable idea' (Geras 1987: 59). There is a certain flexibility, often introduced by means of a neologism or oxymoronic phrase ('regularity in dispersion' for Laclau and Mouffe) which is 'tailor made for facing all ways simultaneously' (*ibid*: 71). As we have seen, 'relative autonomy', and possibly 'struggle', or 'authoritarian populism', can be seen as similarly dubious.

There is a delicate, indirect, glancing, or coded way of dealing with criticism, rather than point-for-point disputation, and a tendency to shift levels of debate, to offer (in the case of Laclau's and Mouffe's reply) a 'theory of discourses' rather than an actual discourse in reply (Geras 1988: 51). There are 'gestures' towards problems, and qualifications, rather than, say, 'desiderata of explanatory adequacy' (in the case of choosing among different hegemonic practices – Geras 1987: 73). As a number of pieces in the debates also show, including the Geras/Laclau and Mouffe interchange, there is also personal abuse, *ad hominem* remarks, accusations of betrayal or fading vigour, in a spirit of generational revolt, and a knowing sense of which way the wind is blowing:

> Everyone who knows where it's really at these days will know that Gramsci just has to win. . .[the contest for most promising marxist]. . .because in a certain relevant left milieu, he confers a moral and intellectual [and academic?] legitimacy.
>
> (*ibid*: 61)

Geras even suggests that the massive effort to gramscianise new work can be the result of wanting to cover a break with one's past allegiances: 'The mantle of Gramsci is vital to a pair of ex-Marxists so they may appear to represent themselves as post-Marxists' (*ibid*: 65). Laclau and Mouffe reply, very acutely, that this is because marxists are particularly prone to see every departure as a 'betrayal', quite unlike bourgeois philosophy, say, where Hegel is not usually accused of 'betraying' Kant!

This discussion will not use terms like 'betrayal', although it is important to identify all the argumentative manoeuvres, not just the rational academic ones. One manoeuvre found especially in academic debates, and sometimes seen at conferences, for example, is a disarming modesty. This is displayed well in written form in one of the interventions in the debate with Jessop *et al.* about Thatcherism, where Hall gives as one of the reasons for developing an admittedly over-ideological account of 'authoritarian populism' an apparently harmlessly scholarly ambition to add a 'sort of footnote to Gramsci's "Modern Prince" and "State and Civil Society"' (Hall 1985: 119), much as an elderly professor might devote his life to a neglected poem. Hall goes on to explain that he felt he just 'happen[ed] to have some competence in that area', although he also feels the political and ideological level of analysis has been neglected by 'the left', so the project was not that academic and innocent! Hall's work also features a number of endearing pedagogical homilies about needing to 'learn lessons', or trying to 'bend the twig', although the same writer is not above more abrasive references to his opponents as 'loony', as offering 'polite intellectual terrorism', or trying to hustle and blackmail (Hall in Alvarado and Thompson 1990: 21).

POSTMODERNISM: A PLAIN PERSON'S GUIDE

The sort of discussion that concluded the section above shows that arguments and debates associated with gramscianism are not always rational or 'philosophical' in the old sense. At strategic moments, a series of techniques that are perhaps best described as 'rhetorical' are deployed to convince the reader. In one tradition of scholarship, these sorts of arguments are deplorable signs of 'camouflage' or evasion, as in the attacks launched by Geras, but again, by one of those strange reversals of value, the same characteristics could promote gramscianism to the very vanguard of postmodernist theory and aesthetics.

Some gramscians seem happy for this to be so, especially in cultural studies (or these days 'communication studies') perhaps: Hebdige's *Hiding in the Light* (Hebdige 1988), or Chambers' *Popular Culture: The Metropolitan Experience* (Chambers 1986) embraces most visibly this new vanguardism in the very layout of the books (and Hebdige's witty introduction on the impossibility of writing books any more has already been cited). Writing an essay, a magazine article, or some other 'fragment', rather than a book is the way to do cultural studies these days. As we shall see, the decline of the authorial voice has also brought with it a more free-wheeling descriptive style, a glossy rhetoric, and a certain 'slipperiness of pronouns' as author and audience cheerfully swap identities (but only in the narrative, of course).

Marxism Today represents another kind of dethronement of the old academic rigour and political 'earnestness', a break into guilt-free consumerism. There is an uneven development of the break even here, though, and some residues remain from the old 'modernist' era: the academic world in particular is not yet ready for postmodernist course materials or assessment schemes. And any reader who has followed this account thus far will be able to predict that there will be one major marxist writer from the old era who will emerge from the postmodernist onslaught pretty well unscathed.

Giving a full description and analysis of 'postmodernism' is clearly beyond the scope of this book and its author, of course. There are several excellent introductions to the debates by now in any case (Foster 1986, Crook 1991, Kaplan 1987, Featherstone 1991, the *Theory, Culture and Society* special – see Denzin 1988, for example). It seems that Lyotard (1986) is the most commonly read formulation of the postmodernist crisis for social science (and Jameson's Introduction in that book is popular too). The discussion here will be fixed by the body of gramscian material which is our main interest: the main question will be how did the gramscians respond to aspects of the postmodern critique of sociology and marxism, and how can we discuss and evaluate their response on their own terrain, as it were?

In general, the impact of postmodernism can be described as posing certain radical doubts about a number of organising assumptions which lie at the heart of 'modernist radicalism', and gramscianism in particular, for our purposes. Some of these issues have been prefigured already in the debates about linguistics and its connection with marxism in Geras and Laclau and Mouffe above, and this might be one way to introduce a more general debate about postmodernism.

Margolis (1989), for example, argues that there are two questions involved – the notion of 'privileged' knowledge or concepts forming some sort of foundation for analysis, and the issue of whether or not there is anything outside of discourse. In a densely argued contribution, he goes on to suggest that the two questions are not necessarily linked. For example, one can admit to 'constative discourse' (where there is something outside of language), without necessarily subscribing to some privileged knowledge. As another example, particular readings may now have to abandon claims to having privileged foundations – but they must still try to legitimate their generalisations. Further, if postmodernism is to develop beyond a mere iconoclasm, it too will have to face issues of legitimation of its readings. Otherwise it will descend into mere linguistic anarchy (Lyotard's solution according to Margolis – and see Sims 1986: 10 on Lyotard's 'aimlessness or at worst opportunism'). Liberal complacency and a 'laissez-faire' agreement to work uncritically, in a coalition, one might say, with the existing theoretical systems of analysis is another option (Rorty's solution, says Margolis).

Crook takes us further along lines like these, and defines the issues as raising significant doubts about both the object and the theory of 'modernist radicalism'. The first doubt arises from a rejection of the view that 'the social' (especially the old social order of capitalism) exists any longer. Generally, social transformation, arising from the new technology, the new electronic information handling, and the decline of the old productive industries in capitalist societies have produced a novel 'postindustrial' society with the decline of the old social classes and the emergence of newer formations (see Foster 1986 especially).

Baudrillard is taken as a particularly insistent critic of the classic notion of the social. As the very clear discussion of his work in Chen (1987) and

Kellner (1987) explains, Baudrillard's view is that the social and political dimensions of life have vanished as individuals suffer from a surfeit of communication and withdraw into a kind of deviant passivity and indifference. The image of social reality on the TV screen, a mere simulation, becomes merged with reality itself – a kind of mass culture theory without the hope, as Kellner puts it. This 'implosion' follows as an ironic and irreversible consequence of the explosion of the mass media and the information industries. 'Society' remains alive only in the activities of opinion pollsters and demographers who do not merely study it, but actively construct it.

More generally, Crook suggests that

> the view has gained currency that the really big problems are not social but involve the interpenetration of natural, technical, signifying and psychic processes. . .[so]. . .'the social' risks being left in the cold.
>
> (Crook 1991: 6)

As Bauman argues, intellectuals dealing with the social lose their influence (Bauman 1987). Intellectuals are also threatened by the predicted decline of the university in Lyotard. Mrs Thatcher's famous dictum that 'there is no such thing as society', and her government's campaigns against social sciences as subjects in higher education, seem to be in respectable theoretical company after all.

Radical social theory gets into trouble, argues Crook, since it began with claims to offer radical new departures from the old ways of thinking about social life (especially merely 'philosophical' or 'ideological' ones). However, as with our discussion of the limited nature of 'breaks' in Chapter 1, a closer examination shows such theory still to be deeply entangled with the old metaphysics or metanarratives (and here Lyotard and Derrida are used as illustrations of the critique), or with the old concerns with social order and discipline. Here, Foucault's notion of social theory as just another of the possible forms of power/knowledge, rather than as some uniquely liberating discourse, emerges strongly.

The apparently special unity of theory and practice in radical theory is supposed to counter some of these objections: the flight to politics or to praxis can appear as a welcome solution to intractable theoretical dilemmas, as we have seen. Radicals claim to be able to guide social change in a suitably 'progressive' direction, avoiding at last the pitfalls of partial changes (in both senses of the word partial). However this relevance to practice or politics still involves a foundationalism – 'claims to have secured guarantees which grant a unique discursive privilege' – in political debate (Crook 1991: 28). This inevitably redirects attention back to the underlying metaphysics or metanarratives in such claims. Radical theories like those of Habermas and Althusser (and gramscianism above all!) try to reduce these

38

embarrassments to the minimum, says Crook, but ultimately fail to avoid altogether these interconnected critiques.

These powerful critiques make a simple absorption of postmodern critique into a radical social theory impossible, even though there can be a superficial similarity with modernist critiques and themes. Foucault in particular was once read as an ally of marxist theory, especially Gramsci's – see Smart (1983) for the most relevant reading of this kind. Dews (1984) suggests that this reading fits best with Foucault's work on discipline and punishment, but that this 'marxist' phase did not last and soon gave way to a fully discursive position.

The postmodernists have been critiqued in their turn, of course, in a number of ways. Postmodernism has been seen largely as a conjunctural development, for example, rather than as a permanent trend (Anderson 1984), as a phenomenon largely explicable in terms of the development of consumer capitalism (Jameson's and allied criticisms are well summarised in Urry 1990), or as a new metanarrative (Callinicos 1985: 96) or as riddled with metaphysics (Ree 1984) of its own. Many critics have pointed to the largely uncritical way in which the postmodernists have accepted the 'postindustrial' theses of earlier sociologists, with their technological determinism or reductionist theories of social change (usually a version of the 'knowledge explosion'). Baudrillard's view of the unmediated bad effects of the media is also startlingly old-fashioned, as we shall see.

Crook is sceptical of many of the critiques, seeing in them a danger that materialism will simply be reasserted, but he holds no brief for post-modernism either, arguing that it is both monist and nihilist. Monisms can be 'physicalist' or 'discursive', but both types involve 'some single principle of world production' (Crook 1991: 18), whether this be some physical mechanism (as in Baudrillard's 'tropes' about explosion and implosions), or some pre-given model of discourse (as in Hindess and Hirst).

Nihilism (basically, an inability to give an account of one's position) arises from the undifferentiated nature of this monism: there is no structured basis for change (e.g. no hope in Baudrillard). Alternatively, if change is posited as integral to the monist substance in question (say in a structured and necessary 'micropolitics'), there is no way of saying what counts as desirable change (or at least no formal way – there is always 'smuggling' as we have discussed it above): 'no reasons can be adduced for engaging in socialist rather than, say, fascist, discourse' (*ibid*: 160). For Crook, the 'foundationalism' in both modernism and postmodernism is the real obstacle to progress and has to be overcome.

GRAMSCI: FIRST PAST THE POST?

When we turn to the reaction to postmodernism in gramscian thought, we have several possibilites. One sort of response is found in Hebdige (1988,

Chapter 8). Briefly, Hebdige sees postmodernism as working with three 'negations'.

First, there is the negation of totalitarianism, both theoretical and political, a negation which extends to include some sociological systems, and the old totalitarian marxist regimes. Second comes the negation of teleology and foundationalism, and all those theoretical systems that depend on privileged concepts and surface-depth metaphors as discussed above, and on claims to authorship/authority. Postmodernists shift to linguistics, information theory and communications as of interest 'in themselves' as it were, as constitutive. A postmodern style, involving parody, simulation, pastiche and allegory, helps to efface teleology, 'depth' and authorship. Lacan and Derrida are the main examples cited of these 'decentring', 'unfixed' accounts of subjectivity, identity and language.

Finally, there is a negation of utopia, criticised as involving a reduction of linguistic complexity. The target here is an approach like Habermas's alleged pursuit of the 'ideal speech act' as a linguistically transparent utopia, where all misunderstandings can be talked out and only the better argument prevails. There is a denial that there will ever be a social 'transparency', to use terms in Laclau and Mouffe, or that one day social life will be free from alienation, social division and ideology (as in, say, the communist utopia in the *Manifesto* – Marx and Engels 1950).

Discourse theory revisited

Sound as it is technically, Hebdige's summary tends to see postmodernism as a kind of revamped discourse theory, and this helps him locate it very much on the familiar ground of already developed gramscian responses. Hebdige seems to be echoing earlier struggles by the CCCS Media Group in particular to fight off linguistic imperialism in discourse theory. Specifically, Hall's 'critical note' (Hall *et al.* 1980) argued that screen theory attempts to exploit a number of mere homologies between Lacanian psychoanalysis and Althusserian theories of ideology, so as to claim the transcendental importance of the former. Earlier, Burniston and Weedon (CCCS 1978) had borrowed from the work of Kristeva to attack Lacan as falsely universalist: briefly, the moment of entry into language is not the crucial moment in the determination of human subjectivity for Kristeva. There is an earlier pre-symbolic phase, one which is not dominated by patriarchal symbolism, moreover.

Other pieces attempted the same sort of argument to reintroduce class struggles as outside of, yet somehow implicit in, linguistic behaviour. Morley, for example, (in Hall *et al.* 1980) wanted to argue for the existence of empirical audiences and subjects which are not coterminous with the 'subject positions' constructed by discourse. This looks very much like an 'empiricist' argument, though, an impression fostered by his use of (rather strange) empirical studies of the *Nationwide* audience – see his Unit 12 in *U203* (Open University 1982), and the discussion of the media audience in Chapter 8.

This sort of empiricism is easily dealt with by discourse theorists, though. Morley's argument against screen theory's specific reduction of meaning to an encounter between one audience and one text might be criticised in this way, but not all discourse theory neglects 'interdiscourse' or 'intertextuality' (briefly, the contexts and meanings provided by other discourses or texts). Derrida's approach, so Weedon *et al.* tell us (in Hall *et al.* 1980), fully accepts that subjects are constituted in a number of textualities – but still there is no other source for subjectivity outside texts as such.

Marxist linguistics

Other linguists are preferred who acknowledge the centrality of social struggle in the very constitution of language – Pecheux, Volosinov, Bakhtin. Callinicos (1985) gives a particularly good account of how one might use Bakhtin, and more modern linguistic theorists, to overcome postmodern objections to a non-discursive context. Here again, though, it is not always clear what is being claimed for these 'struggles' and the 'subjects' who conduct them. Empiricism seems to lurk here too. Macdonnell's account of an empirical experiment by Pecheux demonstrating 'struggle' (Macdonnell 1986) reminds us of Morley's empirical work and is open to the same objections and counters.

Similarly, the fascinating article by Woolfson (CCCS 1976) summarises Volosinov and attempts to ground his concepts (especially 'multiaccentuality') in an empirical anlaysis based on a transcript of a discussion between some Glasgow workers. One of the objections launched by Tolson, though, (also in CCCS 1976) is to reassert that these subjects are themselves constituted in discourse.

Indeed, Tolson goes on to suggest that Woolfson (and possibly even Volosinov) locates 'struggle' in terms of the discredited 'scientific marxism' with its laws of development, its dialectics based in Engels, its old base/superstructure split. This is certainly the way Woolfson reads Volosinov, who was writing, after all, in the 1930s in the Soviet Union.

Certainly to return to a point made earlier by Laclau and Mouffe, it is not all that clear that 'struggle' is an independent entity entirely outside of discourse – indeed, it is easy enough to reply that it requires a discourse to make it an antagonism, as it were, as opposed to a mere misunderstanding or difference. To cite another argument in the same debate it is not made clear why these linguists want to prioritise class struggle, and not other linguistic struggles between other parties – or individuals for that matter (the empirical work by Morley and Pecheux did highlight non-class groups, and Woolfson's focused on individuals). Individual utterances clearly do refer to social contexts beyond the level of the individual sign, and thus invoke an interdiscourse and a potential 'struggle' between speakers, but then every use of a context-dependent term could be dignified with the title 'struggle'. The term works tactically, perhaps, to gloss the hoped-for process whereby individual or local semiotic struggles escalate into a struggle for hegemony.

More persuasive is the view that particular empirical subjects may have different repertoires of discourses (Morley's second argument in his piece in Hall *et al.* 1980). Different repertoires will soon lead us to social class as a determinant of those repertoires. This may be too reductive, limiting and sociologistic, though, for modern political priorities (see Ang's discussion in Seiter *et al.* 1989). Much gramscian argument seems content just to announce that certain Russian linguists have argued that struggle is constitutive, and Lacan or Derrida shown to be partial, thus achieving some kind of tactical draw.

Finally, it is worth noting that Weedon *et al.* placed their faith in Foucault to provide some anchor for the otherwise free-floating signifier in disciplinary practices or power/knowledge forms. The same mooring appears in Bennett too (see his *Introduction* to Bennett *et al.* 1986). As argued above, though, not everyone agrees that Foucault can be just added on to marxism. As Smart says, one of the doubters is Hall himself.

Hebdige certainly wants to see 'struggle' as an essential feature of an adequate semiotics. The apparent incapacity of the subject to live outside of the text in postmodernism shows only that a successful 'war of position' has already 'articulated' the class subject, and Hall's work on Thatcherism is shown to be exemplary. A new phase for the politics of struggle on a linguistic and political front is permitted, and Gramsci restored via the concept of hegemony.

Postmodernising Gramsci

However, Hebdige realises the difficulty too. Only one aspect of postmodernism's critique has been addressed – the issue of 'constative discourse'. What of 'privilege'? There is a danger of anchoring the new optimism to the old notion of a 'master narrative' of working-class emancipation again, or to the deployment of privileged concepts like 'hegemony' and 'war of position' which promise some sort of determination of linguistic and cultural phenomena. There is a danger too of slipping back into a surface-depth metaphor, with the apparent linguistic harmony on the surface only concealing some world-constituting 'struggle' in the deep. It could be that in this respect, the gramscian retort is, like some others, not really a retort at all, but the mere reassertion of a position despite the weight of criticism directed against it, reflecting a desire to 'go on as if nothing had happened', an engagement with some of the substantive issues in postmodernism, but not with the crucial general negations with which Hebdige began.

Hebdige knows that Gramsci cannot really be dressed as a post-modernist, and admits there are problems. There is one solution left:

> The retention of the old marxist terms should not be allowed to obscure the extent to which many of these terms have been transformed – wrenched away from the 'scientific' moorings constructed in the Althusserian phase. . .[Now] nothing is anchored to. . .fixed and certain meanings. . .everything appears to be in flux. . .[H]egemony is a precarious 'moving equilibrium'. . .Within this model there is no 'science' to be opposed to the monolith of ideology, only prescience; an alertness to possibility and [the] emergence. . .[of]. . .fragile unities which. . .act to interpellate and bond together new imaginary communities. . .marxism. . .has gone under. . .and yet it is a marxism which has survived, returning perhaps a little lighter on its feet. . .more prone. . .to appreciate. . .that words like 'emergency' and 'struggle' don't just mean fight, conflict, war and death but birthing, the prospect of a new life emerging: a struggling to the light.
>
> (Hebdige 1988: 206-7)

This extraordinary passage could be interpreted in less lyrical terms, of course, as saving gramscianism, but only by giving it a licence for opportunism, a survivor's marxism indeed. The concepts are deployed here deliberately as a 'game', perhaps, as Geras suspected of Laclau and Mouffe. Hebdige is perhaps not seriously defending Gramsci, but performing a playful 'trumping of a communicational adversary' (Lyotard 1986: xi), as an academic equivalent to the jokes and tricks so much admired by Fiske. His plea is perhaps a tactic designed to cock a snook at a strongly established postmodernist strategy, and thus to keep the old project alive a bit longer.

Gramscianism is again an ideology in this account, though still an uncompleted one (but at least Hebdige spares us the news that we are just beginning again). His relentlessly cheerful and optimistic remaining chapters bring us the good news that postmodernism can be fun, even for progressives, with lots of new social movements about. In this Hebdige squares with the hedonism of Fiske and the whole 'new times' enterprise, and, indeed, he appears again in the Hall and Jacques collection (1989).

However, his attempt to write a happy ending and narrative closure for gramscianism as a force in politics and cultural studies opens up questions yet again. At the very least his readers will want to ask those repressed Althusserian (but also common-sensical) questions: whose interests does gramscianism now represent, now it is an ideology? Why should we prefer it to other ideologies, and what exactly is its practico-social function?

To be even blunter, and to inject a methodological note, it is clear that gramscian concepts can be deployed tactically in a discussion of postmodernism – but why should anyone want to? The concepts are tactically useful because they are ambiguous – a floating referent apologetically identified by Anderson helps Hebdige claim that hegemony is a fashionable floating signifier. Ambiguity can keep old concepts in business for ever – but is this a sufficiently positive basis to think out a new situation (or even to regenerate a research programme, to put it in pragmatic academic terms)? To refer back to Hall's reply to Jessop *et al.* cited above, is it now personal, theoretical or political motives that produce this desire to postmodernise Gramsci?

A measure of what is missed by the insistence on the deployment of the old concepts in the old problematic is provided by the emergence of journals like *Theory Culture and Society* (*TCS*) or the development of cultural studies in the USA (Angus and Jhally 1989, for example). *TCS* does not feel it has to police new developments in the name of gramscianism, or to keep the faith with the old terminology, and its own editions have deployed the work of Elias, Simmel, Durkheim and critical theory (for example) to launch analyses and debates. Angus and Jhally are similarly open and refreshing: one gramscian account is included, but the collection lacks that closure and predictability, that conformity and self-referentialism that we find in British gramscian work.

Gramscianism has been forced to supplement the creaking edifice it has constructed, in cultural studies at least, with new linguistic blood. Again, one can not help but feel there is a certain asymmetry again in the enlistment of the likes of Volosinov/Bakhtin (or Pecheux) to the cause: linguistic resources are being sought that will endorse the priority of 'struggle', fit best with a pre-ordained gramscian world-view that must not be challenged or developed, rather than offering a basis to understand modern culture (precisely the distortion likely in excessively partisan approaches, according to Adorno, as we have seen in Chapter 1). 'Struggle' must come first: despite postmodernism, gramscianism retains its metaphysical centre.

Post-fordism: the gramscianisation of postmodernism

It is possible to see post-fordism as a solution to the problems raised by discourse theory again, this time in a particular political setting. Following the rejection of the 'juridical' notion of power and the new emphasis on 'micropolitics' in Foucault, an equivalent of a 'floating signifer' crisis affected radical politics – what was politics, or rather, what was not? Could politics be fixed to any particular practice, or was it to be diluted to such an extent that organised parties or movements became unnecessary or redundant? Answers in the gramscian camp varied, with the 'cultural studies' wing offering the most relaxed view of dilute politics, as we shall see (sometimes bolstered by an 'escalation' scenario whereby dilute politics coalesced into a 'proper political' challenge).

For the analysts of Thatcherism, still embroiled in conventional party politics, some way to 'fix' politics was required. Jessop (1982) discusses one approach – 'derivation theory', which suggests that the flux of politics in capitalism can be fixed by some basic limits set by the logic of capital accumulation, or of class rule. This sort of derivation model became important in debates about the 'Eurocommunist' option in Britsh circles – and, academically, in the work of Picciotto and others (see, for example, Holloway and Picciotto 1978).

Post-fordism arose from a different solution, according to Rustin (1989) – that offered by the 'French regulationists'. This option is best seen, perhaps, as a kind of 'production-derivation' theory. Gramsci was among the first to realise (and Weber, but we have broken with him) that 'Fordism' was a new phenomenon, embracing not only a new mode of mass production, but the need for a new kind of social discipline, a new man [sic] to work in the new conditions. A loose form of economic determinism is suggested by this formulation, and a new metaphor – 'regulation' – giving due allowance for religious, social and even sexual practices.

Mouzelis suggests that another function is served by such a formulation too, although he does not use the term post-fordism as such – the need for an institutional structure to ground the kind of post-marxist discourse theory we have discussed earlier, as a kind of 'middle ground' between fully floating discursive politics and more orthodox class politics, an intermediate 'mode of domination' to 'guard against the study of economic, political and cultural phenomena in a compartmentalised, contextless or ad hoc manner' (Mouzelis 1988: 123).

Post-fordism involves a speculation about what happens when the predominant mode of production changes from mass production to more flexible forms (see Rustin 1989 for a list of the changes). The concept promised to revitalise gramscian analysis and manage some of the critiques of postmodernism on the political level at least: there is a way of bringing in something external to discourse (still seen as the main challenge, rather than the thornier issue of 'privilege'), and, at last, it becomes possible to steal some of the postmodernists' clothes on the issue of the new technology, the information revolution and so on.

Older marxist themes can be brought back in too, above all the notion of 'struggle'. Post-fordism can be struggled over, so to speak, and full advantage taken by the left of the new social movements and alliances it generates. Gramsci seemed to approve of Fordism as bringing a long-awaited modernisation to Italian society: at least there would be some change, at least Fordism would displace and annoy some of the old class enemies. The 'new times' socialists seem to have the same rather desperate longing for post-fordism. Change and struggle are back on the agenda. New movements have come along just in time to revitalise politics, and the ties to the traditional agents of change, the working class, can be quietly slipped at last, along with 'serious politics'. Cultural politics seems to have come into its own, as postmodernism has broken the old internal distinctions: now the task is to make all those changes line up, as it were, to politicise and lead them. If Hebdige offered a way to postmodernise Gramsci, post-fordism offers a way to gramscianise postmodernism.

CONCLUSION: FROM GRAMSCI TO GRAMSCIANISM

Gramscianism develops from aspects of Gramsci's work, symptomatically read, and often abstracted and thrice distilled. As a result, writers in collections can often repeat simple views that have been qualified elsewhere (as in the pieces that ignore the warnings of McLennan over Althusser in CCCS 1978), or cheerfully ignore readings that are 'unfortunate' (Finn *et al.*, referring to Gramsci's work on education in CCCS 1978). Those accounts of Gramsci which are not compatible can be left 'unpreferred' (see Gilroy in CCCS 1982 dismissing those who read Gramsci as advocating a popular front led by the working class, rather than a distinctively 'black' struggle). Gramscians can cite each other as offering a suitable discussion, rather like the 'man of the people' observed by Gramsci who has 'no concrete memory of the reasons. . .[for his beliefs] and could not repeat them, but he knows that reasons exist, because he has heard them expounded and was convinced by them' (Smith and Hoare 1971: 339). The theoretical wings of gramscianism do indeed offer serious and sustained intellectual scholarship and debate, even if often rather 'asymmetric', as we have seen, but for other writers in the more 'vulgar' wings, a rather ritualistic incantation of the special concepts of 'hegemony' or 'conjuncture' or 'levels' will suffice to legitimise the analysis and the activist politics which follow.

We have to look outside purely theoretical debates to explain the persistence of gramscianism, as a particularly suitable ideology. It is a 'centaur' indeed, as Gramsci hoped, but a centaur needing to reconcile particular and rather specialist opposites, largely drawn from familiar old social science. Anyone with any experience soon knows what these crucial opposites are, and can use them in critique: for every general formal theory, there must be a concrete, historical, practical, political or empirical 'opposite' which has been neglected; every dominant ideology has its points of resistance; every idealism its materialist counterpart; every dualism begets a monism; every settlement a struggle. Gramscianism can situate itself and defend its boundaries against allcomers for ever, given a certain ambiguity in the concepts and a certain tactical nimbleness. In academic terms, this makes it a most successful programme: why do the gramscians want to rebuke Thatcherism or social democracy for using the same sort of nimbleness?

In the course of our specific analyses we will see all the tactics mentioned above, from 'smuggling' to *ad hominem* abuse, including on the way agenda-setting (such as refusing to put Habermas or Bourdieu or Giddens on the agenda), insisting on having the last word and the right to summarise and order arguments, and the tactical pursuit of modesty and moderation. Variations include seeing all strongly argued positions as faulty and thus 'maliciously' equal (gramscianism may be wrong in parts, but so is screen theory or discourse theory, and anyway we all agree Lukács is worse, so let's just agree to disagree). There is also a habit of announcing a periodic and permanent beginning so that no one may evaluate the perspective by its results.

These tactics are not unique to gramscianism, nor are they particularly reprehensible. There is no moral critique or debunking intention here (or not much of one). The point is to argue that gramscianism bears the marks of its context: all theories have political, theoretical and personal *and institutional* aspects. These tactical features of the argument are indeed highly conventional, developed in the desperate struggle to maintain radical theory in highly conservative and competitive academic institutions.

The constraints and determinations located in this academic institutional context have to be grasped as important, however, in terms of the actual development of the project. The gramscians have largely ignored or glossed them in their own self-understandings. There is perhaps still a lingering reservation about the discussion of ideas focusing on anything outside the ideas themselves, but Geras is perfectly correct to suggest that 'intellectuals can be ready to explain the behaviours of the whole world but not. . .their own situation. . .as though they were beyond the pull of motives' (Geras 1988: 60). There is no need nor intention here to offer an account of weariness and betrayal as he does, however. Instead, the 'scandalous' story of the actual institutional contexts in which gramscians work will have to be told (in the final chapter) for a fully 'overdetermined' understanding.

3

STRUGGLE AND EDUCATION

INTRODUCTION

The emergence of a distinctive new left perspective in this area in Britain can be identified relatively clearly. In 1970, at a British Sociological Association Conference, the 'new sociology of education' was announced. The proceedings of the Conference led to the publication of a famous book (Young 1971), and a less famous one (Brown 1973). Some of the participants in the Conference were postgraduate students at the London Institute of Education, and two in particular were recruited to staff a new course in the sociology of education at the Open University (OU). The Education Faculty's course *School and Society (E282)* (Open University 1972) at the OU recruited very heavily among the generation of non-graduate teachers that the OU was designed initially to serve (Harris 1987).

OU courses had an influence even beyond the thousands of OU students who were taking them, and *E282* soon became the basis for many another sociology of education course in teacher training colleges. The 'new sociology of education' became widespread and well-established in a very short time.

The new perspectives were to be developed in a distinctive manner too, one which can be found in many of the areas discussed below in this book. An initial iconoclastic phase announced the new dawn with revolutionary fervour (and more than a hint of youthful rebellion against the earlier generation of 'old sociologists'). A period of uncertainty followed, during which the new approach came to be codified and regularised, and developed in response to early academic counter-criticism. In the third phase, a new well-organised narrative emerged, one which operated primarily to establish the credentials of the new approach with academic critics. Academic respectability, however, is a fragile plant that needs constant care, often so much so that it tends to displace all other goals, including the earlier popular activist intent.

As with other chapters in this book, it is going to be possible only to discuss examples of the wide range of work produced at each of these stages: I have decided to consider what I take to be the most representative and the most popular examples.

THE BREAK

The iconoclastic phase worked very effectively in the sociology of education, which had always been seen by other social scientists as a relatively unsophisticated and largely 'practical' discipline. Its main institutional base tended to be in teacher education, and there it had to struggle constantly against demands for immediate practical relevance to the exigencies of classroom life as they were. The sociology of education that existed in university departments escaped this professional domination, possibly, but sought to make itself useful in another direction – as the research wing of political parties interested in broad policies, and as the discipline that underwrote a number of influential (quasi-) government reports in the 1960s and 1970s. The price to be paid for this 'usefulness' was clear – the sociology of education was driven by immediate practical concerns, not too critical of existing practice at all levels, despite its support for reform, and barely able to generate any momentum of its own, so to speak. Of course, not everyone agrees with this account – see Ahier in Young and Whitty (1977).

At the institutional level, before the OU taught us otherwise, our courses were, as Swift was to argue (in *E282*, Open University 1972), perpetually introductory and apologetic, locked into an agenda set by others, never able to generate enough initial insight or experience into the discipline to offer students a decisive break with their 'professional' concerns or their 'common-sense' perceptions of their tasks. The new sociology of education was to 'make' its own problems and issues, not just 'take' them from others, to use Young's terms (in Young 1971), to ask its own questions and use its own concepts and methods to pursue them.

It is still a very appealing programme, of course, especially among those of us who have seen the wheel turn back to 'professional' courses in the most uncritical and bland sense in our teacher training institutions. As we shall see, the 'new' sociology of education, and its marxist heir, developed very acute critiques of educational institutions, ones that later gramscians would do well to consider.

The old and the new could be contrasted effectively by considering the school curriculum. The old sociology barely studied the curriculum at all, while the new placed it at the centre of its enquiries. An early piece (Young in Young 1971) argued that analysing the curriculum would offer a new insight into the old problems (classically the marked effects of 'social class' on educational achievement), by enquiring how these particular selections

49

from all the socially available knowledge came to be chosen and enshrined as 'proper' knowledge. This 'school knowledge' was obviously partisan knowledge, furthermore, which most of the clients found difficult to acquire because it reflected and encoded the values and interests of dominant groups.

Of course, enquiries into knowledge enabled the sociology of education to enter at last into the mainstream of social theory, and this promised to increase its status, at last, too. All the 'founding fathers' [*sic*] had an approach which could be developed, but the newly popularised work of Marx on ideology could be explored particularly. Other authors were available too, like Karl Mannheim, for example, who had tended to dominate the specialism of the sociology of knowledge in Britain, after his stay at the London School of Economics. There were also the newly fashionable American symbolic interactionists, ethnomethodologists and 'social phenomenologists' (the latter clustered around the work of Alfred Schutz).

It was clear too that Young was engaged in a struggle with his own colleagues at London University, especially those who were advocating some abstract 'philosophical' approach to curriculum, seeing school knowledge as derived somehow immediately from underlying universal categories of mind or forms of knowledge, or universal competencies (see Hirst or Phenix in Golby *et al.* 1975). Although this sort of approach did not necessarily ally itself directly with existing curricula, such efforts usually ended in apology for the status quo. The struggle with the philosophers led to famous exchanges in the pages of a journal (*Education for Teaching* – see White and Young 1975, for example), which in turn established a set of terms for discussion. Critical sociology found itself engaged in a secondary issue as critics in philosophy raised the crucial issue of the foundations of Young's position: in brief, the whole project was accused of 'relativism'.

The implications of social phenomenology were becoming apparent in these debates with the philosophers, and were proving embarrassing, as Demaine argues (1981). Social phenomenology is a perfectly respectable academic stance to take, of course, not without paradoxes and problems, but as a radical politics it presents problems.

Briefly, the phenomenological position left one with a lifeworld divided into 'multiple realities', for Schutz. Humans moved between these multiple realities as between discontinuous worlds, via 'leaps' or 'shocks' (Schutz 1971). One could simply 'leap' from the academic 'reality' of relativist critique to the 'reality' of committed politics. As with all human actions, such leaps were motivated. This position sounds rather more congenial to us in the 'postmodern' era than it did to radicals in the 1970s, however, who, taking their model of radical politics from Marxism, wanted a tight, structured link between theory and politics, with implications in the former committing one to action in the latter, almost despite one's individual motivation or will. This kind of 'foundationalism' was discussed in Chapter 2, via summaries like those in Crook (1991).

The paradoxes had become apparent much earlier, in the works of Mannheim too, of course: relativism, or, more precisely, what Mannheim called 'relationism' (Mannheim 1972) was a plausible and well-founded position, but it did not permit any exceptions. It was not possible to take a relativist stance towards the politics of others, while clinging to one's own politics as somehow exempt from the critique. Mannheim's position ends in an uncritical relativism for Adorno (1978), or a 'pathos' for Vallas (1979), as his own arguments prevent him from embracing any concrete politics. The same fate, for the same reason, threatened to cancel the activist projects of the new sociology of education.

Yet Young did want his readers to embrace his radicalism as a kind of rational commitment (Demaine 1981), for politics to flow seamlessly from theoretical analysis, precisely as in the ideal radical theory discussed in Chapter 1. It is some sort of indication of the relative influence of the political and the theoretical parts of the new sociology that Young decided to review the theoretical base of his position rather than his political commitment.

However, for the new sociology of education, work could proceed at a number of levels, following the exciting flow of ideas over the newly built bridge between sociology of education and sociology of knowledge. At the grand level, work should try to develop the notion of school knowledge as ideology or as the world-view of certain 'powerful groups' or dominant elites. At the 'micro' level, work could follow implications as the administration and management of this school knowledge was developed by actual teachers in classes, and mediated through their professional activities, as in Keddie's early study of 'classroom knowledge' and its role in stratifying children (in Young 1971). At the intermediate or 'meso' level, various curriculum packages were designed, developed, and discussed by bodies like the Schools Council or other 'curriculum mongers', providing more material for the analysis (see, for example, Young's critique of the Schools Council in terms of the conservative criteria it used to police curriculum innovations – in Bell *et al.* 1973).

In those early days, it seemed that the need to dethrone the old approaches permitted or even required a popular front of all the radical alternatives, encompassing symbolic interactionist work and ethnomethodology, as well as Marxism, so that some sort of broad programme was maintained, based upon an intent to expose the 'taken for granted' assumptions in schooling.

The micropolitical or tactical aspects of the popular front approach in the neighbouring field of youth cultures have been described by Hall, and have been discussed in Chapter 1.

E282 had to conform to the conventions of an OU course, however, and the course team were in deep disagreement about the validity of the new approach. So the pioneering zeal of Esland, Dale or Keddie was intended to be 'balanced' by the more cautious inputs of Swift and Cosin in the second half of the course, involving some shrewd micropolitical strategies by the chairperson of the team to achieve this 'balance'. But for various reasons, it was the first half that remained memorable, even if never fully grasped by the OU students who took the course in large numbers (Harris 1987). Nevertheless, the course and its 'set texts' and 'readers' changed the sociology of education for ever: it gained theoretical richness in its journey into radicalism, but it also encountered increasing resistance from (some) teacher trainers and from national politicians.

THE TRANSITIONAL PHASE: INTO MARXISM

By 1976, however, the new sociology had itself split. Reliance on Berger and Luckmann had hidden a conflict that was to energise the split. Berger and Luckmann claimed to be able to locate their approach firmly in mainstream social theory, and wanted to develop a parallel between the cycles of construction and reification of reality in their approach to the notorious discussion on 'alienation' in the young Marx (see the Introduction in Berger and Luckmann 1966: 13–30). However, doubts were emerging about social phenomenology as a suitable base for radicalism: these doubts are expressed very forcefully in Whitty and Young (1976), and Young and Whitty (1977).

In particular, 'social phenomenology' appeared to be far too 'voluntaristic', and too naive politically. All teachers had to do, it seemed, was to recapture their alienated ideas and dereify the assumptions others had built into schooling, and the whole system would lose legitimacy and undergo change. This is a view that implies that politics is a matter primarily of gaining a 'correct' perception of reality, of course, before the 'linguistic turn' of later marxist work like Mepham's (Mepham and Ruben 1979). Despite the recognition of this unsatisfactory problematic, and an attempt by others to incorporate Mepham and other linguistic analyses (see Chapter 7), this 'false consciousness' approach was to haunt much of the later more explicitly gramscian work too. Doubtless, teachers (and OU lecturers) have always overestimated the power of mere ideas to change people's lives: they have a vested interest in 'false consciousness'. Ahier makes this point, and says, in effect, that the new sociology was unable to break with more conventional bourgeois conceptions (in Young and Whitty 1977).

Young, Whitty and the others were keen to develop an adequate radical politics instead, to critique existing educational practices as ideological or conservative, and to try to grasp the features that prevented radical changes when they were attempted by activist teachers: examination boards, school bureaucracies, parents and pupils. These analyses were very acutely aware of the significantly conservative tendencies of schooling, and very self-critical – quite unlike the naive educational or cultural politics of later gramscian work. As brief examples of the insights on offer in Whitty and Young (1976), Hextall, and Whitty, on assessment, offered a rare glimpse of the 'secret garden' of marking work: Hextall argues that the process goes on underneath a misleadingly fair and objective surface appearance, much as in the mystifications of the notorious capitalist slogan 'a fair day's work for a fair day's pay' (Whitty and Young 1976: 70).

In the same collection, Bartholomew analyses the deeply authoritarian 'hidden curriculum' of the teacher training college, justified in the name of a 'realistic' division between theory and practice in education. This allows authoritarian lecturing because colleges do 'theory' which is seen to simply require a didactic approach, and it diverts attention from the practices of colleges themselves. Young, Whitty or Collins outline the dilemmas faced by radical courses like social studies and media studies as they ran into the organisational inertia of the school. Hardy's unusual study of the politics of textbook publishing includes an insightful critique of their sort of phoney participation and involvement, hidden behind a style which presents texts as 'a "body of knowledge" which denies its own production' (*ibid*: 97). Tulloch analyses views of knowledge seen on television quiz shows, argues that these reified conceptions illuminate the educational values of dominant groups, and suggests that they do have an effect on public conceptions of education: in passing, he offers very brief (and very rare) critical comments on the Open University (*ibid*: 104).

Young and Whitty (1977) went on to rebuke their earlier allegiance to the phenomenological new sociology by exploring the new wider economic and social context, and increasingly used marxist terms and models to describe it, especially the 'fetishism mechanism' and, still implicitly, the metaphor of 'real' and 'phenomenal' forms. A marxist activism was emerging to establish a critique of the claims of social phenomenology which apparently ignored the links between certain constructions of reality and the material base (which is how marxists of the time argued for the superiority of their approach). Radical but non-marxist proposals like 'deschooling' were also rebuked for ignoring the necessary structural and collective struggle (Young and Whitty 1977: 23).

But Althusserian and other marxist 'reproduction' theories were also too 'one-sided'. One critical piece became influential: Erben and Gleason (in Young and Whitty 1977). There is no intention here to offer a 'correct' reading of Althusser any more than of Gramsci, but it was implied in Chapter 1 that the initial critiques of Althusser's *ISAs Essay* (Althusser 1971) were rather odd and one-sided. Erben's and Gleason's critique seemed to offer a combination of moral, political and theoretical criticisms, for example, in ways which are still puzzling:

[Althusser's approach] fails to adequately address the processes
through which those who work in schools may act to influence both
the conditions of their work, and the wider social context of which
schooling is a part . . . it is necessary that . . . teachers and students be
regarded as important.

(Young and Whitty 1977: 73)

These are stirring words, designed to appeal to radical readers, but in what
precise sense do they apply? Why is it necessary to regard teachers and
students as important? Politically necessary? Ethically? Scientifically?
Empirically? What processes of influence? What wider social context, and
why the activist one especially? Erben's and Gleason's article goes on to
rephrase Althusser in classic humanist marxist terms, with references to the
need for pupils and radical teachers to be 'given the opportunity to
redefine and reshape that situation in the light of their own critical
experiences' (*ibid*: 75), or suggesting that Althusser works with a process of
the 'fetishism of commodity consumption. . .like the work of Meszaros'
(*ibid*: 76). Erben and Gleason want to deny that their work is a 'retreat into
marxist humanism' (*ibid*: 83), but it is hard to know how else to receive it.

By way of criticism, Erben and Gleason try to show how Althusser's work
is connected to well-known accounts of heresies like functionalism and
positivism, which the 'new sociology of education' had already established
as flawed, of course. They link Althusser, via a 'parallel', to Parsons
(although their own analysis of deviance and contradiction could also be
Parsonian, or possibly Mertonian). To be fair, there is also a recognition of
other aspects of Althusser's work and of trenchant criticisms of them. Yet
overall, the arguments sound like activist 'morale boosting' – pointing to
'black power, women's liberation, civil rights in Ulster' as 'sites of class
struggle'. What they must mean is that they wish these struggles were 'class
struggle', or maybe that they might become 'class struggle'.

As in other areas, the search was on for a suitable marxism. Williams,
Thompson, and finally Gramsci appear in Young and Whitty, but there was
still admiration for the work of Fay (1975) and his ultra-activist
anthropology of 'struggling man': struggle is everywhere and should be
encouraged wherever intentions are frustrated, only activism validates
theory – and so on. Classic British activism (what might be called expressive
or cultural radicalism, mostly done by petit bourgeois groups, localised yet
appearing as universal, and operating without a Communist Party) was to
appear to solve theoretical problems, and to unite theorists in the struggle
with radical teachers and pupils.

Frith's and Corrigan's contribution also openly discussed the
ambiguities and uncertainties toward State education among socialists,
predicted differences between radicals and working-class consumers of

State education, and urged a move beyond mere slogans to a real collective movement (Young and Whitty 1977: 255f).

This move into positive politics raised another question, though – what exactly was being proposed as proletarian knowledge, the alternative to and replacement for the vested interests of powerful groups which dominated existing curricula? Again, Young had found himself enmeshed in a specific pre-set agenda in British educational debates, between 'progressives' and 'traditionals', and he had to try to find a way between both 'curriculum as fact' and 'curriculum as practice' approaches (Whitty and Young 1976). This tendency to translate radical approaches into available polarities in everyday teacher politics was to affect the impact of *E282* too – many students read it simply as supporting the 'progressives' against the 'traditionals' (see Harris 1987).

Young and Whitty were also attacked for underestimating the revolutionary potential of existing 'high' knowledge (Entwhistle 1979). The critique came based on considerable scholarship in the work of Gramsci himself, and proposed reviving an old marxist project to provide for the offspring of proletarians the very best of bourgeois knowledge, so that they may break with the ignorance and mythical thinking that suffuses 'their' culture, and learn to fight the class enemy with its own weapons. This kind of 'organic intellectual' should not be prepared for the task with specially provided 'relevant' knowledge, but should emulate the example of all leading marxists themselves – follow an impeccably bourgeois education, the better to break with it decisively at a later stage.

There is indeed much support for this view in reading Gramsci himself, and it is these sections which gramscians have had to explain away, often by invoking the ambiguities introduced by the context of production of the *Prison Notebooks* discussed in Chapter 1. For Finn *et al.* (in CCCS 1978), these sections were simply 'unfortunate'.

The question of the alternative, and the issue of the difficult wrangles over theory, seemed to be settled and replaced by the new activism. This activism went 'beyond critique' (Young and Whitty 1977). It was for those engaged in the struggle to decide for themselves what they wanted as an alternative. The politics of the analysis emerged as the final test of its adequacy, a development seen, eventually, as gramscian. Despite the reflexive analysis, though, little in the way of positive politics seemed to emerge, and the onslaught on education inaugurated by Thatcherism, the demoralisation and defeat of the teaching force, the new legislation to control teachers all were to reveal the power of a massive counter-force, being assembled even as the radicals were holding conferences and forming the new Socialist Teachers' Alliance.

Of course, everything depends on there being a group of activists willing and able to struggle for alternatives. Here, as in other areas to be discussed in this book, agents to carry out the mission had to be found. Ideally, such agents would be already disaffected, split from existing social formations, ready to acquire new concepts with which to think out their futures. Given a large group of nearly-rebellious almost-activists, something like the gramscian mission, to offer intellectual and political leadership, could be developed.

There were lots of disaffected schoolchildren, already half-aware of the ways in which schools discriminated against kids from certain social backgrounds. There was a tangible grievance, shared by the parents of these children too in the form of low or absent qualifications, and, later, depressed employment prospects after school.

Willis's famous book (1977) (reviewed below) was to demonstrate that children like this were often not without ability, and, in his hands, they became lively, witty, insightful, and rather endearing too (despite being racist and obsessed by machismo). The book was another challenge to the current orthodoxy (and still a powerful one) that working-class kids were 'culturally deprived'. The notion had received a thorough rebuke from Keddie in the 'interactionist' tradition in the new sociology (Keddie 1973), but Willis's work was capable of placing the whole debate in a satisfyingly wide and high-powered context and claiming it even more firmly for marxism. As Hall argued (in Unit 32 of *E202*, Open University 1979), the lengthy sociological and psychological interest in the 'pathological' cult-ures of the working-class child could be reformulated in marxist terms, just by asking how working-class and middle-class cultures came to be like that.

As Riseborough was to argue later (in Ball and Goodson 1985), the struggle betwen cultures of children and teachers at school was a subset of class struggle in its classic sense. Education was, at last, 'brought back in' to the central concerns of social theory, and, more importantly for Young's work, to proper, recognisable, respectable politics. Of course, the dying echoes of the student revolt of the late 1960s had done much to radicalise a generation of social scientists too.

Willis's conclusions in the book were not very encouraging, however, for 'the lads' only managed a 'partial penetration' of the politics of the school, and, in a classic demonstration of what others would call the 'paradox of the subject', 'chose' to cut themselves off from any academic knowledge that might help them deepen their insights, and 'willingly' went off to find 'working-class jobs' (and male working-class pursuits, as the final sentiments of the legendary 'Joey' reveal). This rather depressing conclusion to the book was to lead to further efforts to expand (identify, or encourage) the areas of resistance and struggle among schoolchildren, characteristically in the context of challenging the more pessimistic 'reproduction theories'. Willis himself repented a little and Riseborough argued for extending the powers of cultural production of working-class children still further, to point out their success as 'teacher mincers'.

If those earlier analyses tended to support pupils against teachers in the class war, later on teachers and lecturers were to be auditioned themselves for the role of activist. University lecturers and researchers in the 1980s had no difficulties in finding a link betweeen their particular occupational politics and the 'broader issues' as Thatcherism whittled away at the very heart of higher education. The sociology of education, and marxism, came in for particular attack of course, directly, in the speeches of Government ministers like Sir Keith Joseph, and in the activities of various right-wing think tanks.

SCHOOLING AND SOCIETY (E202)

A spectacular and public turn away from 'social phenomenology' also appeared at a conference in 1976 to announce the remake of *E282* (causing a good deal of confusion to those of us in the provinces who were only just beginning to grasp the perspective). New theorists appeared, including Gintis, and many of those who were to contribute to the Whitty and Young collections. The old alliance with symbolic interactionism and ethnomethodolgy was over. The new version of the OU's sociology of education course, *Schooling and Society* or *E202* (Open University 1979), featured a divided course with two course readers, one symbolic inter-actionist (Hammersley and Woods 1976) and one marxist (Dale *et al.* 1976), and a number of fascinating attempts to gloss over or reconcile the division.

E202 offered combinations of Units from each of the different perspectives, interspersed with periodic 'Revision Units' which openly discussed the differences and similarities, strengths and weaknesses of the different accounts, albeit from a rather academic, distanced stance, in the case of Mackinnon (*E202* Unit 13 and Unit 24) or Woods (Unit 30).

Hall's review of the course (Unit 32) was a different matter, an attempt at a classic gramscian 'last word', like the ones in *U203* (discussed in Chapter 8). The Unit quite properly begins with an open announcement of its partiality, and then develops a series of arguments that was to end in gramscianism in a way which is familiar. In the first section, a number of sociological approaches, including non-marxist ones, and historical work, based largely on CCCS writers, are deployed to argue that liberalism, reformism and individualism look like natural and obvious approaches to education, but are really political, are 'dominant ideology'. The attack on liberal conceptions was a major thread in the course reader too (Dale *et al.* 1976), with works by American theorists like Karier attacking Deweyan liberalism, and Henderson critiquing conceptions like meritocracy (with its accompanying faith in individual intelligence scores). In Hall's review, the categories of bourgeois science are rebuked using Marx's *Grundrisse* (Marx 1973) in a way which we will discuss later, when we consider Hall's work on the 'ideology effect' in the media.

This sort of opening was important for external readers too, and was to form the basis of the course team's defence against well-publicised accusations of marxist bias (Gould 1977). Gould's Report, although pretty lightweight and clearly part of the emerging 'moral panic' in education (see Sarup 1982), did have an effect on the OU, apparently, and brought new arrangements to ensure 'balance' on course teams. Certainly, the External Examiner (D. Hargreaves) for the course felt so worried that he felt it necessary, in a special radio broadcast (reprinted in Unit 1), to caution students to be critical of, and vigilant against, what he called, a 'difficult and dangerous' course (Open University 1979, Unit 1: 34)! Hargreaves, like several other authors, positively recommends students to adopt 'critical' readings and seek their own 'balance', based on their 'intertextual' resources in other OU courses, or in their experience.

Having introduced the idea that all approaches are political (and 'theoretical', to rebuff the easy dismissals of the 'practitioners' in education), Hall then proceeds to review a number of critical approaches, and to end with a solid endorsement of the gramscian approach. The review is very useful and thoughtful, of course, and can only be described briefly here. In perhaps the best section, Hall charts the possible ways in which theorists have linked the education system to the wider social context: briefly, the options range, in order of sophistication and worth, from direct 'correspondence' (Bowles and Gintis), to 'reproduction' (Althusser, Bourdieu, Bernstein), to 'coupling', 'conforming' or 'articulation' (Gramsci, of course). A curious feature of this argument is the decision to lump in Bowles and Gintis, Lukács, and 'critical theory', all as theorists of 'alienation' or 'expressive totality'.

As one would expect, Gramsci runs as a scarlet thread through the discussion, in effect setting the agenda (again, quite properly, of course): improving on Lukácsians and Althusserians as in CCCS (1978) (and see Chapter 1), and if not exactly countering Bourdieu and Bernstein, at least keeping up with them (Bernstein had been favourably reviewed in an earlier Revision Unit). This is the familiar strategy of making Gramsci's work look like a completion of earlier approaches, a 'metadiscourse' that organises the others.

Bowles and Gintis (1976) – another set book for the course – had been pretty heavily criticised throughout the course, even in the first few Units which had been rather favourably disposed to the 'correspondence' approach. Several other Units attacked the approach in some detail, including a fascinating attempt to rework the substantial empirical data in the study (reprinted as an Appendix to Unit 13). Hall's dismissal of their case was on safe ground by now, as the considerable enthusiasm for the first seriously and scholarly marxist account of education had faded. Even so, as in many brief summaries, it is a bit of a straw man who is attacked – the careful empirical analysis is not mentioned, nor the reservations about the unevenness of 'correspondence'.

Bowles and Gintis were really being tried out for the role of early effort which everyone can feel happy about rejecting, as a kind of scapegoat for marxism, much as 'critical theory' was. By having his own approach come last, Hall avoids any critical scrutiny of his position, of course, and one can only wonder what would have happened if gramscian accounts had been subjected to the same rigorous analysis as Bowles and Gintis: if Bowles and Gintis were guilty of relying on incomplete empirical data, for example, Hall's analysis did not seem to have any at all! (Similarly, one wonders what Bourdieu's last word would have been on gramscianism – later discussions try to anticipate this too!). I am not trying to reinstate *Schooling and Capitalist America* specifically, but similar levels of scholarship still would be welcome in both analysis and critique on the left. Bowles and Gintis were to perform an auto-critique and an 'activist' turn themselves, of course (Gintis and Bowles 1980).

We find familiar 'textual shifters' in Hall's discussion, such as when Hall assures us that '[Gramsci] in my view is by far the ablest and most profound theorist to develop this paradigm' (Open University 1979, Unit 32: 53). We find certain slippages of terminology, such as when 'articulation' is used simply in a common-sense way to indicate things being joined together, then in a more specialist way to allude to Mouffe and 'enriched' gramscianism. 'Hegemony' is defined in at least three ways (e.g. on pp. 34, 36, 55), and Anderson's (1976) critique of the ambiguity in Gramsci on the relation between civil society and the State is dealt with in what looks like a very indecisive manner (Unit 32: 54–5).

Finally, Hall's review is also useful for revealing the extent of the links between the OU course in education, and the work of the CCCS. *Resistance Through Rituals* (Hall and Jefferson 1976) was a set book, and was discussed (none too favourably, in fact) in the course. Johnson and Williams appeared in the reader (Dale *et al.* 1976). Hall's review refers to *Resistance* . . . as an example of how to 'manage' interactionist work to reveal the underlying political context of 'culture clash' accounts of working-class underachievment via the 'double articulation' with generation and class (Unit 32: 47). There are several references to other CCCS work at strategic moments, including Finn *et al.* (in CCCS 1978) on education and the 'crisis'.

CCCS WORK

Willis's (1977) study of working-class lads is rather atypical of CCCS work, in fact, although it is one of the most revealing studies in my view. The piece follows a 'reproduction' approach really, albeit in a rather unusual way, and features an ethnographic study of school pupils and various adults, during the transition from school to work, connected to some much more abstract general theory. Willis uses a range of methods and theoretical approaches, including the 'structuralist' work on the subject associated with the *Tel Quel* Group and with Ellis (see notes 8 and 9 – *ibid*: 140). Gramsci's relevance is acknowledged, but Willis has reservations too: he is not so sure that working-class culture will turn out to be as progressive as historicists had hoped (*ibid*: 137), and he has doubts about the concept of hegemony because of the ambiguities identified in Anderson (1976), which we reviewed in Chapter 1 (*ibid*: 170). Willis's doubts were to remain to affect his work in 1990 – but this time, hegemony seems to be too reductive a concept, too likely to constrain the possible meanings of 'common culture'.

Learning to Labour is too rich to summarise with any justice. In 1977, it was received as a marvellous example of the kinds of cultural resources with which working-class lads resisted formal schooling. Many of the examples of resistance pre-date later and more fashionable work on 'raiding' and 'poaching' associated with deCerteau and Fiske (see Chapter 8), and 'the lads' were congratulated for being able to penetrate the ideologies of schooling (especially the individualistic and meritocratic 'bargains' on offer in exchange for compliance).

Willis probably overdoes these insights in fact, especially where he claims that the lads are able to get closer to the true nature of labour in capitalism (as in Marx's account of abstract labour). As usual, we are never really sure whether he has discovered these insights in the ethnographic study, or had them in mind, so to speak as he comments on the transcripts: whether the transcripted conversation on p. 101 *really* shows that 'For "the lads" all jobs mean *labour*', or whether it only takes on this significance following Willis's 'textual shifter' is debatable. (Try also the transcript on p.168, after a rather 'difficult' section on the role of ideology.) These sections seem to imply that theoretical concepts can be somehow 'discovered' in common-sense, and, of course, Althusserians would want to rebuke such 'empiricism'. Willis is optimistic in relying on (Lukácsian?) historicism after all to argue that the working class must get closer to these concepts than the bourgeoisie.

Nevertheless, the work also shows the complexities and the limits of a resort to working-class experience to resist capitalism, an insight which is sadly forgotten in the populist enthusiasms of later work. Willis argues that experience alone is severely limited, both internally (by its 'blocks', to use a Habermasian phrase, especially those concerning sexism and racism), and by its inability to break decisively with dominant ideology which 'confidently strides' into the vacuum left by the lads' deviance (Willis 1977: 160). After all, the lads accomplish only an inversion of official school ideologies. This does demystify those ideologies and lead to insights – like the correct perception that gaining qualifications involves massive sacrifice yet still leads only to limited upward mobility for the few – yet those ideologies gain the larger victory, since the lads are persuaded that inequality and exploitation are inevitable and natural (and even individual), and go meekly to their destiny in manual labour.

Willis singles out careers education and vocational guidance as the most visible manifestation of the official views, which seems rather odd, and the restriction of discussion of the effects of the media to careers films is positively eccentric. Nevertheless, even here, he is alert to the contradictions and strains within and between official ideologies, pragmatic considerations, and resistance in schools.

Willis suggests how sexism and racism can be articulated to the reproduction of capitalism, from the point of view of 'the lads' (he apologises for the omission of women from a central place in the analysis). Briefly, manual labour gets filled with a compensatory meaning by patriarchy and racism – it becomes more culturally significant than it should be (*ibid*: 150–3), as an expression of manliness and of meaning beyond the basic physical level. The ambivalences and contradictions of sexism and racism are well explored, for a change, and this again compares well with the later blanket condemnations of working-class attitudes. The importance of these interconnections is clear – capitalism needs patriarchy and racism to support its class divisions and to enable men to endow their class position with meaning from comparisons with those less powerful even than themselves. It also needs the lads to *choose* manual labour as 'naturally' theirs, which helps the bourgeoisie justify their position by contrast, as 'better than' proletarians.

Much can still be gained from these insights, including some implications for the idea of 'motivation crisis' in Habermas (although this will not be pursued here). As with feminist analysis, a little empirical investigation, however asymmetric, a certain openness to experience, rather then a concern to police a theoretical apparatus, seems to have produced a most insightful study, even at the cost of remaining marginal to gramscianism. Indeed, the ghosts of Durkheim or Runciman, as well as the ethnographers, seem to haunt the study, and, despite Willis's reservations, structuralist work seems to pervade it. Willis does recommend activist 'struggle', however, but even here, his proposals are not at all idealist or abstract (see his Chapter 9), and he does not seem to share the metaphysics of struggle – struggle as a justification of all theory – found in most gramscian works.

However, Willis changed his mind. His 'revisit' to *Learning to Labour* (in Barton and Walker 1983) could have been written by Stuart Hall (and indeed it resembles Hall's review of *E202* in many ways). After a summary of the main themes, the article tries to resolve and manage some of the open-endedness of the book in a familiar direction. There is an attempt to find a middle way between reproduction theories and (unnamed) work which 'romantically and uncritically identifies with, an oppositional or working-class spirit' (Barton and Walker 1983: 107). Much of Willis (1990) would now qualify for inclusion, we shall argue. After an economical review of Bowles and Gintis, Bourdieu and Bernstein (just as in *E202*), Willis ends in gramscianism (although there are no explicit references to Gramsci). 'Cultural production' provides both complexity and struggle. It also gives us grounds for optimism(!)

Willis use neologisms rather than conventional gramscian terms, but the drift of the argument is unmistakable. Instead of concrete politics in the thoughtful Chapter 9 of *Learning to Labour*, a list of actions which seem to me to describe pretty closely what combatants in the war of position in schools and colleges really do, Willis succumbs to the delights of purely abstract cultural politics, based on left-wing functionalist possibilities of structural looseness in the system. This abstract activism solves theoretical problems too, since it alone fixes and interrelates the multiple possible identities offered by the formal properties of race, class and sex. It also solves the old (bourgeois sociological) dilemmas of the relation of subjects and structures – both are culturally produced (a classic 'monist' argument, open to all the problems we discussed in Chapter 2).

To be brief, Willis avoids the conservative implications of reproduction by focusing on cultural production, but at the expense of simply avoiding the issue explored in *Learning to Labour* – what happens after the moment of production? Despite some reservations even now, Willis is set to embark upon the journey that will end with *Common Culture* (Willis 1990) – an uncritical celebration of any form of resistance, even inversions, with none of the subtleties of *Learning to Labour*, a propagandist text, designed to boost the morale of 'struggling' professionals in Thatcherism rather than to investigate the concrete complexities of working-class culture.

Willis's work appears in the later CCCS pieces by Finn *et al.* too. *Unpopular Education*, for example, (CCCS 1981) uses Willis's work as an example of the potential of a continuing tradition of popular education, that is education rooted in a socialist populism. Finn *et al.* want to use this conception to criticise, by contrast, as it were, social democratic versions of State education in Britain in the 1970s. Genuinely popular education had been around before the advent of State education in Britain, the argument went (and the work of Johnson in Clarke *et al.* 1979 was used here), and Willis, and some feminist work too, was used to suggest that that radical tradition was still alive and a force to be reckoned with.

The major error of social democratic thought, either as Labour Party policy or as its analogue in the traditional sociology of education, was to ignore this radical tradition, and offer a substitute instead, based on access to a State-controlled and professionally mediated bourgeois education. Working-class and female reluctance to get involved was rational and understandable, given both a realisation of the adverse class-chances of success while at school, and a well-founded suspicion about the reality of meritocratic or credentialist patterns of selection for jobs after school.

Sociologists failed to realise why their careful positivist research and susbsequent social democratic recommendations ended in what looked like continued apathy on the part of working-class parents and kids: they had spent their time fitting 'increasingly ingenious techniques to a narrowly conservative set of questions' (CCCS 1981: 131), and they lacked a suitable grasp of working-class culture as lived experience (that is they were not gramscians). Politicians too were committed merely to widening access, had no real grasp of the (reproduction) functions of schooling in capitalism, were far too complacent about allowing teaching professionals to define the nature of a 'proper education', and thus lent their support to an increasingly ineffective and deeply unpopular educational system.

Eventually, even Labour politicians realised that this type of education system could not achieve their goals of social justice, however much money was spent on it. And other subdued priorities in the 'dualist' social democractic repertoire were to emerge. Labour had always had to maintain two contradictory platforms – to represent labour and to maintain and develop capitalism. Drawing upon similar arguments in *Policing the Crisis* (Hall *et al.* 1978) Finn *et al.* were to argue that both of these goals could be held together during periods of economic growth, but were easily exposed as contradictory during economic crisis especially in the particularly acute youth unemployment crisis of the late 1970s. Labour's reformism was exposed as conditional, expenditure on education was to be cut, and the demands of 'industry' for 'trained personnel' were to dominate. The people's revenge, for having been excluded and deluded, was to turn to the new right doctrines and support Thatcherism.

The arguments are powerful and poignant for people who lived through that crisis and saw their hopes for educational reform dashed. Indeed, in many ways, *Unpopular Education* looks consolatory, a 'common-sense' account of those events for the middle-class left. Like *Policing the Crisis* (reviewed in Chapter 4) it uses 'quality' press reports and official documents to support its case, to further correspond to the sorts of sources with which a 'concerned' professional reader might be familiar. It is quietly encouraging and hopeful, for example in its tendency to 'talk up' the sort of popular education that is supposedly absent and to which the Labour Party must return. In fact, the sorts of conditions that had led to the emergence of pressures from below for 'really useful knowledge' were probably no longer present, as Stedman-Jones argued (in Waites *et al.* 1982).

The authors of *Unpopular Education* come close to admitting this themselves (in Chapter 2), and in their very acute and ultimately pessimistic analysis of the new vocationalism and the role of the Manpower Services Commission, which was to be explored later by Bates *et al.* (1984).

Willis's work too had indicated the serious 'limitations' of working-class reluctance, and even the sort of feminist work cited in *Unpopular Education* tended to be largely pessimistic: in neither case is the pessimism allowed to intrude, though, lest readers be downcast. The idea of a latent radical popular education remains as an absent presence (to coin a phrase), as a version of the latent 'struggle' that appears so widely in gramscian work.

As in other accounts, the modern 'respectable working class' hardly featured at all, and although the social origins of some of the new right writers are attributed to this group, there is no real exploration of working-class conservatism, although there is a recognition that one is needed (a gramscian one, that is). This may be due to the premature rejection of bourgeois sociology again: as an obvious example, the dismissal, with only a cursory discussion, of the Nuffield social mobility studies (Goldthorpe *et al.* 1980, Halsey *et al.* 1980) missed a chance to explore the views of successful working-class males, and Hopper's (1981) study is invaluable for an account of the meanings and effects of different rates of social mobility.

An over-ideological explanation substitutes. There is an underlying 'articulation' argument, which surfaces when contrasting the radical popular with the conservative populist views of education (Chapter 1), or when nominating Laclau to analyse the elements in the discourse of educational reformism (Chapter 5). The familiar story of the right disarticulating and rearticulating popular elements is present in the account of the demise of social democracy, but, despite the apparently obligatory newspaper analysis, the work is not done as formally or as fully as in *Policing.* . . . There are references to 'authoritarian populism', and hegemony as a discourse. Unlike later work, though, the main goal of the left is not so much to rearticulate a popular discourse as to tap back into that subterranean (mythical?) radical current, a version of the argument that says activism decides policies.

There are other political proposals that were to become more famous later – to form alliances with various new social movements, for example – and echoes of the older yearning for 'organic intellectuals' and some common ground for researchers, teachers and taught. The Socialist Teachers' Alliance offered such a possibility, perhaps, although its most tangible outcome seems to have been to keep CCCS alumni in touch with each other and to act as a forum for planning new jointly written books. Perhaps the most significant political pieces in *Unpopular Education,* though, concern some prescient warnings about the dangers of allowing too much penetration by professional managerial radicals: there is an uncomfortable reminder of modern issues of *Marxism Today* in the examples of scorn, indignantly cited in *Unpopular Education,* directed by those intellectuals against working-class culture: 'popular attitudes were stripped of much of their good sense and realism' (CCCS 1981: 140) as a result.

Further CCCS annual specials featured pieces on education too. CCCS (1982), for example, shows how the school system helps to develop the general issue pursued in the book – the construction of black people as a social problem in Britain. Chapter 5 of that book argues that the racism inherent in British society and schooling is not examined, and, instead, black culture and language is seen as deficient, a further example of CCCS analysis supplying the missing political context of much bourgeois sociological work on educational failure. The Women's Study Group's special (1978) features McRobbie's chapter and her analysis of how girls are able to resist some of the patriarchal structures in school only to willingly submit to their intended careers in the family, an argument which follows Willis (1977) in its 'reproduction' implications.

The work by Bates *et al.* (1984) on the new (for the eighties) MSC schemes has been cited, but will not be reviewed in any detail here. It is more convenient to consider in more depth the latest CCCS special *Education Limited* (Education Group II 1991).

This piece is a fascinating mixture of approaches, really. Johnson's contributions, as befits a veteran CCCS member, try to settle accounts with a number of critics of gramscian work (he has made some criticisms himself, of course – see Tolson in Maccabe 1986). He admits, for example, that the analyses of Thatcherism fail to account for the internal tensions and the failures of what is now called new right thinking. A much less abstract detailed history of the crises and settlements within Thatcherism is offered instead, with attention given to the individual 'articulations' of named politicians. In the process, politics is treated as a specific area, with no real attempt to render it as a level, or as an epiphenomenon, and something of the world of the professional politician is grasped in the recognition of the 'heroic' skills of policy makers in winning the consent of warring factions in their own parties and responding to the opinions of the public.

Although Gramsci and Foucault are acknowledged in footnotes (see, for example, p. 109), there is no real attempt made to lead the reader towards the discovery of hegemony or articulation as in earlier pieces (especially *Policing the Crisis*). The specifics of the development of English education are developed by Green's chapter, for example, instead of using history as an illustration of some pre-established schema of crises and class conflict (although a thesis looking remarkably like the original *New Left Review* accounts of the failure of Britain's bourgeois revolution emerges now and then). However, these accounts could be bourgeois history!

Some new right thinking is examined in detail for the first time, in Johnson's contribution, and the negative aspects of the policies are seen to have produced a crisis when it came to positive proposals, a version of the impasses and dualisms that afflicted social democracy. It is pleasant to see gramscian writers thinking of Thatcherism as incoherent and crisis-prone too, for a change, but Johnson fails to develop a material account of the roots of these impasses and dualisms as Habermas and Offe do, and so there is still a danger of an over-ideological emphasis (see Chapter 9 below). There is a brief reference to an implicit theory of motivation crisis, as market forces lead to 'radical disaffiliation at the moral and cultural level' (Education Group II 1991: 84).

There is an attempt to clarify the relationship between the new right critiques of, say, State bureaucracy, and the equally hostile stance of the New Politics (which seem to be a version of the 'new times' approach). An unkind critic might well see this attempt as successful, but only, via the dubious process of inversions, mere 'slot rattling' between the old bourgeois poles of individual agency and social regulation. I suggest in Chapter 9 below that 'new times' writers would do well to read some J. S. Mill if they must try to reinvent a liberal relation between individual and social interests.

The other contributors to *Education Limited* restore a concrete 'ethnographic' or case-study approach to radical work, one omission for which *Unpopular Education* is rebuked. These are fascinating and illuminating, reminiscent of Young and Whitty at times, showing the dilemmas and struggles of radical teachers as they are forced to respond to the new 'vocational' initiatives in education, and the compromises and incorporations they face. Vickers' and Hollands' chapters show the complexities of trainees' responses to Youth Training Schemes, and argue that remnants of 'really useful knowledge' still serve as an intertextual resource in the parental community (as do other contributions). These chapters show that, on the whole, youths are not at all taken in by the Government's claims for these schemes.

However, these penetrations (Willis's vocabulary is not explicitly used) are marred by limitations too – there is a pervasive ideology of individualism among the trainees, with little awareness of the structuring influences of class, age, race, gender and local labour market factors, and precious little evidence of any radical critical response. Indeed the long-term inadequacy of a 'laddish' approach is revealed nicely in Carspecken's insider's account of the conservatism of Liverpool parents, who, having launched an occupation of a school threatened with closure, insisted on 'traditional' education for their offspring (at first at least), complete with examinations, discipline, and proper school subjects. The complexity and the difficulties lead to a suitably modest, localised and realistic view of politics, as in Whitty and Young again, especially in Johnson's charmingly reflexive 'ten theses on a Monday morning'.

However, *Education Limited* represents a return to the earlier traditions in another sense too. Reading some of the pieces, it is almost as if all that theoretical struggle over ideology had never happened. Contributors seem to want to work with humanist marxist accounts of ideology, with notions of dominant ideology, reification, and false consciousness in their most elemental senses. As examples: Johnson accuses new right thinking of falsely universalising specific interests, and the joint Introduction to Parts 2 and 3 modestly aims to demonstrate the illusory nature of individual choice and to lay bare the political processes that structure it. Avis too accuses the training schemes of working with abstract and empiricist (almost reified) knowledge, offers a basic critique of positivism, and, later, focuses on individualism as the key ideology. Hollands' critique of Training Agency materials accuses them of being dominant ideology, masking 'real working-class issues such as decent employment rights' (*ibid*: 190). Carspecken's account comes close to accusing working-class parents of false consciousness, of being 'conditioned' (*ibid*: 262), and seems to believe that true consciousness can be achieved by correct perceptions following dialogues with experts.

If this represents a tactical decision to minimise theory in order to maximise solidarity with teachers, it seems unwise, or dangerously patronising, or just bad faith: gramscians began rebuking these views some twenty years ago. The whole vocabulary of false ideas masking true interests must surely seem suspicious to any modern reader, let alone any who have traversed the fiery brooks of debates on postmodernism or 'new times' marxism. The failure of the CCCS theorists to confront these 'spontaneous' accounts seems like an example of that quietism that characterises 'progressive education' (or modern teacher training).

It seems impossible for CCCS work on education to get right the academic, theoretical and political balance in any one piece – *Education Limited* advances in one direction only to retire in another.

OTHER RADICAL WORK

The ending of *E202* marks the high point of an attempt to accomplish the gramscianisation of the new sociology of education via the 'last word' strategy. Writers in the sociology of education at the OU or in the USA, or at London University never fully gramscianised their accounts, though: doubtless a conventionally academic context preserved a more open relation between gramscian and rival work. It is difficult to decide whether attempts to incorporate other writers serve to widen the debate beyond gramscianism or to collaborate in the processes of enrichment and elaboration, and thus preservation, discussed earlier. Readers must decide for themselves whether the two rough tests I have provided to spot a gramscian (in the Introduction) fit the examples I am going to mention below.

In Sarup (1982), for example, gramscianism blows hot and cold. A major part of the analysis is developed using Foucault, for example, without a sustained attempt to use him merely to 'elaborate' gramscianism. Yet after some specific criticisms, Sarup's overall conclusion is that '[Foucault's] concept of power is inadequate . . . power cannot be separated from capital and the state' (1982: 25), which seems to give marxism the last word again, at least in this section.

Feminist perspectives in Sarup are ably and openly summarised, but around an agenda of 'radical' versus 'socialist' feminisms. As with Foucault, it is not clear that Sarup simply gives marxism the last word here, although perhaps he thinks it might triumph in the end, after marxism is 'further developed, transformed' (1982: 92) (a fuller discussion of the ways in which marxism has tried to incorporate feminism is provided in other chapters). When discussing racism too, Sarup sees marxist anlysis as offering an account of the roots of racism, but not of all its specific forms.

By comparison, the collections of conference papers in Walker and Barton (1983), and Barton and Walker (1983), on gender and race respectively, and their relations with class, are more open, inevitably, and show the range of possible radical work in these fields. It is clear in both collections, for example, that empirical work was beginning to show some of the specific complexities in, and interactions between, different categories and groups, posing difficulties for any simple attempt to 'articulate' all the aspects of oppression together. The work on female resistance in Walker and Barton anticipates some of the similar work on the female audience in media studies that was to have such an impact on some of the more ambitious 'interpellation' accounts, as we shall see. The same collection features Culley's and Demaine's Hirstian critique of marxist feminism (applicable to much gramscian work generally) which is reviewed in greater depth later. The readers for the Open University's MA course on gender (*E813*) also reveal a wider range of approaches – Arnot and Weiner (1987), Weiner and Arnot (1987).

'Reproduction' accounts could still be found elsewhere, though, especially in American work like Apple (1982). In Whitty's account (1985) of such work, it becomes clear that a 'linguistic turn' had revitalised reproduction accounts, rather like the one associated with early 'screen theory', in the work of Wexler especially (see his piece in Apple 1982). Whitty says that colleagues writing about media education had used an aspect of the *Screen* 'realism debate' to critique educational discourses for their ideology effects, and I have used this work myself to critique distance education materials (Harris, in Evans and King 1991). Perhaps the best example of this work, though, is found in the collection assembled by Giroux *et al.* (1987), reviewed briefly in the concluding section. An OU postgraduate course *Language and Literacy* (*E815*) represents some of the later debates on critical linguistics reviewed in this book, and the readers include pieces by Williams and Bakhtin (Mercer 1988), although the applications seem to be those of concern to conventional sociology of education – pupils and their dialects and other linguistic competencies, and the effects of these on attainment.

Sarup's chapters on the State seem to follow the agenda set by gramscians really quite closely, drawing upon work in *On Ideology* (CCCS 1982) and *Policing the Crisis* (Hall *et al.* 1978) in particular. Whitty (1985) suggests, however, that an interest in the State in marxist theory did deliver many analysts to gramscian readings, but that an interest in Jessop or Offe also persisted – e.g. in the work of Dale *et al.* (1981), a reader for a subsequent OU course (*E353*) (Open University 1981). However, Whitty himself seems to attempt to order these perspectives against an 'activist' problematic, defining interventions, for example, as 'radical only when they have the potential to be linked with similar struggles to produce transformative effects' (Whitty 1985: 168).

There have been conversions back into gramscian 'struggle' too, as we have suggested above – Willis, Gintis and Bowles, and Apple (e.g. see his Introduction in Dale 1989). In many ways, this could be an understandable move from reproduction theorists as the teachers' 'struggle' to save the education system emerged.

TEACHERS AS PROLETARIANS

Given work like that summarised in *Education Limited*, the era of the struggling pupil seemed over. Gramscian work turned to struggling teachers instead, but only to face new issues and problems. Briefly, a number of conference papers revealed that the position of teachers offered contradictory possibilities as the Conservative 'educational offensive' gathered steam (Walker and Barton 1987). On the good side, so to speak, teachers began to look more and more like workers rather than professionals, and this had both theoretical and political payoffs for marxist analysis. However, resistance to the Tory onslaught took new and specific forms, at least after the phase of industrial action, and seemed to be grounded in localised, organisational opportunities to do micropolitics. Some of these are described in ways which are as penetrating as, and rather similar to, those in CCCS work (see Evans and Davies or Sikes in Walker and Barton 1987). Unfortunately, the study of educational organisations and of micropolitics were dominated by non-gramscian approaches – leading to another struggle, despite some early attempts to compromise (see Ozga in Walker and Barton 1987).

The tensions were reflected, inevitably, in Open University Education Studies courses. Although Ozga's article mentions an undergraduate one, it is a postgraduate one, chaired by Ozga and Westoby, that will be explored here, briefly – *Educational Organisations and Professionals* (*E814*) (Open University 1988). The course readers are Ozga (1988) and Westoby (1988). To declare an interest here, I am a regional tutor for, and an admirer of, this course, probably one of the last critical ones the Open University will run. I have written an account of my experiences as a tutor in Evans and Nation (forthcoming).

A gramscian approach is outlined in the first half of the course, focusing on the 'macro' or structural forces at work on the teacher's job, followed by a very different set of critical perspectives designed to analyse educational organisations in a number of specific ways in the second half.

In brief, the first half subverts the notion of teacher professionalism (and the concept of teaching as a bourgeois career). Feminist and marxist critiques are offered, drawing upon, for example, Lawn and Ozga (in Ozga 1988), and Apple (*ibid*). In the former, the attack on teaching as a profession is carried by two powerful arguments: first that teachers do play an important role in modern capitalism, in the superintendence and the valorisation of labour, and thus can be considered in marxist terms, as members of a definite social class; and second that teaching has been subject to a process of deskilling, just like other occupations, and with the same intents. There are implications for the class location of teaching, and Lawn and Ozga go on to advance the case for deskilling/proletarianisation as an explanation of recent developments in teaching.

The use of terms like deskilling or proletarianisation is designed, quite explicitly in Apple's case, to link in the position of teachers with a more general theory, ultimately to 'wider crises of accumulation and legitimation' (Apple in Ozga 1988: 112). There was also a more general struggle to join, to resist State-inspired campaigns and moral panics (in the USA too, Apple argues), and emerging threats from commercialised alternatives to schooling, in the shape of pre-designed teaching and assessment packages.

Gender is deeply implicated in the process of proletarianisation too, mostly via a 'dual exploitation' approach. Apple's attempt to locate himself in the debate displays, like Willis, the construction of new metaphors to reconcile class, gender and race: these are 'not reducible . . . but intertwine, work off, and co-determine the terrain on which each operates' (*ibid*: 101). Many Open University students seem to find this evasive(!)

These issues lie behind the specific struggles faced by teachers, Apple wants to argue. Following Braverman, Apple wants to see Taylorism as not just a rationalising technique but as a movement that 'brought acceptance of a larger body of ideological practices to deskill . . . workers' (*ibid*: 105). This kind of Bravermanian argument had been widely deployed earlier in the sociology of education, reflecting the considerable impact Braverman had had in revitalising marxist analysis (despite his use of rather 'orthodox' terminology). This work had long been discussed in radical circles, and all of the pieces reviewed above relate themselves to it. In general, gramscians found Braverman to be too deterministic and unsound on 'struggle', insufficently sensitive to the relational aspects of class – see, for example Thompson's work (in Young and Whitty 1977: 231). The US new left also pursued Braverman with mixed feelings as we shall see in Chapter 9 (see the Ehrenreichs' chapter in Walker 1979).

The proletarianisation thesis is critically discussed in *E814*, of course, and there have been 'second thoughts' about it as a general explanation (Ozga and Lawn 1988). The best direction lies in concrete investigations of the teacher's work, including the effect of gender, resistance, and organisational variables. Teaching as work, as a labour process, would also restore the connections between the sociology of education and the sociology of work, as in Tipton's influential piece (in Ozga 1988), and clearly facilitate the linkage of teachers with other workers in a collective struggle.

This sort of analysis is carried by Grace's article on the role of the State (in Lawn and Grace 1987), which plays a prominent role in the first half of *E814*. Grace begins with a history of the struggles between the State and the teaching profession since 1870. Using a series of familiar reservations, he denies any simple conspiracy on the part of the State, or any simple solidarity in struggle on the part of the teachers but argues for a set of constant objectives in State policy – the control of an occupational group which can legitimate or threaten the structure of popular consciousness.

Apparently, the struggles can be considered as occupying four phases of 20 or 30 years each, running through State condescension and teacher bitterness (1900–20), the political unification of teaching, leading to the incorporation of teacher unions via an 'ethic of legitimated professionalism' (1920s and 1930s), a period of 'organised consensus' between teachers and the State (1940s to 1970s), and then a return to confrontation in the 1980s. This attempt to periodise history into phases of settlement and crisis is characteristically gramscian, and can be found in other work like Clarke and Critcher (1985), or Langan and Schwartz (1985), all of which draw upon *Policing the Crisis* (Hall et al. 1978). It seems a good way academically to manage complex histories.

We have no independent access to the history of teacher politics in this article, though, and thus it is difficult to judge how well the events really did fit the periods in question. There seem to be so many currents at work – quiescent partnership and the emergence of Rank and File are both found in the third period, while both a successful campaign against the Minister of Education and a continuing condescension by government towards teachers can be found in the first. It is hard to see what gives each period any coherence or internal consistency. Finally, it is never clear just what causes each period to yield to the next – some universal logic of the social relations of capitalism as in some predestined class struggle, perhaps, or a series of responses to purely political struggles, strategies, temporary victories and defeats, as in a long war. Or perhaps these are purely tactical shifts of policy designed to ensure governmental popularity with the public or with important pressure groups? Sometimes the analysis seems circular

– the weakness of the National Union of Teachers is explained partly by the relative decline of education as an important area (Lawn and Grace 1987: 221). There are also some omissions, inevitably, like the interesting case of occupational closure achieved by a combination of pressures from below and from above, when teaching became an all-graduate profession after 1972. Mostly the analysis seems able to explain everything, though: there are complexities, Grace tells us, but there are also themes (so anything can be explained as either one or the other), but we are not given any 'desiderata' to judge whether any one episode should be judged as a theme or as a complexity.

Having presented a classic gramscian concrete analysis, Grace then decides that 'legitimated professionalism' is a symbol of the understanding of the whole relation between teachers and the State. The concept of professionalism that has developed in teacher politics is clearly flawed for Grace, and ought to be abandoned. The depoliticisation which legitimated professionalism implies has to be overcome by what looks rather like a popular front strategy of alliances with other opponents of the State.

Grace's work was not uncontested on *E814*, and Shipman's debate with Ozga (on an audio tape to accompany the course) covered some familiar ground – what of the contradictory elements in the State, revealed by battles between the Department of Education and Science and the Inner London Education Authority, for example, or what of the role of activist teachers themselves in changing the patterns of teaching against the wishes of the State? Ozga's responses followed Grace's (and those in many other gramscian pieces) – while not denying complexity, and while wishing to dissociate from the old orthodox determinism in marxism, Ozga also saw a need to avoid pluralism. She still felt that an underlying general role for a partisan State could be detected, much as Grace had argued for a continuity of 'theme' somehow 'under' or 'behind' the complexities.

It is worth saying that Shipman's critique hardly dented these arguments either, based apparently upon a simple point that some of the episodes in the recent history of teacher politics appeared to contradict some of the predictions of some marxist readings. Much the same basic ground assumptions seem to inform his points as well as Ozga's: both alike seem keen to correct the excesses of 'orthodox marxism'. No detailed analyses of any actual incidents or policies were discussed, certainly not at the level of detail of, say, those in Salter and Tapper (1981) (mentioned briefly in the Grace article). Salter and Tapper concluded that no underlying struggle for hegemony could explain the complex, contingent and emergent qualities of their case studies. In many of the debates, the arguments are rarely hammered out in detail, though, especially in this kind of specially constructed OU didactic piece.

Although there had been clear implications for studies of the school as an organisation in the 'labour process' approaches of the first half of *E814*, the second half did not simply lead on from the first, but turned into a much more eclectic examination of some of the debates about educational organisations. What gives this section of the course its (substantial) critical impact is the opportunity for readers to juxtapose these critical readings with actual management practices and 'theories' that are increasingly familiar in schools and colleges. The former enthusiasm for 'scientific management', for example, is subjected to a range of historical, feminist and psychoanalytic, and what was probably originally functionalist criticisms (see Westoby 1988, and Morgan 1986). Serious doubts are raised about the current fashion for management as a matter of maintaining a good ethos or sense of mission (see Ouchi and Wilkins in Westoby 1988). Organisational theories are exposed as ideologies in the sense of cloaking the real political interests of specific individuals or groups, defined as micropolitical ones, and managers are accused of attempting to impose an apparent universality upon what is, in actuality, a mass of 'loosely coupled' sub-systems (see Weick in Westoby 1988, and Ball 1987).

Indeed, the style of the second half of the course could not be more different from the first half. Managerialism is critiqued instead of professionalism, no real attempt is made to sort out and order the critiques or the object of critique into some overarching perspective, no attempt is made to manage or ignore the negative aspects of the critiques or to tie up alternatives into some activist politics. There is no premature closure of the debate here (which, as we shall see, raises further implications, not all of them 'good'). This relatively unmanaged material would also be worth organising as a test for gramscian perspectives, but, as in many OU courses, an academic division of labour substitutes for a debate.

The impact of such work, in so far as it is possible to judge from tutoring students, can be to relativise and help to critique management as a claimed area of neutral expertise in schools and colleges. This work badly needs to be extended away from the inadequate notions of ideology and from an excessively 'micro' level of analysis. However, while marxist analysis is more welcome to modern teachers, it is still subject to some suspicion, and it can look simply propagandist. A less committed approach can be more effective in achieving critical insight.

CONCLUSION

A brief consideration of the work of Giroux *et al.* (1989) raises important issues about the relations between analyses of education and other areas covered in this book. It is clear that schooling has always considered it necessary to deal with popular culture, for example, usually negatively, as a source of illicit meanings and identities, as Aronowitz's chapter suggests. Giroux and Simon, though, in their contributions which top and tail the collection, argue that it might be possible to see popular culture as a source

73

of critical meanings, to be used in the struggle to revive the idea of schooling as cultural politics.

Specifically, they argue in their Chapter 1 that the left should not just dismiss popular culture but see its positive side as providing a series of affective pleasures and subjective identities, investments among the young as well as external ideologies imposed upon them. Teachers could use these, specifically to empower and involve excluded groups of pupils.

Further chapters continue the theme: Willis rehearses the arguments for seeing young persons developing a 'grounded aesthetic' that he was to develop in *Common Culture* (Willis 1990); Corrigan, in a poetic piece which is difficult to summarise, celebrates aspects of punk subcultural style, connects them to academic techniques (also a 'theft of signs') (see Giroux *et al.* 1989: 73), and proposes we learn (five) pedagogic lessons from the experience. Grossberg's chapter makes a familiar claim that 'the Left' must learn from popular discourses how to tell more effective stories of its own (Springsteen's popularity is his teaching piece). Aronowitz proposes that radical pedagogues not only celebrate aspects of popular culture but actively encourage students to do productive work with video and music, especially to relearn how to represent the American working class (Giroux *et al.* 1989: 207).

The book addresses these issues in familiar gramscian ways, on the whole, but with important exceptions (especially Smith and White). There is heavy reliance at times on Hall's work on the popular and on articulation, in that rather ambiguous American sense discussed above (Chapter 2). There are serious reservations to record, therefore, about the idealism of the approach: unforgivably, for example, Giroux and Simon do not mention student assessment as a major constraint, and, as usual with gramscian work, seriously overestimate the political power of a plausible articulating discourse, and underestimate the tendency of the system to incorporate radical initiatives (despite some brief remarks on the dangers of voyeurism, or the colonisation of the private by the official that a move to study popular culture in school might bring). An over-reliance on Hall leads to a premature dismissal of critical theory as usual, and there is little substantive analysis in the establishing pieces of the organisational base of academic work (not so in Smith, though, as we shall see).

Nevertheless, the general thesis seems acceptable – education is not confined to schooling, and the distinctions between educational media, popular media, and popular culture have diminished if not imploded. For this reason alone, I hope readers who are interested in education will also go on to read some other chapters of this book. There they should find work of some significance in considering the 'production formations' and the 'reading formations' of educational materials.

If they read McLaren and Smith in Giroux *et al.*, they will also find striking parallels in the account of televangelism and its success in involving the audience. There are 'lessons for the left' here too! For those tempted to simply try to 'apply' the techniques of popular media to educational discourse, however, Ellsworth's chapter serves as a caution and as an introduction to some of the critiques of those forms and techniques that specialists in education will rapidly recognise.

That brings me to the second reason for joining together education and popular culture and media. The sort of critical work reviewed in this chapter badly needs to be read by some of the critics in other fields, who seem to have ignored the specifics of educational organisations and the tensions and dilemmas confronting any radical educators or writers, even though they are often lecturers or pedagogues themselves.

To rely on Giroux *et al.* again, for now, it is clear that work in popular culture on interpellation or positioning, for example, leads to a critique of much educational practice itself as working with a

language that ignores its own partiality, that refuses to engage . . . ideological assumptions . . . [and] understand its own complicity with those social relations that subjugate, infantilize, and corrupt.

(*ibid*: viii)

The acute critiques of educational and popular media in Ellsworth apply superbly to Open University materials, in my view, including those that try to convey gramscian arguments. Smith's doubts about radical practice, including his own, raise all sorts of critical possibilities for the practice of the Open University Popular Culture Group (and for *my* own!): is a focus on popular culture merely a lure to engage students, then quietly to position them passively in some discourse? Does the attempt to empower persons, and 'talk up' popular activities lead only to a quietist celebration of individual perceptions and common-sense? Is progressive practice really designed primarily to manage or postpone the guilt or embarrassment one feels at that awful moment when an 'academic' discourse has to be introduced into what was a pleasant discussion?

As later chapters show, criticisms can indeed be levelled at gramscian educational discourses, especially those at the OU, but also in some of the CCCS specials. Radical education does not stop at getting a suitably radical content, as most practising educators know, and some of the forms used to carry gramscian argument look suspiciously 'ideological' themselves.

Finally, I hope it is clear that I have no intention of claiming to be above these criticisms myself, nor to see them as originating in a simple flaw or oversight on the part of others. All educators, lecturers in colleges like me, and writers of books like this, as well as the researchers and writers criticised here, face serious dilemmas in developing their educational strategy – as Grossberg (in Giroux *et al.*) suggests, it is very difficult both to make a statement to persuade or motivate an audience *and* to signal that there is no intention to hold that view absolutely, and that contributions are openly invited. It is also true, though, that some styles are more open than others, and some teaching systems: compared to many writers, reviewed in this chapter especially, far too much gramscian work eagerly embraces the conventional pedagogic repertoires for closure, and remains complicit with the constraints of the system.

4

YOUTH AND SYMBOLIC POLITICS

INTRODUCTION

On rereading *Resistance Through Rituals* (Hall and Jefferson 1976), it is easy to detect the same kinds of struggles that affected the developments in the sociology of education charted in the previous chapter. First, marxism had to relate somehow to earlier traditions in the study of youth subcultures, especially functionalism and symbolic interactionism, both in their formal modes, as academic studies, and in their more popular journalistic or 'common-sense' versions. Early statements led to other kinds of criticism, often from near-colleagues, and these criticisms led to a second-order attempt to restore harmony, involving a clarification of the kind of marxism required, and a turn to gramscianism as a synthesis.

What makes *Resistance Through Rituals* so interesting is that one can see these processes of construction at work, assisted by the very style of the collection (the contributions are still 'working papers', sometimes rather brief notes, or pedagogic diagrams).

The Theoretical Overview that precedes the main pieces (although it was clearly written after them) shows the familiar, rather strained attempts to work through the different traditions, respond to them, and then somehow claim them for the new approach. Sometimes the strains emerge as debates between alternative focuses – 'class' versus 'youth' as a category, for example – sometimes in terms of tensions between 'determinism' and 'specificity', and sometimes as debates about specific sociological 'paradigms' like symbolic interactionism, or methods like participant observation. There are more obviously internal debates to be managed too, with feminists, with different members of the Birmingham Centre, and with colleagues working in other institutions (especially Murdock and McCron).

Although this collection was not to highlight the issue, debates between different marxisms were clearly immanent too: the Overview displays a cheerful eclecticism characteristic of preliminary work before the influence of the Althusserians, as it quotes freely from Althusser, Marcuse, Marx and Engels, the young Marx and Sartre, as well as Gramsci. This promiscuity was soon to earn a purist's stern rebuke, as Chapter 1 explained.

Because the book is so important and so revealing in terms of this interest in debates and their resolution, it is worth considering some of its arguments in more depth.

There is, for example, an interesting relation to the non-marxist sociological work on youth and deviancy. As with the 'new sociology of education', there is a need to make a break with this earlier material. This is attempted largely through the critiques of a body of work, which apparently had tried to offer 'youth' as a new significant social grouping, either classless, or even a new class in itself. Analysts who adopted this view of youth were either too optimistic, seeing youth as an idealistic agent of social change, or too pessimistic, seeing youth as the victims of a consumerist culture industry.

SOCIAL CLASS AND THE PARENT CULTURE

Both optimists and pessimists, however, had neglected the crucial structuring role of social class, the rather misleadingly named 'parent culture', which offered a fundamental shared 'problematic' to young people – 'that matrix of problems, structures, opportunities and experiences which confront that particular class stratum at a particular historical moment' (Hall and Jefferson 1976: 44). This class problematic was mediated to young people differently from their parents, however, and this is where the specifics of age and generation have their effect: young people encounter specific 'paramount realities' of education, work and leisure in ways which are quite different from their parents.

In the famous formulation, youth subcultures are, therefore, 'doubly articulated' to class and to age. Conventional analyses of 'youth' failed to grasp this double articulation, and thus remained at the 'phenomenal level', the level of myth and metaphor, the descriptive rather than the explanatory level (see pp. 15f). The methodological claims for marxism are strongly advanced here, in other words, in passages which owe much to the discussion of the fetishism mechanism in Marx (although this is not made explicit), and we shall return to these claims below.

This essential articulation to class is argued in a number of the specific pieces in the collection, possibly inconsistently. Thus Clarke sees skinhead style as resulting from an 'image' of the working-class community, especially of its collective social life ('mobs') and its toughness, a kind of ideological or cultural legacy. Corrigan and Frith, on the other hand, see the problematic more in terms of political tactics and strategies of resistance, a kind of political experience which somehow leaks into the activities of the young. P. Cohen, whose influence is acknowledged, had seen the influence of the decline of community 'sociologistically' (i. e. as a kind of sociological determinism) in terms of the structured opportunities it bequeathed to the young (including the 'upward option' of apparent social mobility into the new affluent worker stratum).

The discussion on middle-class youth also stresses the material aspects of greater leisure time and prolonged childhood bequeathed from the parent culture, and the emergence of new strata in the middle class itself. While some of the central bourgeois virtues persist in this counter-culture, like individualism, many of the old values have been subverted and replaced: hedonism replaces deferred gratification, permissiveness replaces the old sexual economy and so on.

However, the legacy from the parent culture is not always as easy to spot as this (nor are the mechanisms of transmission always clear, as has been suggested above). Sometimes, youth does interesting things with its legacy, and creatively adapts its problematic into seemingly autonomous cultural forms. However, the analyst can still 'decode' these adaptations, using especially the guiding concept 'homology', as we shall see.

The analysis is extended in interesting ways via the discussions on black subcultures and female youth. For the former, it is asserted that inherited experience (of slavery and subsequent 'alienation' from living in racist societies) can be detected in the music and subcultures of black youth, even more so than for working-class white youth according to Chambers, but the connection with current class position is left largely undiscussed, apart from pointing to the obvious economic functions of slavery and imperialism, and an oddly 'bourgeois' statistical appendix to Hebdige's article on economic growth, unemployment, and its differential impact on Jamaican black youth (Hall and Jefferson 1976: 154).

Both Hebdige and Chambers go on to develop cultural histories of subcultures and black music that barely refer to the double articulation, except in indirect ways: despite their apparent adherence to the gramscian framework of the whole collection, and despite their beginning with marxist-looking accounts, their articles would fit equally well into figurational approaches (see Chapter 8).

The piece by McRobbie and Garber lies outside the overall focus on class too. This piece, sharpened a good deal in a later version (McRobbie in Bennett et al. 1981b), pointed to the relative invisibility of the politics of gender in the mainstream work, and proposed different forms of female subcultural resistance or style, and different concepts with which to locate or make visible females in the mainstream work. The responses from the rest of the collective ranged from an apology (Corrigan and Frith) to an attempt by Powell and Clarke in an appended Note to argue that the apparent marginality of females is better explained by a 'doubly structured subordination' (another 'double articulation'?) between gender and class.

This device might secure at least some of the influence of class again, and form some kind of link with the main body of the work, but it looks very tenuous, or even tokenistic. Powell and Clarke also have to give ground rather riskily to the notion of 'reproduction' in their central argument that girls must be managed through the 'dangerous passage' from one family to another, and the routine plea for more (ethnographic!) research at the end of the Note cannot really disguise the very abstract nature of the discussion, designed to settle acounts with the McRobbie and Garber critique rather than to focus on female youth.

It is perfectly possible, therefore, to see the feminist critiques as pointing to examples of an insufficient break with conventional sociology, at least with its phallocentrism, despite the claims to be founding a new programme.

INVERTED BOURGEOIS SOCIOLOGY?

The hidden connections with the old work after all are also displayed by Critcher's analysis of the reaction to a particular court case involving black youth. This is the embryonic 'mugging project' that was to be developed as *Policing the Crisis*. In attempting to explain what the press and judiciary obviously saw as inexplicable and thus as 'savage', Critcher invokes a number of standard 'old' sociological explanations including differential association and social strain theories: doubtless the labour of integrating these into the new marxist perspective had to wait until after the immediate political struggle. At the moment of struggle, though, the old sociology would do, apparently: given the complaints about the conservative or apolitical nature of this sociology, this is an interesting development.

These attempts to recapture women's and black peoples' struggles for marxism are examples of several attempts discussed under the section on women and black people as 'alternative proletariats' (next chapter).

References to the old sociology are all over the new work. To quote the most obvious case, to be examined in more detail below, the ethnographic tradition persisted in the radical work, not only of the Birmingham Centre, but in the National Deviancy Conference material too, as Butters' review reminds us (in Hall and Jefferson 1976). Throughout the Theoretical Overview, and in many subsequent pieces, ethnographic material is cited in support of the central arguments.

Less visibly, 'bourgeois' sociology slides in behind many of the apparently new themes: the notions of structured opportunity echoes the classic American material of A. Cohen and Cloward and Ohlin, and the subsequent critique by Downes (Downes and Rock 1979), although the relationship to this kind of material is glossed very briefly in the Overview. As argued above, Critcher's piece echoes a number of American approaches, including Merton's famous piece on anomie theory, with its five possible responses to 'strain', especially in the passage that introduces what seems to have been taken as the major theroretical innovation of Critcher's piece – the three-level model of 'structures, cultures and biographies'.

P. Cohen's seminal piece also draws upon a vocabulary based in functionalism as in 'The latent function of subculture is this . . . Mods, parkers, skinheads, crombies all represent in their different ways, an attempt to retrieve some of the socially cohesive elements destroyed in the parent culture' (P. Cohen, quoted in Hall and Jefferson 1976: 32). The discussion which follows claims to be reinterpreting this anomie theory in gramscian terms as a matter of winning space, one of the many tactics in the struggle over hegemony, but this looks like one of those inversions described in Chapter 1.

Downes and Rock suggest that:

> [Anomie theory]. . .is the invisible prop to the Birmingham Centre for Contemporary Cultural Studies' radical work on class, youth, and deviance in Britain . . . Hall, Clarke, and Hebdige of Birmingham could be labelled the radical anomie theorists.
>
> (Downes and Rock 1988: 113)

Of course, as Downes and Rock point out, this continuity is only a surprise to those who think the functionalism of a Durkheim or a Merton is a rather crude apology for the status quo, incapable of yielding a sustained critique of capitalism. An open recognition of these writers, and discussion of their work, instead of the classic glossed or stage-managed 'break' with them, would have brought other benefits: Durkheim's work on the sociology of culture might have rounded out the discussion of homology, while a proper discussion of Merton and his critics might have prevented the late rediscovery of the problems of 'understanding precisely how the impact of certain forces on a parent culture is filtered through and differentially experienced by its youth' (Overview in Hall and Jefferson 1976: 33).

The failure to explore bourgeois sociology before confidently replacing it is a feature we have noticed before. In this case, it lies behind the sympathetic critique of Murdock and McCron. They refer to other American work which seems very similar to the main CCCS argument about homologies between experiences and subsequent cultural responses, and they mention another ghost lurking at the feast – Mannheim and his work on the 'sociology of knowledge', and, specifically, his work on generational consciousness. Unfortunately, Mannheim's work is dismissed even before it has had time to be explored, by Murdock and McCron insisting that Mannheim needs a specific theory of class (and hegemony, inevitably), and should abandon his 'value-free' methodology: Mannheim, it is implied, somehow simply omitted these aspects. It is relatively easy to supply them, though, and thus Mannheim can be worked in by being claimed as a naive proto-gramscian.

Murdock and McCron can be pushed into a more thorough critique, though, as they indicate when discussing class and class consciousness. Important existing studies on this topic have been ignored, they insist, referring to Mann's work on the structuring of adult class consciousness by 'situated' and 'mediated' forces.

This work came to full fruition in Giddens' 1973 study, in fact, where the 'structuration factors' were redefined as 'mediate' and 'proximate' types. The former consisted of social mobility chances, which affect social class both in reproducing the 'common life experience' over the generations and in confining individuals to particular ranges of occupations. 'Proximate' factors were more localised practices like

> the division of labour within the productive enterprise; the authority relationships within the enterprise; and the influence of . . . distributive groupings. . .[which are] . . . those relationships involving the common patterns of consumption of economic goods.
>
> (Giddens 1973: 108)

This important work was to be developed in a number of pieces in fact, such as those studies of working-class conservatism in Jessop (1974) and Bulmer (1975). The latter study in particular contains much of interest for a work interested in how types of experience get 'coded' as 'images' of class.

A decade or so later, Hall's work on Thatcherism was to meet the same charge of having failed to consider empirical studies of political consciousness, as we shall see, but while that survey material could be managed as irredeemably 'bourgeois', it is strange that this earlier material on class was overlooked, especially as, according to Giddens himself, this work is compatible with the classic marxist concerns for the forces and relations of production and their determining effects upon political consciousness (see his Chapter 8 in Giddens and Held 1982). The idea of local determinants of 'imagery' was never fully addressed in the CCCS work, though, despite a belated acknowledgement of some of the work in *Policing the Crisis*.

ASYMMETRY

The real difficulty, explaining the absence of this sort of work, Murdock and McCron suggest, lies with the 'asymmetry' of the CCCS analysis, which has led analysts to focus too narrowly on rebellious youth, and not enough on studies of class (and culture) more generally, including conventional youth or conservative proletarians, one of the early criticisms made by Marsland (1978). The theoretical aspect of this charge seems to have been lost in the only limited attempt to respond to it within the collection (Powell and Clarke), which thinks that adding women in will somehow restore the symmetry. Hall too mentions the charge in his account of 'problematics and problems' at the Centre (in Hall *et al.* 1980), and points to the rather odd study of Boy Scouts by Grimshaw (there is an extract in the same volume) as an example of how the Centre has studied 'normal youth'. In fact, Blanch's study (in Clarke *et al.* 1979) would have been a much better one to cite, and it will be reviewed in Chapter 8.

It is not just a matter of adding in extra studies like these, however, especially if they just reproduce the framework or help inoculate it against criticism by introducing a weak version of a critique. It is the method that is asymmetrical, proceeding from the chosen subculture to work back to some supposed characteristics of the parent culture (via homology), and failing to demonstrate an ability to test out the analysis by operating it in reverse.

The first step in any reverse testing of the homological method would involve gaining more knowledge of working-class culture at large. There are different possible reasons for the failure to do this, it will be suggested. As one possibility, the peculiar notion of political commitment has affected the work and given it an openly ideological or partisan nature. As another, the work has reproduced a quiescent stance towards the conventional academic division of labour that isolates specialisms like 'juvenile delinquency', and 'sociology of culture' or 'sociology of work'. No doubt this happened during the course of the 'break'. It might be possible to see in the isolation and narrowness of at least the early CCCS work, and that of other gramscians, precisely that accommodation with academic convention underneath the fiery radicalism.

ETHNOGRAPHY

Members of the Centre had simply used ethnographic methods in their substantive studies before realising the need to discuss methods more precisely, according to Butters' article (Hall and Jefferson 1976). Ethnography in some seminal American work, especially Becker's, had seemed radical and 'on the side of the underdog', of course, but the method had become controversial. There had been a series of discussions in the National Deviancy Conference (NDC) volumes (discussed below).

Like the NDC writers, Roberts (Hall and Jefferson 1976) argued that participant observation had not split sufficiently with positivism, and had accepted an accommodation within it instead, agreeing to operate as a purely descriptive humanistic focus on the exotic and the outsider. This had involved a mere sidestepping of the 'larger questions' of power, at least until the political upheavals of the 1960s put on the agenda the issue of rule-making as well rule-breaking, and thus directed attention to the issue of who has the power to make rules. Roberts refers to the debates within the NDC as an indication of the difficulties of reconciling even radical ethnography to specifically marxist accounts of the origins of power, and wonders whether this is the right way to conceive of the theory/practice relation. Although useful, however, this piece is almost silent on the problems faced peculiarly by the CCCS writers, as distinct from the NDC ones.

Butters' piece in *Resistance* . . . argued that the methods of participant observation were internally incoherent, with central dilemmas (such as how to maintain normal contacts with respondents while managing the 'surplus' knowledge of the situation gained from research) unclarified by the apparently unambiguous technical procedures advocated by the latest writers like Glaser and Strauss.

Butters argues that the CCCS project features instead a Sartrean dialectic of regressive and progressive moments. Normal research is either 'progressive' or 'regressive' rather than both. The 'regressive' mode merely subsumes data to existing general theory deductively, while the 'progressive' mode uses data to explore, modify and extend the theory inductively. We are to read the 'mugging project', Butters suggests, as one which investigates mugging using marxist theory for the first time, and thus locates it in a political context. However, it combines this deductive investigation, uniquely, with a progressive phase which strives to 'open up and reorganise the received account of monopoly capitalist hegemony . . . so as to accommodate a new social history of law and order versus "delinquency" in the theatres of ideology and politics' (Hall and Jefferson 1976: 271).

Reading Butters, again, it is clear that every one of the stringent tests for coherence he applies to conventional participant observation would also find the CCCS work wanting: neither Willis's work nor the finished version of the 'mugging project' reassure us that the researchers have managed the issues of 'ego-detachment' and instrumentality, for example. We shall have reason to doubt the apparent rational progression from early hunches to confirmed theory in much of the work too (especially the work on the media, perhaps – see Chapters 7 and 8). There are doubts too about the elimination of observer effects, the way subsequent write-ups reduce and code experience, and how they make available the processes of data-gathering and analysis for 'critical testing'. Butters seems to share some of these doubts: at the end of a lucid analysis, and after a noble attempt to talk up the Centre's work, even he could only point to the central role so far of 'analogy and metaphor', rather than any explicit accounts or procedures for such a dialectical method, even in the mugging project.

The third explicit piece on participant observation and ethnographic methods is a puzzle. It consists of a critique of the famous findings of Becker that the drug subculture has a crucial effect on the perceived results of drugtaking. Pearson and Twohig want to suggest that this 'cultural high' is overestimated and want to point to different usage practices ('technologies of ingestion') as having a mediating effect. From this finding, the authors draw some general conclusions about 'sociological imperialism', and the ways in which certain views of the world of the deviant in sociology (ethnography especially) correspond to those of 'left-liberal intellectuals' (who want to legalise dope), or 'bourgeois intellectuals' who want entertaining accounts of triumphant subjectivity in an anonymous industrialised world. It is hard to see where the alternative offered by Pearson and Twohig fits into the gramscian project, except simply as another critique of Becker, however, and, if the idea was to clear the ground for the CCCS project, the critique looks dangerously unstable since 'gramscian imperialism' is open to very similar rebukes.

Finally, some people at CCCS kept faith with the possible radical uses of ethnography. Feminist writers used ethnographic techniques to discover a range of interesting activities by the media audience, as we shall see. Willis's project on the symbolic creativity of everyday life (Willis 1990) also provides ethnographic material to document the new leisure pursuits of the young, and we shall discuss that work in a later chapter.

Hobson, Willis and Grimshaw were still to defend the use of ethnography as part of the Centre's work more generally too. Willis, for example, argued that ethnographic material was essential to avoid the premature theoretical closure of investigations, by providing a source of 'surprise'. Ethnographic data are also being tried out as an anchor or fix for the more free-floating theoretical speculations.

However, 'surprise' also depends on the researcher's ignorance or naivety in the first place. Willis seems to register surprise when he encounters the complexity of working-class cultural responses, for example, but then the less one knows initially about the group, the more surprised one is likely to be, and this may tell us more about Willis or his assumed readership than about the proletariat. Grimshaw too contrives to be surprised by the horseplay among Boy Scouts: 'I was unused to this sort of game. I chose to wrestle with the least threatening of the boys' (Hall *et al.* 1980: 103). After this novel experience (!), Grimshaw tells we surprised readers that he had witnessed 'an element of boyish sporting aggression in which the differences of the respective statuses of the boys and the controllers [*sic*] were temporarily suspended, to the satisfaction of all concerned' (*ibid*: 104). We know, of course, that this kind of 'surprise' is also the effect of a writing technique that lay at the heart of ethnography's early claims to scientific status (see Clifford 1983).

Incorporating conventional sociology or ethnographic data was difficult to manage partly because there is no clear account of how to do it in gramscianism. The emerging relation seems to be homologous (!) with 'popular front' politics: a broad amalgam of critical or radical sociologies and traditions can be assembled with a quiet intention to give them some kind of marxist leadership. As a result, CCCS treatment of bourgeois sociology seems to vacillate between penetrating critique and rejection. Because total rejection leaves few options except a monastic retreat from academic work, or the endless repetition of the same critique, there is still room for conventional sociology. This leads to an attempt to argue that, nevertheless, sociological work can be seen as a kind of proto-gramscianism after all, as we have seen before in other examples.

There seem to be hints of classic marxist strategies underneath this attempt in CCCS work: claims about the theoretical or explanatory advances to be gained by thinking of the social formation as a complex totality. The use of concepts like 'double articulation', 'double subordination', the need to operate on the specific and general levels, to explain action and social reaction, to use progressive and regressive logics, can all be seen as attempts to invoke 'the dialectic' in Marx, to echo the famous discussion on commodities where Marx shows how the apparently simple commodity is a complex unity of both use-value and exchange-value, and goes on to show how this insight can be developed to explain the contradictory nature of capitalist labour markets and the flaws in bourgeois economics.

There is, of course, a tremendous debate about whether this was Marx's method. However, even if this were an acceptable model to borrow, it is pursued with far less rigour than in Marx, and with far less a sense of discovery. Not too far down the critical track lies a model of the social formation waiting to be endlessly rediscovered – it is one where cultures are structured according to the power which derives from the class position of their originators. This certainty demotivates a critical scholarship, providing a pretty pragmatic and 'asymmetric' asset-stripping of bourgeois sociology, compared to the more rigorous (still problematic) 'immanent critique' of Taylor, Walton and Young and the NDC which we shall discuss shortly.

For CCCS work, the struggles between the opposing cultures provide a certain complexity to the social formation, but, to paraphrase Althusser, it is still a bourgeois complexity, traceable in the last instance to a fundamental or essential struggle which does not have to be discovered, but which can be asserted (hence the many statements that there must be struggle – e.g. 'The struggle between classes . . . thus always assumes the form of a continuous struggle over the distribution of cultural power' Hall and Jefferson 1976: 12). We have a fairly standard reproduction model, in other words, despite the introduction of 'struggle'. Here again, although Althusser is mentioned, his work is still kept carefully subservient to gramscian terms.

AN ALTHUSSERIAN CRITIQUE

Of course, the Althusserian general opus had surfaced in the characteristic forms developed by Hindess (mentioned in Butters' contribution), and, later, in 'screen theory' (Coward 1977). The National Deviancy Conference writers were the first to experience the challenge though, in the celebrated interchanges between Hirst and Taylor and Walton (Taylor *et al.* 1975). The interchange is instructive as a signal of the crisis that quietly dogged gramscianism (and all 'radical modernism') for the next fifteen years, finally appearing in the struggles over 'new times' and 'postmodernism'.

The NDC trajectory had its own specifics, of course, (see the commentary in Downes and Rock 1988), and there are significant differences of substance between NDC and CCCS work. NDC had been concerned from the start with crime and criminology rather than subcultural deviance focused on leisure and style, and despite the overlaps, 'critical criminology' had moved along a clear path focused upon the law and illegal behaviour. As with CCCS, they had scoured the sympathetic American sociology of deviant subcultures, and had tried to preserve its critical impact by politicising it. The NDC project, however, focused on the political struggles over the law and the judicial system, and the practices of criminalisation as a form of social control. The orthodox view of the law in criminology had been a functionalist one, whereby the law simply represented the real interests of all, but that was to be replaced by a 'conflict' perspective. This conflict perspective was to develop increasingly as a marxist one (despite some early flirtation with 'conflict sociology', especially with Dahrendorf).

The emphasis on criminalisation had enabled the NDC writers to offer a more plausible marxist 'immanent critique' of bourgeois sociology, it has been suggested. As the Conclusions to *The New Criminology* (Taylor *et al.* 1973) put it, it was possible to restore a social context for the classic sociological work, by exploring the political economy of both the criminal actor and the juridical reactor. How had the problems for both been created and defined? How had the resources (including power) been differentially provided to both types of participants? We saw Hall using the same argument against sociological accounts of 'cultural deprivation' in the previous chapter.

Capitalism itself was criminogenic, and deviancy and crime could be seen as an attempt to reassert a certain cultural diversity against widespread alienation (and, via Matza's work, to rationalise the consequences of being caught): bourgeois sociologies of deviance described the activities of the culturally diverse, and had stumbled upon the importance of a context of structured conflict and power, but they had no adequate theoretical resources to develop their insights. By contrast, Marx himself had written a good deal on law and jurisprudence, and indeed in the process had developed much of his general theory about civil society, science and ideology, and the connections with political economy (the concept of alienation had a juridical meaning, for example).

However, scarcely had the ink dried upon the manifesto of the 'new criminology' than a powerful autocritique developed, under Althusserian influence. *Critical Criminology* (Taylor *et al.* 1975) was published, just before *Resistance*... In it, Young was to argue that a critical inversion of orthodox criminology was insufficient, for example, and that the theoretical resources of the new criminology were too slender to sustain a proper analysis of the State and its judicial arm: these resources were largely a single 'control' perspective and a naive usage of the term 'alienation'.

Young argues that the celebration of human diversity, encouraged by ethnography and by the need to form a broad front of radical splinter groups, ran the great risk of acting as mere voyeurism or 'zoo-keeping', and as a kind of consolation for powerless radical criminologists. Finally, Young goes on to offer some projects for a revitalised radical criminology, including taking an offensive against bourgeois practices, instead of defending working-class ones: undertaking an exposé of the rich and powerful and how they bend the rules while avoiding decriminalisation (using official statistics to do so if necessary, despite the earlier abhorrence of 'positivism'), taking on the definitions of crime in propertied societies (e.g. demanding a focus on fraud rather than theft, or harmful non-crimes), and, finally, undertaking a proper analysis of law and the State in marxist terms (moving, ironically, away from the very specific focus with which the project had started). The latter project offered the only proper course to take.

It was this latter project that revealed the difficulties, though. Hirst argued that there could be no real marxist deviancy theory (or any other 'applied' marxism), since marxism was a science of the social formation, with concepts like 'mode of production, the class struggle, the state, ideology etc' (Taylor *et al.* 1975: 204). These could not simply be applied to a field constituted by some other discourse like 'the established social sciences'. Hirst elaborates his point by tracing the different stages in Marx's writings, treating the early works on law as moral critique of specific laws rather than a general theory, discussing the 'Feuerbachian' work on 'alienation' as not specific to law, and arguing that the 'historical materialist' phase offers little hope for radical criminologists hoping for a theory which predicts a 'crime-free' communist society.

Hirst goes on to reinterpret Marx's discussions of crime and law as matters of politics not abstract theory. Crime and delinquency might be forms of political protest, but more often are forms of 'reactionary accommodation' to capitalism, or a source of division among the proletariat. Similarly, laws are indeed predominantly the laws of the ruling class, but no society can be law-free, and some laws are more useful politically than others. Finally, and even more significantly for our examination of CCCS work, Hirst argues that crime is generally politically marginal to capitalist societies, and that the real purpose of the legal system is to contain the threat from organised labour: in this sense, radical criminology serves the purposes of capital by talking up crime as a major political challenge.

The ensuing debate between Hirst and the radical criminologists took the familiar form of a contest between advocates of a radical ideology connected to activist politics, and those of a rigorous marxist theory. As we have noted before, these contests look like simple ones between activists and theorists in British academic circles. The peculiar nature of 'modernist radicalism' means that both theoretical and activist political imperatives have to be followed in the work, sometimes in an interestingly defensive manner as we shall see.

In a more direct criticism, Coward (1977) rehearses many of the points associated with Lacan's decentring of the notion of subjectivity, his turn from representation to signification (see the section on women in Chapter 5). Coward commends the same project of working out the materialist determinations of particular subjectivities instead of the emphasis on cultures and hegemony. The 'culturalist' approach was to be defended subsequently, by the Media Studies Group at the Centre, as we have seen. The substantive criticisms (of *Resistance* . . . and some work on the media) are worth summarising here, however.

First, Coward argued, the term culture is an old liberal-humanist one, not easily grafted on to marxism: where this graft has been attempted, marxism itself has had to be read in liberal terms, as a theory of alienation or an historicism. Second, cultures assume an 'origin' in strange collective subjects – the fundamental classes. These somehow underly specific social divisions, which are mere 'phenomenal forms' and are thus insignificant (hence the absence of women in *Resistance* . . ., for example) and are assigned abstract world-historic roles and purposes. Third, the classes are destined to be locked in permanent struggles, producing a predictable history of crisis and settlement until the working class triumphs. This underlying struggle is somehow directly represented in a number of social phenomena including (for the working class) organised labour, socialist parties, and youth cultures (and in the existence of a number of culture clashes – e.g. in schools for the working classes, as in Riseborough). For the ruling class, the 'Ideological State Apparatuses' (ISAs), including the media, transparently represent dominant ideology. Homologies reveal these simple representations.

Fourth, cultures are ranked in order reflecting the supremacy of the ruling class, and hegemony describes a state when an imposed ideology replaces genuine cultures. The State and its ISAs reproduce this hierarchy: any complexity arises for CCCS writers from the uneven effect of the attempt to impose hegemony. They do not consider any tensions inside ISAs themselves, on the one hand, nor have they thought of the interpenetration of dominant ideology into apparently 'pure' working-class representations on the other. Oppositional meanings arise from the necessary inadequacy of dominant 'codings' (and are thus properly speaking merely 'deviant' – we will explore this in more depth in the discussion of Hall's piece on encoding and decoding in Chapter 7).

Fifth and finally, the role of analysis is to dispel 'false consciousness', expose the ideological distortions of 'reality' in ideology, and correct the 'misrecognitions' of real objects (rather than to generate any specific knowledge of its own).

Despite some attempt by CCCS writers to close with 'screen theory', and despite the eventual demise of the approach, some of these criticisms can still be seen to have force, as we shall see. Coward's critiques were dealt with by the CCCS Media Group, as we have seen. Hirst's had a more immediate effect in altering the focus of CCCS work on youth cultures and deviance. This now began to follow the trail blazed by NDC writers into an account of the State (in *Policing the Crisis* – see the next chapter).

YOUTH SUBCULTURES: POLICING THE CHAOS

This section reviews some of the later work on youth subcultures that developed themes in *Resistance* . . . . Willis's work on the culture and resistance of working-class schoolchildren has been discussed in an earlier chapter, together with his subsequent paper 'bending the twig' back to activism and away from what can look rather like a classic 'reproduction' account. His *Profane Cultures* (Willis 1978) had also deeply influenced the work of the writers in *Resistance* . . ., as much by its methodology as by its substantive concentration on bikers and hippies.

One aspect of the methodology that Willis uses so well is his 'incantatory' language, and there are many examples to be found in both pieces, but more formally, *Profane Cultures* was also noted for its use of a range of methods including the new way of transcending ethnography – homology. Using a familiar marxist trope, Willis argues that ethnography provides an insight into concrete subjectivity, 'the forms in which men become conscious', and then proposed additional levels of analysis to investigate the 'symbolic structures' underneath these forms.

Of these new levels, the homological has become famous as an account of how particular items reflect the structured concerns and typical feelings of a group, as, say, the black leather jacket does for bikers. Each homology arises from an 'integral' process of selection and cultural work on an object or item, in a complex dialectical way, naturally. As a result, current members of a group are not subjectively aware of these structural meanings, embedded in the history of the black leather jacket in previous cycles of provision, transformation and resistance.

As Hebdige argues (1979), the figure of the homology was to play a major part in *Resistance* . . . to explain how certain 'sacred objects' lay at the heart of, and provided a coded value-system for, a coherent subculture. To push this further, homology also seems to be used to explain the fairly simple symbolic connections between the lived experiences of groups and their chosen styles too, as in the ways in which the Teds' 'upper class style of dress "covers" the gap between. . .unskilled. . .real careers and life chances, and the '"all-dressed-up-and-nowhere-to-go experience" of Saturday evening', or as in how the skinheads '"re-present" a sense of territory and locality which the planners and speculators are rapidly destroying' (Hall and Jefferson 1976: 48). Willis too is in this tradition with his insistence that the constant mechanical tinkering with the motorbike, that all owners of British bikes had to do, can be seen as a symbolic way to dominate work by 'taming a fierce technology', or 'mastering the alienation of the machine' (Willis 1978).

Hebdige's work was to cast doubt upon this central process of symbolisation in several important ways. First, there was an assumption that the groups were in a position to perceive the correct position, the real (poor) prospects of the unskilled, the real effects of planners and speculators, or of the impact of advanced mechanisation and alienation. Second, these correct perceptions were somehow presented as 'raw materials' to a subculture – but Hebdige argues they were already mediated, in a mixture of 'real' and 'ideological' forms in the mass media: the media provide those images of the decline of class and nation, or the options available to youth. Subcultures are thus 'representations of representations' (Hebdige 1979: 86), and their critical perceptions and insights are often widely shared by 'straight' society too. Finally, Hebdige wants to suggest that there are much more complex processes of signification at work in subcultures, especially and primarily in punk. Far from groups symbolising their experiences in a transparent manner, so as to make things easy for the analyst, punks chose to make their styles 'noisy', impenetrable, deliberately arbitrary, not based on any central sacred symbols, designed to shock and confuse the bourgeoisie, much as Dada had done in the 1930s (see his Chapter 7). With such material as this, Hebdige finds the use of homology 'too literal and too conjectural' (*ibid*: 115).

The method cannot be defended by pointing out the exceptional nature of punk. Hebdige refers to the quietly ironic ways in which mod subverted the idea of neatness and pushed it to parody. Irony and parody are chronically likely to be missed in the use of techniques like homology, and the researcher runs the risk of dealing with 'extrapolations from the subculture's own prodigious rhetoric'. This rhetoric is 'always ambiguous', there is often a 'double and triple take'. Hebdige went on to argue in his later work that all youth subcultures are always both a demand to be seen and a refusal to be watched – they are 'hiding in the light' (Hebdige 1988).

Hebdige extends the possibilities of what might be called sophisticated signification by reworking his material on the influences of black culture and black music on white youth, going so far as to identify the relation to black youth as the defining characteristic of white subcultural forms, of at least equal significance as class. McRobbie was to argue the same case for women (in Bennett *et al.* 1981b). Doubtless, a skilled analyst could argue that the same kind of absent presence characterises the role of many other groups – Celts in mainstream British culture, perhaps.

White and black youth culture and musical styles are connected by a whole series of sophisticated significations described variously as inversions, miscegenation, 'deep structural adaptations which symbolically accommodate or expunge the black presence' (Hebdige 1979: 45), mythologisation and displacement. Although Hebdige was too polite to say so, the old notions of direct symbolisation in 'homology' looked like they involved a rather conventional underestimation of the intellectual, cultural and signifying powers of working-class youth, one shared by generations of kindly (or hectoring) bourgeois.

The openness of signification in music was to be taken still further by Chambers (1985) who, while acknowledging the structuring influences of class, race, sex and commerce, proceeds to demonstrate how musical styles are complex combinations of artistic, technical, political, experiential, personal and commercial influences, best understood as a kind of internal conversation between adjacent styles rather than as a direct expression of the lived experience of a coherent group in the old sense. The flexibility of the musical form itself, with its complex transformations of transposition, inversion, counterpoint, harmony and the rest, breaks the old notion of homology. The same complex analysis is developed by Frith, who points to the errors of 'subcultural theory' in mistaking the role of the 'continuous cultural exchange . . . between different social fantasies, differently mobile dreams of "making it"', and in equating the amateur audience with the professional musician (Frith 1988: 4). To be fair, both of these writers, and some others we will examine, are writing from a position after the 'end of youth'.

Popular music is a specialist field, and I lack the expertise to pursue it any further. Yet it is clear that an examination of popular music suggests that signification, even critical signification, became universal and sophisticated rather than the expression of a radical tradition in youth culture. The specificity of the term 'ideology' slipped away, despite some desperate defence by Hebdige (and Chambers), and, as Hebdige acknowledges, 'post-structuralism' was hard on the heels of the work of the early Barthes, with its denial of the 'preferred readings' and 'positioned audiences'.

THE END OF YOUTH

The 'end of youth cultures' was at hand. In real life, the youth of the 1980s in Britain ceased to be the metaphor for change and stylistic innovation, and became victims of social and structural change instead (Frith in Haralambos 1985). Hebdige in his later piece, which marked his own 'farewell to youth studies' argued that the stylistic dimension disappeared to be replaced by a simple confrontation between 'desire and the absence of means, a brick and a shop window' (Hebdige 1988: 35). Style had become disconnected from class, and from youth, and from politics, and style represented or coded more than just the lived experiences of a definite group.

Much of *Hiding in the Light* is a journey into and out of the postmodernist crisis as we have seen in Chapter 2. Barthes had led the way into a new kind of structural linguistics, no longer marxist, but focused on the signifiers themselves rather than what they signified, and driven by a number of linguistic manoeuvres (motivated by a search for pleasures ranging from simple hedonism to those playful linguistic sophistications of the 'second degree'). Chapter 8 explores the similar shift signalled by the work of Fiske, and discusses his 'linguistic imperialism' more explicitly.

We can clearly see the displacements in Hebdige's later concrete analyses. We are offered a discursive 'genealogy' of youth, instead of a political history of youth as resistance to powerlessness, showing how youth has become an object in different sorts of gazes (a problem in different sorts of discourses). We get a rather pathetic obituary of Sid Vicious and Nancy Spungen, and with them, of punk and thereby of youth cultures generally. Punks were victims not of simple commercialism or alienation, but of the process of symbolisation itself: 'Compelled irresistibly by the dictates of an image they'd in part constructed but in larger part had constructed for them, they were in a sense, victims of their own drive to coherence' (Hebdige 1988: 40). That coherence had a 'bad' end for Sid and Nancy in that they ended up playing out the final stages of a sensationalist press saga where they met a 'fitting end'. (Hebdige reserves a nicer, homelier, fate for the academic adventurer in the vertiginous depths of linguistic analysis in a return to the normal values of their class of origin, as we shall see.)

The book proceeds to analyse 'structures of taste' as objects, rather than the bearers of them, tracing the meanings of 'English taste' by reference to the perceived threats (decadence and feminisation) of American and continental influences, rather than the class problematic as the privileged centre. The scooter is intensively analysed rather than the mod, to reveal the technical problems of accounting for the sedimentations of meanings in the object at the stages of production, advertising and consumption, rather than to reveal the hidden political coding in the style, or the homologies with the 'upward option'.

Pop Art is analysed very persuasively, as a movement which questioned the barriers and distinctions in the field (of art this time), and broke them as effectively as did the avant-garde, despite an insistence that connections were also to be made with the low-status areas of design, graphics and commerce (thus risking Americanisation). Pop Art, like punk, displayed a critique of art via self-parody. We can still see, even in these rather abstracted analyses, an echo of the earlier interests – Hebdige is still analysing and celebrating mods and punks, but now at one remove, so to speak.

Hiding in the Light is also significant for its discussion of the impact of postmodernism, and its relation to earlier CCCS projects. As we said before, even the style of the book reflects the aesthetics of postmodernism. Typically, the debate is introduced via concrete analyses of *The Face* and Biff cartoons (parodies of contemporary culture). The piece on *The Face* sees the magazine as the postmodern archetype, refusing notions of 'representation' and 'depth', discussing issues in a characteristically fragmented and non-earnest way, so that readers can take what they want (via 'cruising') without any necessary commitment to any underlying critical discipline: 'the "reader" can take pleasure in a text without being obliged at the same time to take marriage vows and a mortgage on a house' (Hebdige 1988: 162). The style uses parody, irony and ambiguity, partly from fear of 'naming' objects directly, and thus domesticating them. *The Face* operates only in a 'now', incorporating past and future by reducing them to the same 'flat' superficial surface. Readers of *The Face* ('a significant minority' in 1988) draw from it the cultural capital necessary for survival in this continuous present.

We shall suggest that British academic courses in cultural studies offer the same service for 'cruising' students and lecturers. Hebdige's text contains many fertile suggestions for understanding the modern academic audience too.

Hebdige's journey into postmodernism is a fascinating one. He emerges from the crisis with a renewed faith in British gramscianism (unlike other contemporaries like Chambers 1986), as we have seen, and his work seems to underpin or converge with many of the themes discussed by Fiske and Hall and Jacques, even though he recognises hedonism as only one stance available to the postmodern populist. These stances will be critically discussed later. Postmodernism does seem to have had the effect of removing internal distinctions between the formerly separated specialisms of youth cultures and other aspects of popular culture, though. Youth has 'imploded' into lesiure and media, as subsequent chapters reveal, and analysts seem to have agreed upon a new interest in consumption as culture. Hebdige represents a work of transition in this respect.

At the very end of his book, though, Hebdige commends to us modesty, self-criticism, anti-climax, and a curious return to origins: 'We all come down to earth in time; we all come back "home"', or, earlier, 'but in the end we are – as Gramsci said – all of us philosophers, which means we are all homesick, yearning backwards to the source' (*ibid*: 244). This could well be an epitaph for the whole journey of the scholarship boy into academe and then out again, finding solace in the old community (even if it is imaginary), and finding a source of strength in the capacity to 'have a laff', albeit refined with a knowledge of Bakhtin's work on Rabelais.

CONCLUSION

The work on youth subcultures can be used to illustrate the strengths and limits of two major aspects of gramscianism – the break from social sciences and the flirtation with linguistics. Both have left gramscian work looking rather lopsided instead of more complete, and have helped the underlying wishful thinking of the work to come through. Of course, it is easy to see the absurdity of the claims made for the political significance of 1970s youth from the vantage point of 1990s Britain. Symbolic politics was never likely to resist real politics, as a series of events showed: the police occupation of the London School of Economics in 1969 after the revolutionary carnivals of 1968; the increasingly expert surveillance and policing of demonstrations and protests, football matches or street carnivals in the 1970s and 1980s; the policing of the miners' strike; the management of youth protest by a combination of containing riots and providing softer apparatuses of social control. The turn to coercion seems not to have been theorised, just as Anderson warned in 1976. Worse, Hirst's warning was ignored too: perhaps those (of us) who celebrated youth styles as oppositional politics helped only to justify that turn to coercion. There must be lessons (!) for those who want to prioritise cultural politics today.

5

THE CRISIS AND ITS CONSEQUENCES

POLICING THE CRISIS

Many of the criticisms following *Resistance Through Rituals*, including some of Hirst's, were to be addressed in this famous work. Ostensibly, the book represents the successful culmination of the mugging project mentioned in *Resistance . . .*, and can be read as attempting to move beyond what Butters had mentioned as an attempt to hold both regressive and progressive moments together, still using analogies and metaphors. *Policing the Crisis* (Hall *et al.* 1978) can be seen as a much deeper, much better researched and much more developed effort to go beyond these mere metaphors into something like a fully marxist account of the politics of crime.

Policing . . . is in fact a very complex and densely argued book, with sections on the role of the media, and theories of the State, but also with chapters on the state of 'normal' working-class consciousness, and on student revolt (as an attempt to complete a 'symmetrical' analysis, perhaps?), an account of then current Parliamentary policies, and sustained attempts to think out the position of black people in marxist terms.

This involves the use and transformation of a good deal of academic work, and some journalistic accounts, not all marxist, and not all turning upon the attempt to reconcile ethnographic and marxist accounts of crime. Indeed, even though the book has gone down in some sociology teacher circles as an attempt largely to settle accounts with labelling theory via the politicisation of the concept 'moral panic', this is not really a major theme. Unlike the earlier paper on mugging by Critcher (Hall and Jefferson 1976), the book almost entirely omits the notion of 'biography' and individual accounts and motives in favour of an almost exclusive reliance on the themes of structure and culture: this is an indication of the Althusserian aspects of the work, despite much reference to Gramsci. There are some rather strange methodological consequences of the turn away from

96

biography, though, and subjective data is smuggled in via the use of 'typifications' based on selective second-hand data, or the development of a curious 'insider' documentary reporting technique.

The focus on crime clears the issues a little as argued above, since it is not difficult to see crime as a matter involving the State, especially in the 1970s, when a number of controversial attempts were made to criminalise certain forms of industrial action or sexual conduct, and these were widely discussed and debated. The book also has a nicely concrete mediating agency in the mass media which acts to 'focus' (a well-used word) the connections between lay conceptions and obviously political ones, which solved one of the problems with *Resistance* . . . (identifying the transmission mechanisms whereby experience was 'coded').

Nevertheless, the book attempts a most ambitious project, which can be phrased in terms of a more explicit rerun of the issue of science and ideology in marxism (whereas *Resistance* . . . had been more concerned with an earlier stage of 'breaking' with bourgeois sociology).

Briefly, Marx had been read as offering, in a number of places, but especially in the Introduction to *Grundrisse* (Marx 1973), an account of the phoney methods of ideology, and a suggestion of an alternative method. What political economy and philosophy had in common, Marx was to argue, was a system of operating with strange abstractions as basic facts or concepts (like 'the individual', a 'population', the spheres of 'production, distribution and exchange') which could then be combined or linked into whole models of 'an economy', or whole conceptual systems and schema. Critique took a two-fold course – to reconsider the initial 'surface' or 'phenomenal' facts or concepts as being the product of 'many determinations' rather than as being some immediate, given data, and to tease out these hidden determinations. Then the phoney connections between superficialities, inevitably simple and ideological ones, were replaced with scientific ones between the 'deep' or 'real' determinants, which would embrace the full complexity of the initial objects and produce a suitably 'complex' unity.

A modified version of this method produced the much discussed 'Generalities' model of the science–ideology relation in Althusser (1966), but, despite a number of Althusserian references (especially to the 'levels' model of the social formation), the first version seems to underpin *Policing* . . . Incidentally, Althusser insists that Generalities II is best seen as a 'mode of production', working on the dubious concepts, facts and ideologies of Generalities I to produce science at Generalities III – yet he is silent about the concrete dynamics and form of this intellectual production process. With *Policing* . . . too we see largely the results of this intellectual labour to produce the critique, or at best a rather stylised account of the struggles with non-marxist concepts, rather than a concrete one.

The immediate goals of *Policing* . . . can then be sketched. First, to deconstruct the obvious and apparent 'facts' about mugging (and, later, other activities of black youth like 'hustling'), and offer alternative explanations and accounts. Second, to expose the phoney 'correlational' or 'metaphorical' connections established between, say, race, crime and the inner city, as demonstrated largely in media coverage, but also in a number of other ideologies, both lay and official. Third, to explain the real 'facts' and connections, by giving an account of the broad political 'context' in which the moral panic about mugging came to gain force, using a battery of marxist concepts, principally those of economic, political and ideological 'levels' and their role in reproduction and, inevitably, hegemony.

Before we discuss these steps, it is worth considering the place of the other issues also raised and discussed, at great length, in the book. We will discuss their substance later, but the first question to answer is why they are there. Why discuss matters like 'explanations and ideologies of crime' in such depth (Chapter 6), or the technical issues about the relations between race and class (Chapter 10)? Why such a detailed account of Government policies (Chapters 8 and 9)? All these are matters of 'context' and background, of course, but who needs such a detailed survey of the field? This sort of question is not intended to be frivolous – it addresses the issue of the intended audience of the book.

All the complications, summaries of masses of evidence and debate about matters like whether black people are a lumpenproletariat or an underclass (for example) make for a very 'difficult' piece of work, whose central themes are convoluted and heavily qualified. The book provides clues as to the intended audience in its Introduction – 'The courts, the police, the Home Office. . .the media. . .Academics. . .Liberals. . .active in the cause of penal reform or improving race relations' (Hall *et al* 1978: ix). Of these possibly conflicting groups, it seems that 'academics' have received the most attention: all those asides and interventions in debates between different authors (and all those careful qualifications and reservations) are for them. In this sense, the book makes another kind of 'advance' compared with the original piece in *Resistance* . . .

It is not now primarily the groups campaigning against the sentences on the Handsworth muggers in Birmingham that are to be addressed and supported, but those who have been hurt, puzzled, or left unbalanced by Hirst's critique of radical criminology mentioned above, perhaps: certainly, they get almost an entire chapter designed to comfort them. *Policing* . . . represents the transition of 'the mugging project' into a fully fledged working academic text. It also marks the deepest point of a rather esoteric 'crisis' caused in left-wing academic circles by the full flowering of the Althusserian critique of methodology: it is this crisis which is being policed here, it could be argued.

How successful is *Policing* . . . in its progress from ideology to science?

The first two parts successfully demonstrate the inadequacies of popular, media and judicial conceptions of mugging. These conceptions are clearly partial, selective, and heavily underpinned by prevalent 'images', despite their rationalised appearance, of race and crime on the one hand, and respectability, order and Englishness on the other. The book demonstrates the ideological work done by the media (newspapers exclusively) in constructing accounts of mugging that connect it with other anxieties about social disorder (via a process of 'convergence'), and which amplify or escalate these anxieties in the process. These convergences are 'rhetorical', abstract, and, as the examples demonstrate, absurd and sometimes hysterical, especially if the trigger word 'violence' is attached.

The media also act to construct a consensus between the official ideologies of spokespersons and powerful authorities, and the lay ideologies of the reading public, including the respectable working class.

We shall discuss work on the media later, but the role of the press here is interesting. Using existing work on 'news values', and borrowing from work already done at the Centre, although this is barely mentioned, the authors of *Policing* . . . are able to demonstrate a neat coincidence of 'relative autonomy' and 'reproduction'. The very values of press professionals on neutrality and balance permit the official definers of reality (the 'spokesmen' upon whom so much media coverage depends) to dominate discussion and set agendas. In this way, dominant ideology is popularised, and particular interests represented as universal public ones. Similarly, the press's connections with its reading public permits it to act as a ventriloquist for that public, to pose as a conveyor of 'public opinion' up to the dominant groups, who can then claim merely to be responding to pressures from below.

However, the views of the publics for the newspapers concerned also appear in the press as readers' letters, and these can exceed the limits of the press discussion in both 'left' and 'right' dimensions, so it is clear that the press cannot be the sole determinant of readers' views.

No other source of these views is discussed though, nor is much discussion devoted to the idea that it might be in the real interests of proletarians too to support law and order campaigns, although it is acknowledged, rather briefly, that there is a 'rational core' to white working-class anxieties about street crime. Here as elsewhere, the voices and views of respectable proletarians are not taken as authentic reports of their relations and experiences, not even in a symbolic or homologous form: they are neglected in favour of 'second-order' sociological accounts. They appear ready-managed, so to speak.

The point really is that the term 'ideology' is used differently to explain the views of the different classes and groups – 'lay ideologies' arise from 'false consciousness', despite reservations about using that term for youthful rebellious groups, while official ideologies arise from an accurate perception of class interests, and, presumably, professional ideologies of newsmen from specifc occupational interests.

What these ideologies have in common is a selectivity, demonstrated in the narrow range of discussion about crime. Here, *Policing* . . . seems to offer a rather abstract 'Kantian' critique, a 'critique of knowledge', directed at the claims made by these ideologies to be valid. However, with official ideologies real political interests are engaged, and *Policing* . . . offers a more political critique, one directed at raising questions about the rights of official groups to dominate in the interests of capital. Whether these two sorts of critique can be run together is highly debatable (see Bubner, for example, in Thompson and Held 1982), and objections to this undifferentiated notion of 'ideology' were to swell into the 'postmodernist' crisis. *Policing* . . . is certainly grist to the mill of those who want to argue that gramscian critique is over-concerned with ideology as the key to politics.

In concrete terms, it is not clear exactly what the media are being accused of – selecting from the available accounts a populist one with insufficient attention given to marxist explanations of crime (an inevitable outcome, given their role), or offering a dominant ideology as a direct expression of ruling-class interests (much less forgivable), or both. In their desire to hold on to both ends of the relative autonomy/reproduction chain, the authors of *Policing* . . . do not want to decide: the first version relativises so much as to break the apparently tight and concrete transmission mechanism between ruling interests and 'popular consent', the second looks like conspiracy.

Despite their vigilance when politicians or moral entrepreneurs effect convergence between different phenomena, Hall *et al.* seem to have done the same thing here with the concept of ideology. At one level, all accounts are partial, all involve bricolage, convergence, escalation, the deployment of rhetorical images, the CCCS account as much as the media accounts being criticised, so one cannot label some pejoratively as 'ideology' on the basis of form alone. Usually, of course, the political goals of the project then appear, to make the distinction between science and ideology sharper, but this begs many questions too: is a partial 'ideological' account harnessed to a 'good' politics more 'scientific' as a result: can 'good' politics overcome 'bad' methodologies? These questions too were put by Hirst to Taylor *et al.* earlier, but they are not confined to Althusserians – Adorno asks the same questions of partisan accounts, as we saw in Chapter 1.

The last two parts of *Policing* . . . outline the 'scientific' alternatives to the ideological accounts deconstructed earlier. There are many intriguing and fascinating arguments, and a variety of argumentational techniques designed to convince the reader. The most fascinating of these consist of the documentary-style analyses of 'Englishness'. These give an account of life in England that is highly reminiscent of the skilled reporting of 'key informants', knowledgeable ex-members of the working-class respectables like Hoggart or Williams. Other ex-members (like me) can find an immediate moment of 'recognition' in the accounts of work and its role in self-esteem, or the pride in 'discipline'. These plausible stories seem no less 'ideological' or more 'scientific' than the ones they intend to replace. They serve a different purpose, of course, to bind the reader to the 'realism' of the account in a literary, essentialist, humanist way, one which the 'ideological' media also use to great effect.

Can press stories and features be critiqued as ideology in Chapter 3 and deployed as major sources of supportive evidence in Chapters 8 and 9? There almost seems to be a belated distinction between ideological 'popular' newspapers and more trustworthy 'quality' press behind these shifts.

The use of typifications at selected moments, in describing the typical motives of a mugger, for example, must also be controversial. Another dilemma seems to be revealed here: 'structural' marxism places little weight upon biographical accounts, but there seems to be a lingering anxiety that omitting all reference to individuals and their motives would either mimic the official acccounts of mugging as 'irrational' and 'incomprehensible', or run the risk of ascribing deep political meanings from the outside, romanticising deviance. These odd typifications seem a most unsatisfactory compromise with journalistic or literary forms of expression, though.

There is a confident attempt to explain the reaction to mugging as one of the moral panics which facilitated the slide to a 'law and order society', but considerable uncertainty about how this society can be explained in marxist terms. Is it normal or abnormal for advanced capitalist societies to be as authoritarian as this? In Chapters 7 and 8, it is not clear that 'hegemony' still is applicable to describe societies that seem to be in a state of 'managed dissensus' or 'authoritarian consensus'. Perhaps there is there some (functional? conspiratorial?) 'deep structure' of control which has moments of rule by ideology and rule by coercion, as Chapter 9 implies (see for example pp. 276f, p. 285).

Whether 'civil society' is still autonomous or whether it has been fully colonised by the state is in doubt, despite the confident intervention at the level of theory elsewhere (CCCS 1978). (Althusser's critique of Gramsci insists that the distinction is a contingent one in the gift of the State, but Hall *et al.* argued against this view.) The model of the social formation to be developed in *Policing* . . . was Althusser's one of 'levels' (useful, via Poulantzas, to explain the articulation of race and class). It is doubtful that this model can be isolated from the rest of the opus to avoid the unpleasant aspects of Althusserian marxism (like the 'purism' of the methodological work as in Hirst's critique, or the party politics, or the pessimism towards social change), however.

101

I wonder, looking back, if it was worth all the effort to incorporate Hirst on Althusser, when Hirst himself was already on the next stages of his amazing 'odyssey' (see Elliot 1986) which led to deep and permanent damage to Althusserianism, and the introduction of the thin end of a very damaging wedge. This 'post-Althusserianism' rapidly widened to a full-blown postmodernist critique which swept away Althusser too.

More concretely, there are questions even about the basic aspects of mugging, such as whether it can be seen as an adequate symbolic politics, or whether it is necessary to develop a strategy to politicise black youth in more desirable ways. This latter uncertainty surely is a result of Althusserian pessimism, and follows a shift in the way in which the struggles of black youth are now thought out, as an effect of historical structures rather than as one of some inherently rebellious and alienated grouping.

To find all these questions at the end of a substantial venture could be seen as a demonstration of an appropriate openness characteristic of proper science. There seems to be no stage-managed 'discovery' here, at least, no premature reduction of the 'complex unity' to some easy slogan about hegemony.

Yet the piece can also look like a conventionally 'balanced' academic piece, riddled with cautious qualifications and reservations. This is a way of attempting to disarm critics, perhaps, by generating *ad hoc* hypotheses to protect the central concepts from falsifcation, as in the classic Popperian critique of marxism. Thus we find the authors dealing with specific examples which appear to go against their general argument by using terms like 'A throwaway humanism, marginal to the argument' (Hall *et al.* 1978: 101) (to handle an unusually sympathetic press item), or the long passage (pp. 137–8) where differences in specific ideologies are acknowledged to deny a 'single, coherent, unified, consistent English "public ideology of crime"', while concluding that 'we also insist that. . .[there is]. . .a structured field of ideological premises'. These sentences may contain valid distinctions of great power and subtlety (e.g. between an 'ideology' and a 'field of ideological premises'), or they may indicate a common academic desire to want it both ways.

Sometimes a concluding section to a chapter will modify and qualify after a fairly simple account (it is hard to illustrate this in a short review – but see Chapter 10), perhaps because another member of the writing team or a sympathetic critic has expressed doubts. Some of the sections seem to have been included to meet demands from invisible contributors. Some sections are simply evasive, or so wrapped in double negatives as to be deeply equivocal: 'It is not merely coincidental that' language used to oppose dissenting groups often tries to criminalise them (*ibid*: 70), or 'Despite these reservations, however, it seems undeniable that the *prevailing tendency* in the media is towards the reproduction, *amidst all its contradictions,* of the definitions of the powerful, of the dominant ideology' (*ibid:* 65–6) (original emphasis).

A common feature too, as in the example just given, seems to be apology in the Barthesian sense – after a number of reservations, qualifications, considerations of alternatives, and the careful weighing of opposing points of view, the writers will announce that nevertheless they believe something to be the case. This is a way of claiming an objectivity and a spurious identification with the doubts of the reader, as Barthes makes clear (Barthes 1973). It is a common pedagogic technique, as well as one used by advertisers. As a brief illustration, on p. 305 there is a list of qualifications of the main argument that 'the mugging' reaction grows out of the drift of the State, under the crisis of hegemony, into an exceptional posture, and we are told that 'it is not in a simple sense the *direct* product of that evolution' (original emphasis). Yet, after a page of qualifications: 'We believe, then, that the nature of the reaction to "mugging" can only be understood in terms of the way society. . .responded to a deepening economic, political and social crisis' (*ibid:* 306).

The claimed narrative integrity of the piece is in doubt even at the level of the basic strategy. It is not at all clear why mugging was chosen for such detailed treatment, for example, when other issues would have done just as well to ground the drift to the law and order society (Ulster, the Angry Brigade, student revolt, or working-class militancy like the miners' strikes are mentioned in the book as marginal accompaniments to the main theme). There is a danger of continued voyeurism or zookeeping here. As argued above, perhaps the intended political alliances with local black people privileged the choice of topic initially, although there is little reference to that audience in the final version.

The impression the authors give is that they just moved, under the pressure of their own argument, from one level of analysis to the other as their discoveries unfolded, but this looks suspiciously like one of the 'logics of enquiry' identified in Butters' piece earlier (Hall and Jefferson 1976). In that piece, Butters argued that researchers often claim to have encountered some novelty, unexpected development or shock on entering the field, which somehow wipes out preconceptions and guarantees the groundedness of the theoretical apparatus. Phrases like 'our analysis can no longer remain at the level of analysing ideologies of crime. . .The "problem of authority" directs us to a different level of analysis' (Hall *et al.* 1978: 177) must not be read at face value, then. As Chapter 6 (below) reveals, the authors had known for some while where they were going.

At the end of the day, despite the academicised developments, the shift between levels is still pretty simple in fact. Ethnography no longer had to be transcended with the turn to Althusser, and Becker could be dismissed with a lofty view that the 'larger forces' at work in labelling are to be preferred, following an apparently innocent 'felt need' (*ibid*: 185), while Lemert's notion of a 'societal control culture' is hijacked for marxism (as is much else) by translating 'culture' as 'ideology' and adding a hierarchy of ideologists (*ibid*: 194). The shift to gramscian terminology is accomplished largely by the use of 'point of view' quotes or sections 'bolted on' to non-marxist description (as in Chapters 8 and 9). It is indeed a rhetorical connection, a secondary level of analysis, hardly mentioned during the substantive pieces, and mixed with Althusserianism (and even at one stage 'critical theory'), to 'cover' the specifics.

Policing the Crisis also raises the issue of the agents of revolutionary change. The right seem to be organising to manage the crisis. Gramscian logic suggests there must be resistance and struggle somewhere too – but where?

WOMEN AND BLACK PEOPLE: ALTERNATIVE PROLETARIATS?

CCCS writers discovered the importance of women fairly early. McRobbie and Garber, and Hebdige raised the issues in the very first published collection of working papers, as we have seen. The Centre also soon established separate working groups to focus on women and black people, and their efforts were soon to emerge as 'annual specials'. When we review them below, the main interest will be in terms of how they fit into the gramscian project. It has already been shown that one initial way to react to the challenge of feminist and black activist work was to consider a form of articulation to link in these issues to conventional class politics, and it is this model and its fate that will be discussed: apart from other considerations, I claim no independent expertise in these fields, certainly not enough to review the whole span of available work or to offer any kind of authoritative guide to the issues in their own right, as it were.

There is no intention to deny Hall's assertion that the work of the Women's Study Group in particular changed the work of the Centre as a whole profoundly (see his piece on 'problematics' in Hall *et al.* 1980). There are signs of clear efforts to consider studies of women and black people as part of the main themes: in the overall review of British history, for example, (Clarke *et al.* 1979, or Langan and Schwartz 1985), or in the study of fascism by Mercer (in Donald and Hall 1986); and both groups (especially women) have been in the forefront of attempts to rethink modern politics, from Bridges and Brunt (1981) to Hall and Jacques (1989). The work of feminist writers on the media audience has been eagerly adopted by Fiske (1987, 1989a, 1989b), and we shall discuss this work in more depth in Chapter 8. Nevertheless, the relationship with women and black activists has not always been an easy one, and there have been some sharp disagreements. These have been revealing for the construction of this book for the light they shed on the strengths and weaknesses of gramscianism.

Women

The Women's Study Group at CCCS clearly stood in a relation of some tension with the rest of the members of the Centre, as Chapter 1 of the main book (Women's Study Group 1978) makes clear. It was not simply that women had remained marginal to the main concerns of the Centre as objects of study, as the piece by McRobbie in *Resistance . . .* had explained – the women analysts had also experienced difficulties in deciding how precisely to position their work. Should it be seen as a reaction to the whole of cultural studies and its failure to theorise women, or as a more modest attempt to address the missing women within the framework, as it were? On a more personal level, 'either we had something to say and should say it, or else we didn't, and so we should stop making everyone feel guilty' (Women's Study Group 1978: 10).

The feminist work had its origins in a different politics and in a different kind of marxist or materialist tradition. The experience of participation in the Women's Liberation Movement (WLM) of the 1960s and 1970s had broken with the conventional British socialist concerns and debates that underpinned much of the work of Hall and the other 'mainstream researchers' (including the focus on hegemony). Briefly, as Brunsdon's chapter explains, experience in WLM had foregrounded the ideological issues, and developed from women's consciousness of their oppression in sites like the family, images of women, sexuality, the emotional as well as the economic division of labour. Since personal experience was the only common ground in all these sites, the slogan 'the personal is the political' emerged as a major rallying point, as did the emphasis on consciousness-raising, awkward as these might be for the newly sophisticated marxism.

The personal and the ideological and the major sites of struggle – the family and the media – began to be investigated and theorised independently of the 'line' being taken by CCCS members on youth, style and culture. Now, for the Women's Group, the issue had become one of trying to connect that work and that experience to the CCCS line, both for good theoretical reasons (to theorise oppression as a whole not just sexism, to further develop theories about how individual positions were reproduced), and to address the local micropolitical tensions mentioned above.

The actual work displayed by the Group in this collection follows the usual pattern of careful research and argument, working out some of the major implications of Marx's economics, especially his attempts to theorise notions like 'reserve army of labour', 'productive and unproductive labour', and the reproduction of labour in families, in ways that had simply not been done in *Resistance* . . . (where the economic dimension of youth had not been addressed), and which has never really been equalled since. *Policing* . . ., for example, in attempting to explore the economic dimensions of black labour, (and to reply to Hirst's attacks by showing some uses of some proper marxist concepts) could only admit a debt to this feminist analysis, and reproduce [*sic*] one aspect of it.

Perhaps the most striking example of the relevance of the family to these economic analyses centres upon the work of Beechey (elaborated subsequently, like many of the insights, in Kuhn and Wolpe 1978). Thus, although it had not been theorised directly in marxist economics, the family performs a number of functions like regulating the entry of females into waged labour, or permitting the employment of women at wages lower than the costs of reproduction. This is possible since there had been established the existence of the notion of a 'family wage' allegedly congealed in male wages, a ploy adopted by organised male labour bargaining over wages and welfare, but one which involves 'the defining of labour as male' (*ibid*: 47).

Of course, the family exhibits determinations at the ideological and political levels too, and examples of State legislation are discussed in detail for the latter (e.g. in Chapter 3): this work too was to be borrowed for *Policing* . . . Discussions of the ideological levels involved a more radical departure from the mainstream work, though, and were to reopen the general debate raised by Hirst, or even more pertinently by Coward.

Once again, issues arose from Freud's work, which had been investigated and much debated by early feminist writing, partly because Freud is an obvious source of theory on what seemed to be the particular issues for women – sexuality, the family. Chapter 6 of *Women Take Issue* (Women's Study Group 1978) summarises some debates in much more detail than can be attempted here, but briefly, Freud's account of sexuality and its connections with kinship systems, and thus with social order, can be linked with marxist work, as long as we are prepared to read Freud as not offering a biological account, nor one based on a view of sexuality and kinship as separate areas somehow with their own set of discrete determinations (although both of these readings have some substance).

We also have to subject Freud to the 'linguistic' reading offered by Lacan, which, among other things, radically changes the notion of the subject and intentionality. The 'law' that operates to structure consciousness, subjectivity, and the whole social and cultural manifestations of 'the Symbolic' is seen as a neutral one with respect to any actual existing concrete system of kinship or social order, however: whichever particular forms develop, including patriarchal ones, depends upon historical and material relations between the sexes (*ibid*: 117). Thus Lacan can be claimed by feminists as denying the naturalness and inevitability of patriarchy found in some other Freudian readings. As for the material practices which operationalise and concretise 'the law', Althusser is seen as offering a fruitful 'homology' (in his essay on Lacan), but, apart from an agreement on the importance of the family, much work remains to be done to tease out the complex conjunctural links between economic, political and ideological functions in actual families. There are strong echoes here of Coward's critique as discussed above.

In *Women Take Issue*, the argument returns again and again to the family as a specific organisation whose importance has been drastically underestimated by marxists. Even Hindess and Hirst failed to theorise adequately the kinship system in their discussion of pre-capitalist modes of production, for example (1975) (one of the failed journeys to locate a specific definition of the marxist term 'mode of production'). Basically, since kinship systems had the effect of subordinating women, not merely distributing surplus to an undifferentiated 'community', the whole analysis has to be reworked to include 'the political' level in social formations at a much earlier stage. Bland *et al.*'s essay (Chapter 8) argues explicitly for an anthropology to supplement marxist concepts, and demonstrates implicitly the tremendous value of comparative work to avoid the 'asymmetries' and tautologies we have identified before.

Of course, like many such collections, not all the pieces in *Women Take Issue* are fully consistent with the theoretical models on offer. The concrete analyses seem much less concerned with material theories of the constitution of the subject, and seem quite happy to work with subjects as classically defined, complete with 'intentions'. They offer ethnographic analyses of isolated housewives, for example, (Chapter 4), teenagers at youth clubs (Chapter 5), or what came to be known as 'redemptive' analyses of the hegemonic strategies and counter-hegemonic resistances of *Woman* magazine or of a Brontë novel.

This 'inconsistency' is also a feature of the subsequent collection in Kuhn and Wolpe, and led to a characteristically Hirstian critique by Adlam (1979) which will serve as a comment on the whole project to unite marxism and feminism. The general strategy will be familiar from the consideration of Hirst's work, and the arguments might have contributed to that fragmentation of socialist feminism described by Rowbotham *et al.* (1979).

The review article reflects the deep suspicion felt towards all totalising projects by the post-Althusserians. Adlam argued that attempts to unite Althusser on ideology and Lacan on the Symbolic merely glosses the different discourses in which the terms are located – basically, the former uses concepts like social divisions, while the latter talks of abstract differences. They cannot just be added together as in schemes which use a basic framework of 'sophisticated economic functionalism' with the concept of ideology 'to take care of the residue'.

There is no way to join the concepts of capitalism and patriarchy. The solutions on offer either ultimately reduce one to the other, or offer an 'oscillation between an economic reductionism or a sexual essentialism', or reduce the objects in marxism, semiotics and psychoanalysis to mere sociological variables which happen to cluster together, empirically, in different ways, sometimes supporting each other, sometimes balancing (as in 'double determinations' of women's oppression).

Adlam, like Hirst, having demonstrated the failure to develop a general theory goes on to deny its relevance. It is the specificity of women's oppressions that need to be grasped, and this specificity is lost by holding to a general theory based on a single underlying antagonism – 'a duality can not be stretched into a diversity' (Adlam 1979: 99). A 'calculative politics' is needed instead, recognising that men and women are not always opposed, and realising that 'women' as much as 'the working-class' need to be decomposed as an essentialist unity. Much of this argument seems to have been accepted, in the USA as well as in Britain, and a coalition of interests replaces the former attempt at a full theoretical integration. The awkward issue of choosing political and theoretical priorities among struggling groups is thus averted, but all parties remain coy about the actual calculations of interest involved. To put this at its sharpest, it is not at all clear what the women's movement actually needs from gramscians, especially these days.

Whatever the fate of its general theory, socialist feminism in the Women's Study Group had the greatest importance in leading to the subsequent work of CCCS graduates in analysing the media (see Chapter 8), or in grasping the specifics of women's leisure in its connections with the dominance of men – see, for example, McRobbie and Nava (1984). Again, the methodological implications are crucial in these pieces, not just their capacity to 'add in' women: this work has generated a much-needed openness towards the specific, the personal and the subjective in gramscianism. Davis (in Bridges and Brunt 1981) reasserts the need for women's oppression to be grasped specifically, and for women to lead any socialist alliance. Given the way in which the women's movement has set practically the entire agenda for 'new times' socialism, this claim is a very strong one.

Black activists

Black activists too had to find their voice within the overall projects at the CCCS, and they did so with a special publication *The Empire Strikes Back* (CCCS 1982). The opening pieces in the collection round out and develop some of the insights in *Policing. . .*, and bring the story up to date to include reactions and developments following the urban riots of the early 1980s in Britain. One change is in the language of racism in Britain, which switches from a concern with 'strangers' and 'immigrants': black people are now seen as a problem within British society, and thus 'race' can be used in new 'articulations' of Englishness (e.g. as part of the 'threat from within'). Indeed, 'race' becomes one of the key sites of struggle in the crisis, enabling several writers to claim that the 'leading edge' lies in the black activist struggle.

This struggle dominates the analysis even more so than for earlier gramscian work. Much of the work on attempting to counter existing conventional accounts of the entanglements of race and various social problems has political goals, and the arguments seem aimed at the British left as well as at police or media racists. Black persecution, and the ensuing resistance, are seen as properly political, rooted in the endogenous crisis of the British State, operating at each of the different Althusserian 'levels', requiring no special additional explanations other than those of gramscian marxism. Even Hebdige's account of the cultural significance of Rastafarianism could be seen as missing the political significance of the movement, and thus having to operate with an 'extra' dimension outside of the usual gramscian vocabulary.

Much of this is directed very acutely at bourgeois sociology, with its ethnocentric insistence on seeing 'race' as somehow a matter of deviance or social pathology, and Chapters 2, 3 and 4 of *The Empire*. . . do much to expose this ethnocentrism, not only in sociology, but in 'common-sense' and in various official practices, especially in education and policing (even its liberal and then fashionable form – 'community policing'). The whole terrain is a good example of the play of the 'ideology effect', as Hall named it (in Curran *et al.* 1977): phoney and abstract divisions and categories are devised, and then value-laden theories are produced to connect these categories into some overall account. Even black researchers are liable to this kind of ideology effect, if they are of bourgeois origin themselves (see p. 133) or are in some other way isolated from the struggle in the streets: Lawrence's Chapter 3, and Gilroy's two chapters argue that direct experience in the 'front line' struggle is a more suitable source of knowledge than mere academic research.

However, some backsliders on the left are also rebuked. *Policing* . . . itself had been rather ambivalent about seeing street crime as political resistance, as we have seen, but Gilroy argued, in Chapter 4, that insufficient attention was given to the role of police practices in defining street crime, and, for that matter, to the widespread occurrence of police crime itself, in the form of assaults on black people, wrongful arrest, official harassment in massive stop and search operations and so on. In that context, the political nature of black street crime is much clearer!

Other researchers are rebuked for excessive zeal, though, in wanting the black struggle in alliance with, but led by the white proletariat. As with the women's movement, black activists in the USA were to reject such political or intellectual leadership too, as the discussion in Walker (1979) reveals. Gilroy's Chapter 8 uses 'enriched gramscianism' based on Laclau to argue that discourses are not reducible to class, yet to deny that 'race' is merely a cultural or ideological problem. In an attempt to hold together both ends of this chain, to argue that race is both a class phenomenon, yet also a specific struggle, warranting its own leadership, Gilroy concludes that black people occupy 'racially demarcated class fractions' (CCCS 1982: 284). Only in the 'rarest moments of revolutionary rupture' are these fractions likely fully to unite (*ibid*: 307).

Gilroy especially was to go on to develop a deeper analysis of the discourses of racism (Gilroy 1987), and to display in the process that steady slide away from conventional marxism, which we have seen before, into the new linguistic cultural politics. Briefly, the 'class fractions' became 'urban social movements', emerging from the demise of the conventional working class, and their role is symbolic, defensive, or at best progressive, rather than revolutionary, as in 'new times' marxism generally.

More orthodox activism remains with former colleagues of Gilroy in the Institute of Race Relations (producers of the journal *Race and Class*). The Institute had already become famous for its combative dismissal of bourgeois approaches to race and race relations, and had managed its own version of a workers' takeover in order to break the ties with its capitalist and State sponsors and get closer to the black struggles.

The Institute's work is not the main topic here, but its Director, Ambalavaner Sivanandan, has produced a collection of major pieces, including a magnificently polemical counterblast to the 'new times' approach which begins 'New Times is a fraud, a counterfeit, a humbug. . .a mirror image of Thatcherism passing for socialism' (Sivanandan 1990: 19). Sivanandan darts some of Gilroy's own barbs at 'theoretical practitioners', including those who get committed only at the level of culture and discourse, changing the focus of the struggle to theoreticist practice (by this time, probably Gilroy himself). In the 'new times', the 'Third World' especially appears only as a 'site for popular culture and popular politics. . . "the famine movement"' (*ibid*: 48). Sivanandan's style is irresistible – he summarises brilliantly the shift to cultural politics as a move 'from changing the world to changing the word' (*ibid*: 49).

He offers his own account of the economic forces still at the base of the new social order, and urges socialists to focus on the eternality of poverty, rather than the alleged universality of 'identity' or consumption: 'Class, even as a metaphor, is still the measure of a socialist conscience' (*ibid*: 44). In global terms, the poverty and misery of the Third World is still the major political issue. In parochial terms, the struggle is still visible in Britain's inner city streets, among the new underclass: thus struggle is still the articulating mechanism rather than any new discourses, and cultural politics remains a luxury, or a diversion. Of course, such activism has its own difficulties, as Chapter 1 suggested.

CONCLUSION

While the State organised itself for an authoritarian turn, popular opponents seemed less and less likely to emerge. Both black people and women present problems for any attempt to designate them as part of some overall proletarian struggle. There is no easy articulation with gramscian theory, although, of course, in skilled hands it can be done. Unlike youth, however, women and black activists demanded at least a say in their own articulations, and, in the process, came to modify gramscianism almost beyond recognition. Both sets of theoreticians and activists are still sources of critique and development, so even the gramscians must be grateful that no easy integration and subordination took place, at least in so far as their academic interests are concerned.

Politically, the crisis for gramscianism was to deepen still further, as Thatcherism came, with some electoral support, and lasted far longer than anyone on the left expected. An even more desperate search for possible revolutionary agents was to ensue, as Chapter 9 reveals.

6

THE MASS MEDIA:
POLITICS AND POPULARITY

INTRODUCTION

The Birmingham Centre developed a characteristic, and rather limited, interest in modern mass media. In brief, the study of television in particular usually had been subordinated to other agendas – a theoretical struggle concerning the status of the subject (a contest with 'screen theory' in particular), and a project to consider the 'articulation' of particular political discourses on the three central 'condensations' of class, gender and ethnicity (see Hall's 'Introduction to Media Studies at the Centre' in Hall *et al.* 1980). The cultural aspects of popular television and film aside from these interests were relatively neglected until rather later, in courses at the Open University like *Mass Communication and Society* (*DE353*) (Open University 1977) and above all *Popular Culture* (*U203*) (Open University 1982).

The media were discussed very unevenly in *Resistance Through Rituals* (Hall and Jefferson 1976), as we have seen. The press had been seen as an important factor in the generation of a moral panic about rebellious youth by Cohen (1987), and this had been acknowledged in the long Overview. McRobbie was beginning to develop the concerns that would lead to her (and other women at the Centre) raising the issue of teenage magazines too. Yet, apart from these beginnings, there is a long silence, as Hebdige pointed out in his later review (Hebdige 1979): both *Resistance* . . . and Willis's *Learning to Labour* (1977) identify some sort of direct, unmediated experience of working-class life as crucial in the symbolic reworkings of youth cultures. The work on the supposedly still active subterranean traditions of 'really useful knowledge' in education come close to this too (CCCS 1981, Education Group II 1991). Hebdige suggested that the media had already symbolically reworked these experiences, it will be recalled (Chapter 4). To paraphrase Hall's later rebuke to the tradition of studies of television and violence, television was responsible for a considerable

112

number of messages about class and community, and national decline, and it seems almost inexplicable that the analysts would not have noticed them. It seems incredible that ethnographic studies had not also pointed to the growth of television watching as a major activity among youth: of course, Hobson's work on women soon did – but did none of Willis's 'lads' watch television?

It would be almost too neat and ironic to attribute this omission to a simple contempt for popular television among the Centre's staff. After all, such élitism is supposed to be one of the characteristics of critical theory and its 'mass culture' approach (critical theorists had written about radio and television as growth points in the culture industry, of course). Buckingham certainly feels such élitist disdain was widespread at the time though, among all radicals (Buckingham 1990).

Hall offers this account of early CCCS priorities:

> At this time [early 1970s?] the preoccupations with the questions of cultural trivialisation and violence in mainstream research high-lighted television as the privileged medium and the entertainment materials provided by the media as the most relevant for research. But, stimulated by. . .[work on coverage of Vietnam]. . .by the Leicester Centre. . .[Birmingham] Centre work took a lead in shifting the emphasis. . .away from entertainment to the heartland of 'political communications', especially in the news and current affairs areas.
>
> (Hall *et al.* 1980: 119)

There is much to discuss in these sentences, with hindsight. Who was so preoccupied, and why should this preoccupation prevent an intervention by the Centre? Perhaps it was one of those territorial disputes Hall tells us about earlier in the same volume? How important is 'taking a lead'? How did this set of priorities square with, say, Hobson's work (some of which was summarised in the same volume as this Introduction) that showed, among other things, that news and current affairs programmes were seen by the working-class women she studied as men's programmes? Or, more generally, whose view was it that news and current affairs represented the heartland of 'political communications', and what sort of agreement, tacit or otherwise, with the media's penchant for Parliamentary party politics is involved?

The theoretical debates that focused on subjectivity and its construction in this CCCS Media Group collection have been summarised in Chapter 2, and they seem to have followed a familiarly ironic path. Semiotics was seen as a way out of the American version of the 'mass culture' approach, which seems to have been especially behaviouristic and functionalist, and as offering a suitably impressive theoretical and political rebuke to the value-laden pessimism implied in the 'cultural trivialisation' theme (located in the English Faculty again? or in Hoggart?).

113

However, the trail into semiotics was also a trail along which lay Lacan and the *Tel Quel* group, and screen theory, with its deep suspicion about the concept of 'culture', and its insistence on the construction of subjectivity in language, for political as well as theoretical reasons (see Ellis in Hall *et al.* 1980 for general marxist, and specifically Maoist, reasons for considering the 'politics of subjectivity'). It is interesting to note that at a fairly early date, Volosinov and the notion of linguistic struggle were being discussed at the Centre (Woolfson, Tolson and Ellis in CCCS 1976). The turn to a version of discourse theory as in Laclau was one way to preserve some sort of defence to the charges made by 'proper linguistics', as we have seen.

EARLY WORK ON THE MEDIA

The work at the Centre in that period does seem to have been remarkably fruitful, and rather long-lasting. Although the chronology is not important, one of the first pieces, on class and the media, had been written in the 1960s (Hall in Mabey 1967). Hall had also written two early pieces in Cohen and Young (1973). Although these were focused on radio news, and the news photograph, all the major themes for the later work are present, including the relations between news values, particular 'inflections' and dominant ideology (called the 'political culture' or 'the consensual view' in the first piece), the notion of 'English-ness' (referenced to Barthes), and how the various double movements or double articulations between the two levels provided a misleading and naturalised objectivity.

A scan of the collection in Hall *et al.* 1980 shows that Heck and Connell also both produced papers on political discourses that prefigured more famous pieces later. Heck it was who argued that the media work through an ideology effect as in Poulantzas, and this also appears in the longer piece by Hall reviewed below (in Curran *et al.* 1977). I am not suggesting, of course, that Heck came before Hall, chronologically or conceptually. Heck cites an unusual Spanish source for her reading of Althusser's conception of ideology as a structure or 'set of [communicative] rules', which leads to the interest in codes in media messages, and she lays out the arguments for 'aberrant decoding', and a discussion of connotation and denotation, that were to become more famous in the Hall article on 'encoding and decoding' in the same volume (also reviewed below).

Connell's study of television coverage of the debates about the 'Social Contract' (a planned agreement between Government and Trade Unions on pay levels and other matters in the 1970s in Britain) anticipates (not literally), and might have been useful to, the authors of *Policing the Crisis*. Connell had collaborated with Hall and Curti on the working paper on the notion of national unity in current affairs programmes (in Bennett *et al.* 1981a). This sort of collaboration is an example of the claimed benefit of the kind of collective labour pursued at the Centre in those days, according to Hall's opening Chapter in Hall *et al.* 1980, although it is also responsible for a considerable repetition and convergence. At the risk of still more, it is useful to summarise two major articles by Hall himself, to set a general theoretical context.

Hall on the 'ideology effect'

In his piece in Curran *et al.* (1977), Hall offers a general introduction to some of the debates about culture and ideology which had raged at the Centre, and which we have largely covered before (Gramsci as offering an enlarged and political reading of reproduction compared to Althusser and so on). There are some new points of interest, though.

Mepham's work on the structures involved in ideology is given a central place with references to a CCCS Working Paper completed by Mepham – presumably this is virtually the same as his later published piece (in Mepham and Ruben 1979). Mepham offers a very clear way of rejecting the earlier work on consciousness in Marx and Marx and Engels, especially in *The German Ideology* (Marx and Engels 1974). This work saw consciousness and material reality as separate entities, and offered terms like 'inversion' to explain the ideological relation between them, as in the famous 'camera obscura' metaphor. In brief, ideology in this early work takes the form of 'false consciousness', inverted reality, 'illusions' or 'phantoms'.

Rather as in the Heck piece summarised above (and, again, the chronology is irrelevant), Mepham reads ideology as a matter of discourses. He characterises the new model, discoverable in *Capital*, as a 'serial' one, rather than a model of 'base/superstructure', with categories like 'real relations', 'phenomenal relations', 'ideological categories' and 'discourse practices' connected by structured practices – 'transformation', 'representation', 'generation' and 'reproduction'.

Reality in this model is not simply inverted or mystified but 'misrecognised' as an effect of discourses which, to be brief, work on the 'phenomenal' level, deal with deceptively simple surface forms, and maintain an account which leaves out the complexities in the depth. Mepham's analysis is developed in terms of 'common-sense' or 'spontaneous' thought, and formal ideas – political economy and philosophy – which incorporate the distortions of everyday life and make a science or a system out of them. In both science and common-sense, dubiously phenomenal categories support each other to create a whole 'semantic field'. However, this self-sustaining field is subject to disruption from the very dynamics of capitalism itself which continually corrodes the boundary between the real and the phenomenal as it forces social change.

When post-Althusserianism and postmodernism hit the fan, these notions of real and phenomenal forms, and the accompanying 'surface-depth' model, would be seen as irredeemable signs of 'metaphysics' or as sources of 'incoherence', but they met a need for Hall who relies heavily upon them for a theory of the mass media. After a long detour through some discussions of language (the usual authors), Hall decides that the media are one of the major transformational devices to erect 'maps of meaning' based on the interconnections of the 'phenomenal' categories found in common-sense and in bourgeois formal ideas.

Drawing upon Poulantzas's conception of ideology as turning upon 'separating and uniting', Hall proposes that the media be seen as the site of a sustained 'masking' of the contradictions in reality, and the construction of an 'imaginative' social order instead. We are not far from the 'imaginary resolution' of contradiction in *Resistance . . .* , of course, as well as the 'imaginary lived relation' of Althusser, and, for that matter, Macherey's 'imaginary reconciliation of irreconcilable terms' (see Burniston and Weedon in CCCS 1978).

Categories like 'the individual', especially, are abstracted from their class position, and reconnected in an

> imaginary unity or coherence on the units so re-presented. . .[for example in the]. . .various ideological totalities – the 'community', the 'nation', 'public opinion', 'the consensus', 'the general interest', 'the popular will', 'society', 'ordinary consumers'.
>
> (Hall in Curran *et al.* 1977: 337)

Finally, the media do this in a particularly compelling even if unstable way, making the 'preferred reading of events credible and forceful' (i.e. very nearly pleasurable) (*ibid*: 344).

The overall 'line' is clear, and the specific analyses develop it, as we shall shortly see. But before we leave this piece, it is interesting to note some points about the diversion through some theories of language mentioned above.

For one thing, Hall tries to situate his own work in relation to the Lacanian work on language and subjectivity. Specifically, he mentions this work (on p. 330) to guard against a view that 'the individual subject be conceptualized as the source or author of ideology', since this would deny the importance of the effects of linguistic practices themselves in the construction of ideology (including the specifics of the codes and conventions of television). Then a sentence introduces the work on 'positioning', in a rather brief way. The next sentence says that

> Important as this line of theorising is. . .it is of critical importance to stress that ideology as a *social practice* consists of the 'subject' positioning himself in the specific complex, the objectivated field of discourses and codes. . .what C. Wright Mills calls 'situated actions' and 'vocabularies of motives' [original emphasis].

It is really hard to decide whether Hall is subscribing to the view that there

116

are empirical subjects or not in this passage. Mostly, he seems to be doing just that – but then there is that curious bracketing of the word 'subject', just to hedge the bets slightly, perhaps. The same confusion can surround the use of the term 'unconscious', which often means that users are unaware that they are using loaded terms which have been 'naturalised', but which also flirts with Freudianism, of course.

Barthes is used to suggest that denotations still denote real things, even if signifieds as well as signifiers 'float' (Curran *et al.* 1977: 328), and Volosinov grounds the 'multiaccentuality' of the sign in class struggle ultimately (*ibid*: 329). However, more effectively, here and in his 'encoding' piece, Hall offers a plausible argument to refute the fully discursive approaches he was soon to encounter.

Coding and discourse theory

In 'Encoding/decoding' (in Hall *et al.* 1980), Hall develops some notions that were also clearly 'in the wind', and that had surfaced in earlier work (e.g. in Williams, according to Clarke and Critcher (1985), or in Eco's early Working Paper at the Centre, according to Moores 1990). Basically, the media operate when real events have to be coded, when they enter the 'relay of language'. Hall uses this figure specifically to argue that this is why discourse looks as if it constitutes everything – discourse does indeed have a 'determinate' moment, and once an event is coded, it becomes subject to dominant discursive rules and professional practices which together can 'rearrange, delimit and prescribe' relations between signs (Hall *et al.* 1980: 135).

But the event still exists, and coding is only one stage in a whole communicative system which includes the production, consumption and circulation of meanings too, and there are other determinations as a result. However, even the production of meanings also involves a 'discursive aspect' (*ibid*: 130), so there is the customary complexity. Nevertheless, the actual signs used in the media reveal that 'the dog in the film can bark but it cannot bite' (*ibid*: 131), a reference to Barthes, I think, which simultaneously reminds us both that filmic signs are not simple representations of reality, and that reality cannot be swallowed up in discourse (or not in specific discourses, that is). This is the source of that polysemy (multiple meanings) that many critics have praised as an example of Hall's break with dominant ideology theses (e.g. Moores 1990).

The article brings us up to date with the debates about connotation and denotation (already discussed above in Heck), and insists that polysemy is not pluralism, since some connotative codes can be imposed in 'preferred' or 'dominant' readings (so dominant ideology is soon reintroduced). These are not simply propaganda for the ruling class, but consist of 'rules of competence and use, of logics-in-use. . .[which]. . .actually seek to enforce or pre-fer one semantic domain over another' (Hall *et al.* 1980: 135). As with many of these articles, and as with Lacan's (filmed) lectures for that matter, one can spend hours puzzling over the significance of these peculiar stresses and emphases on words or syllables, but the importance of splitting 'pre-fer' still eludes me.

These dominant readings have become institutionalised, and have the 'political and ideological order imprinted in them' (*ibid*: 134), but they can be resisted, since the broadcasters do not have perfect control over decoding. Decoding is the process at the other end where 'symbolic vehicles' are taken from the realm of language and related back to real life. Decoding too possesses a discursive aspect. In fact, as Morley argues, and as we have seen, the specific discourses in programmes encounter alternative meanings in the 'interdiscourse' inhabited by the audience (see his Unit 12: 42f in *U203*, Open University 1982 for a clear reassertion of this point). Despite all their infernal art, the broadcasters cannot guarantee a congruity between encoding and decoding.

Although much is made of this point, however, this is more or less exactly the way in which functionalists account for deviance or social conflict, and the piece is very coy about the source of such decodings in any kind of structured conflict or contradiction. Indeed, the importation of anomie theory, even as in *Resistance . . .* , probably would have helped enormously.

Instead, at this point, Hall's argument takes a rather Parsonian but 'left-wing' turn, and he, like Morley, refers to Parkin's early model of value systems to ground his notion of decoding (Parkin 1971), despite another reservation about Parkin as insufficiently interested in linguistic aspects of these value systems. (This reservation is much better developed in the two pieces by Morley – in Hall *et al.* 1980 and in Unit 12, *U203*). Parkin's model is actually rather simple in Hall's hands, and proposes that working-class values be either congruent with dominant values, mixed, or oppositional. At least Parkin goes on to use the model to discuss possible sources and sites of oppositional values, but Hall leaves it as a purely abstract and formal possibility. When Morley tries to relate the model to his actual audience research (*U203* Unit 12), some of the simplifications become apparent.

Parkin's model is pretty sparse as far as models of audience competencies go, as later work demonstrates, and its use opens Hall especially to charges of sociologism or economism (reducing possible cultural and political meanings to effects of one's social or class position). It is chosen, perhaps, by a wish to police pluralism in terms of audience meanings, since not to do so would make the serious political content of the media seem irrelevant. Perhaps there is also a desire to write an early footnote to Gramsci's work on hegemonic or corporate consciousness, with a field of struggle in between. Whatever the reason, the article became famous and oft-quoted, and even appeared in Fiske's summary of the strengths of British cultural studies in Allen (1987), or in Jensen (1990). I even used it myself, briefly, in Harris (1987): like many admirers, I had not really read it, though.

Hall's article also mentions an unpublished critique by O'Shea (note 11, p. 295) of 'preferred reading', which I have not pursued. There may be traces of it in the Critical Postscript to Unit 12, *U203*, where Morley discusses whether these coded and decoded, preferred and oppositional meanings are located in the text itself, in the broadcasters' and audience's comprehensions, or in the analysts' critique. The whole discussion seems to be vague in terms of the different concepts of ideology deployed – is a preferred meaning one which shows an inevitable selection of meanings or one which privileges a ruling-class view of the world? As the discussion of *Policing the Crisis* showed, the two uses may not be compatible (see Chapter 5 above).

Some more recent sociological work on news suggests that there is no easy and unproblematic transmission of the views of the authorities in news production: the authorities vary among themselves in the use of certain strategies to brief and control the media, and their activities stretch well beyond the media themselves (Schlesinger 1989). Clayman's (1990) detailed study of the ways newsmen use quotes and 'sound-bites' to insert them into stories shows the role of mediations in the movement from talk to text, and argues that these specifics make it difficult to sustain a hegemonic reading. And other researchers have pointed to the specific micropolitical processes that go on within media organisations to interpret, manage and construe the utterances of official sources (see Glover in Haralambos 1985).

TELEVISION AND DISCOURSES OF NATIONAL UNITY

The work on two particular British current affairs programmes is well-known partly because the CCCS papers were collected in, and the work developed by, the legendary OU course *Popular Culture* (*U203*) (Open University 1982). The context provided by the introductions to these articles in the CCCS reader (Hall *et al.* 1980) and the OU one (Bennett *et al.* 1981a) do differ, though. Whereas Hall's introduction to media studies at Birmingham stresses the substantive issue of the political discourse, the introduction by Bennett *et al.* takes more interest in the 'technical' issues concerning the representation of the 'real world' and the way in which television 'installs the viewer within particular positions of knowledge in relation to the discourses it mobilizes' (*ibid*: 86). This may reflect an attempt to reach a rapprochement, perhaps 'unity' would be a better term in the circumstances, with 'screen theory' (the early *Screen* debate about realism is also highlighted in the reader and the course).

Naturally, only a brief summary of this work can be considered here.

119

One item of context might be helpful: Britain in the 1970s saw a resurgence of Scottish and Welsh nationalism, reviving the whole debate about Britain as a nation, and threatening to become a major party political issue. Certainly one of the founding fathers of the new left – Tom Nairn – was to develop the idea of this nationalist tension as a major mechanism of change (see, for example, his contributions in Bridges and Brunt 1981, or Hall and Jacques 1989).

There was another issue too – the 'crisis election' of 1974 had been staged by the Government as an issue of the 'national interest' versus the National Union of Mineworkers' pay claim and industrial action, and had taken place after the infamous period of the 'three-day week' (short-time working and domestic power cuts designed to 'save electricity' and to thwart the miners' action of picketing coal supplies to power stations).

Panorama

The article on *Panorama*, a 'serious' current affairs programme, (Hall, Connell and Curti in Bennett *et al.* 1981a) uses the notion of unity to address a number of themes. First, there is the unity between the Government's version of events and the underlying organisation of television coverage. The authors deny a simple conspiracy between Government and broadcasters in the usual way, and advance the theses found in the later Connell article too (in Hall *et al.* 1980): that the practice of television professionals, even when following their ethics of neutrality, serves to construct an ideological reality with a set of classifications and forms of address to the television audience that underpin and reinforce the 'deep' preferred view of the national interest and their right to represent it. Both pieces address the issue of the power struggles over ownership and control between the 'independent' BBC and successive British Governments eager to forge even more of a unity. All this was before the Thatcherite attempt to saturate the BBC with placemen, of course.

Second, specific unities or 'inflections of unity' are analysed, like the one represented by the Parliamentary system of government in Britain, which lies underneath the obvious party differences. This unity is secured by excluding or labelling (as 'extremist', for example) any views that do not support Parliamentary politics. In another specific unity, the Conservative Party especially is positioned so as to appear to be 'on the side of the people' (Bennett *et al.* 1981a: 107).

Third, the unity between different parts of the programme is discussed, including the ways in which the actuality material, the interviews and the interventions by the presenter construct a unified narrative, so to speak. This helped *Panorama* deliver a seemingly authoritative account with 'facts' and 'comment' in their proper places. The presenters in particular had a key role in addressing the audience directly, acting as a link between the viewing public and the experts and politicians in the studio, acting as a representative of the 'Plain Man' as (Sir) Robin Day put it (*ibid*: 95). This constitutes the audience as passive onlookers, who occupy a kind of middle ground between the political groups. Both articles give some close analyses of sequences from actual programmes (Connell includes news in his analysis) to illustrate these mechanisms of 'orchestration' of debates.

Finally, the programme serves as a further illustration of the important concept of 'complex unity in difference' (*ibid*: 95).

A notion of resistance to these messages is also developed. There are possible 'breaks' in audience decoding, for example, and this is often overlooked by marxist critics and television professionals, we are told. The politicians or members of the public that appear can also have their moments, even when the most seasoned presenters are trying to 'orchestrate' them, and Hall *et al.* note an interchange when the then leader of the Labour Party was able to seize the initiative, break the frame of the interview, take the chair, and launch his own discourse (*ibid*: 109–13).

Coward mentions this example in her critique of CCCS work mentioned earlier (Coward 1977). She sees in it the influence of the party political allegiances of the writers themselves in tacitly supporting the idea that Labour can be a genuine 'threat' to the system. There could be echoes too of Anderson's reservations (1976) about the 'neutral State' assumption in so much cultural politics (discussed in Chapter 1).

There is also a detectable element of the early 'media literacy' worries of the left, identified by Buckingham (1990), that proletarians will be rendered falsely conscious by televisual devices, despite the abstract possibility of aberrant decoding, unless they were specifically trained to be 'media literate'. There is no systematic discussion about whether this sort of analysis bears any relation to the actual readings achieved by the audience, however. Indeed, despite the anxieties about likely proletarian viewers, the intended audience for the analysis is the usual largely academic one for CCCS papers and publications, presumably. Whether any members of the actual popular audience for *Panorama* were being addressed in the pieces is unclear.

For Hall *et al.*, though, these breaks are used to deny simple reproduction theses and to argue instead for the superiority of the concept 'structure in dominance', with relative autonomy (actually 'relative independence' is the term used) for the State and the media from the ruling class. This shows the complex ways in which 'the media. . .do some service to the maintenance of hegemony, *precisely by providing a "relatively independent" and neutral sphere*' (original emphasis) (Bennett *et al.* 1981a: 115). This formulation is in great danger of circularity, though, unless there is a clear way to recognise just what is the difference between this sort of hegemonic independence and neutrality and *real* independence and neutrality: certainly this distinction is not clear in *Policing the Crisis* either, we have argued.

This general conclusion is repeated almost word for word, of course, in *Policing the Crisis*, so it is obviously too good to waste. The reader has to 'rediscover' it there, after some considerable concrete analysis of the news coverage of mugging in general and the Birmingham incident in particular. Whichever of these closely connected pieces came first, there must be a suspicion that the conclusion was waiting to be discovered all along in the later ones, of course, and that we should therefore read the 'concrete' analysis in the later ones as a kind of narrative device to engage the viewer (common in academic writing) rather than as an empirical method.

Racism and nationalism

Briefly, by way of context, there had been an interest in the images of race conveyed in the media which had already generated much interest (e.g. Hartmann *et al.*, Hartmann and Husband in Cohen and Young 1973). This work had focused on the stereotypes and negative representations of black people found in the press and on television, and had argued that black people were seen almost exclusively as a threat, as connected with violence, as outside society, or as simply absent from the main events of history (see Julien and Mercer 1988 for a similar account of black people in film).

This list of stereotypes corresponds quite tightly to those affecting the representations of women too, of course, although sexual identity had its own specific forms of stereotyping.

However, in both cases, discourse theory had offered another dimension too, one which offered a break from purely moral critique about inadequate representations (no representations are 'fair' on television). Bennett and Donald cite the work of Pollock (*U203* Unit 25: 61) to argue for the advantages of shifting to a discourse theoretic approach which would begin to consider the ways in which women (in this case) featured in conflicting discourses in mass media. This approach would fully embrace the idea of contradiction (instead of having to maintain that stereotyped images were somehow dominant or more prevalent, or pursuing some other partisan approach), would generalise the ideas of discrimination away from the obvious areas, and inform a deeper struggle against it. This sort of approach was to influence feminist work too – see below, and Walkerdine (in McRobbie and Nava 1984).

Although there is no time to investigate it here, the programme *It Ain't Half Racist, Mum*, made by a consortium including Hall, follows a similar line. A brief summary of the ensuing debate about the programme is in order, to show the development of Hall's work upon the notion of a discourse of national unity in the British media. According to the account in Alvarado and Thompson (1990), a slightly different version from the one that also appeared in Bridges and Brunt (1981), Hall *et al.* set out to investigate the 'chains of meaning', the 'different ideological discourses' involving racism specifically.

In defending the programme, the influence of Laclau is by now clearly in evidence, firstly to argue for the specificity of 'race' by denying the necessary 'class belongingness' of ideological discourse (Alvarado and Thompson 1990: 9–11). Drawing on a rich vocabulary and syntax of race, an organising 'absent but imperialising "white eye"' (a clear parallel to the famous Mulvey work on 'the male look' – see Bennett *et al.* 1981a) interprets events and positions viewers.

Basically, we are offered a 'grammar of race' with typical figures of the slave, the native or the clown/entertainer which can be worked and reworked in particular stories, in news, current affairs (even *Nationwide!*) and fiction and comedy (the political ambivalence of racist comedy is particularly well-discussed, pp.15–18). Hall denies that the media are racist because the personnel are racist, resisting sociologism here at least. The piece ends with an interesting discussion on the significance of realism for critical work (the *Screen* realism debate) and a rather abrupt dismissal of the political significance of avant-garde forms, using the critique of Kristeva Hall had developed in his short Critical Note in Hall *et al.* 1980.

This kind of argument about race and racist discourses, although not this particular example, was discussed rather critically in the earlier OU course on the media (*DE353*, Open University 1977), though, especially in Braham's Unit 14. One aspect of the critique turns on the assumed effect on the audience, and so that can be postponed until we discuss the whole issue below. However, Braham had other critiques to make, pointing out that the media sometimes dampened down racism as well as amplifying it, for example (much the same point is made by Hebdige 1979 in his discussion of the amplification effect in moral panics about youth). Braham also thinks that the often relatively crude, unspecified even, methods chosen to do content analysis might miss subtler differences between apparently similar discourses about race, and he claims to find some.

He argues that identifying a set of news values in general 'does not enable us to predict what will happen in a particular case' (*DE353* Unit 14: 24). Omitting the specifics also runs the risk of comparing news against some notion of a proper discussion based on academic criteria – but 'News is not sociology' (*ibid*: 36), and so it will never be as detailed or explore as much of the context as critics would like. Indeed, Braham goes on to say in effect that news is not marxism either, and asks of Miliband's study (of media views of capitalism) why there is so much surprise and concern that radical viewpoints are omitted from popular news coverage when there are so few marxists in the population at large! (*DE353* Unit 15).

Whatever the merits of Braham's particular critique, there are issues raised for the CCCS approach. In effect, we can see the political strengths and the academic weaknesses of an 'asymmetric' analysis, again, one that takes 'worst cases' and argues towards an exposé of the deep ideological contaminations of an apparently neutral or natural practice or discourse.

Nationwide

Nationwide was a more 'light' and popular current affairs programme, broadcast during the 1970s and 1980s, and subject to a number of interlocking analyses (including important work on the audience) by Morley in Hall *et al.* (1980), and Brunsdon and Morley (see the extract in Bennett *et al.* 1981a, and in Unit 12, *U203*, Open University 1982). Before we summarise the work, it is worth mentioning that Brunsdon and Morley appeared briefly on a BBC item about *Nationwide* broadcast on 25 August 1991 as a 'retrospective'. Whether the programme helped popularise their critique or absorb it into the 'self-parodying' style they identify as a characteristic, is an interesting question. In my personal view, for what it is worth, they also ran the risk of letting popular television construct them as 'academics', as rather unworldly and slightly eccentric, exactly as the programme itself used to do.

Brunsdon and Morley analyse the characteristic 'popular discourse' in *Nationwide*. It is a discourse about everyday events and current affairs, and it offers a 'preferred structure of absences and presences'. Present are references to 'home, leisure, consumption [then a dubious activity for left-wingers], individuals (bearers) and effects', while absent is any representation of 'world, work, production, reproduction, workers (functions), structural causation' (Bennett *et al.* 1981a: 134).

Within this structure, many of the characteristic stories of *Nationwide* found a place – its campaigns on consumerist issues, its stories about British eccentrics and 'ordinary' people, their problems and their quietly heroic ways of coping. And of course there is an image of the nation, or of 'Britishness', a combination of 'national(-istic) politics, concern with our craft traditions and national heritage combined in a peculiarly *Nationwide* inflection: an oddly serious yet self-parodying chauvinism' (Bennett *et al.* 1981a: 139). The recognition of parody in *Nationwide* is interesting, of course, for anyone who might think that it was a special technique invented by postmodernists and found only in *The Face* (see Hebdige in Chapter 4).

Brunsdon and Morley are very perceptive about the techniques used in the programme to foster the audience's involvement with the discourse, and this marks a useful departure from the work on the more 'serious' programmes. At least they are aware of the pleasure that television watching can bring: to paraphrase a comment by Fiske (much later), Hall *et al.* gave no reasons for anyone wanting to watch *Panorama* in the first place!

In *Nationwide*, the presenters adopt a direct address, and a '"populist ventriloquism". . .which enables the programme to speak with the voice of the people' (*ibid*: 123). There is an apparently a-political 'common-sense' vocabulary, popular terms of speech and deliberate amateurishness, speaking on behalf of the viewers when interviewing experts, incorporating actual viewers and their comments into the programmes in a variety of ways. These range from the use of the 'co-optive we' (*ibid*: 129) to the television equivalent of a correspondence column. Using some familiar metaphors (but not really any of the Lacanian theory that originally deployed them), Brunsdon and Morley say *Nationwide* attempts to 'mirror' back to its audience events in the same voice and gaze. (See a very similar analysis of *TV-AM*, from a 'phenomenological' point of view by Wilson 1990.)

Brunsdon and Morley do run the risk of displaying their own incredulity at the complexity of mundane popular culture, a phenomenon which has appeared before, but their analysis was to lead to more recent work on the pleasure of the viewing audience, and, indeed, to audience competencies. The analysis was influential enough to lead to similar efforts by the course team in some of the television programmes on *U203*.

National unity and the ideology effect in *U203*

A number of television programmes made as part of the teaching materials for *U203* (hereinafter referred to as OU programmes to distinguish them from ordinary non-pedagogical broadcasts) continue the gramscian theme, together with discussions of the specific topics under consideration. The OU programmes in this case use clips of ordinary television programmes or films, together with special pedagogic materials – interviews with experts or participants, or commentary (mostly behind camera) – and students receive special 'Broadcast Notes' to assist them to 'decode' these programmes. For *U203*, these notes ran to some 97 pages of summary and commentary on the sixteen television and eight radio broadcasts, and the six additional audio cassettes. Students were told about the aims of the programmes, sometimes were given something of the context, were told 'what to do during the programme', and were supplied with a list of points to discuss afterwards.

Programme 1 of *U203*, for example, discusses the special *Nationwide* Christmas programme of 1979, and shrewdly combines some of the themes of Brunsdon and Morley with Hall on national unity. Christmas as a festival had been the subject of the first Block (of written correspondence teaching material) on *U203*, to begin the analysis with a familiar example (and a recent one since OU courses start in February), and one which would display a range of ways in which one could analyse popular cultural festivals.

As *Nationwide* covered Christmas in its populist ventriloquist way, it offered us a picture of the nation as a family, coming together to forget our

125

differences (regional, racial, socio-economic) in a 'magical resolution' of our difficulties, says Bennett in Programme 1. The imaginary resolution was even shown to us, in popular television's literal manner, in the shape of the Salvation Army's Christmas charity campaign, run jointly with *Nationwide*, in the presents given to the old and needy at various Christmas parties, and in the persons of black adults dancing with white infants at a party in 'the Bristol Region'. In one striking sequence, to match the famed 'skateboarding duck' (an eccentric item now immortalised in the folklore about the programme), Christmas *Nationwide* that year offered us a hang-gliding Santa!

The course team's commentary behind and between the clips focused on the 'serious' issue of how the figure of the family is used to unite the nation, and the television audience (also gathered as a family, the BBC presenters assumed) with the 'family' of and on *Nationwide*. A further *Nationwide* Christmas story on location in the 'Holy Land' provides a means of offering the same 'imaginary' view of the 'family of nations', as political differences between Israel and her neighbours are rendered as religious ones, various national stereotypes are tried out (Palestinian society as unchanged since the time of Christ), and the Christian festival is seen to unite people (mostly 'kids' and middle-class Arabs and Jews) from different nations.

Programme 2 set out to illustrate the thesis advanced in Units 1/2 that Christmas as a festival involves a selective construction of the past, one based, inevitably, on 'struggle' between various popular forces and certain 'authorities'.

The programmes on football as a spectacle (15 and 16), to take another example, show how the BBC and ITV try to make televised (Association) football involving and pleasurable, by employing new techniques (like the low camera-angle shot, situating the player against the crowd, or the action replay), and to make 'stars' of individual players, managers, (or even television comentators, one might add: there are hints of the old populist ventriloquism idea in the course team's remarks on commentary and its role). Critcher also gets a chance to outline his thesis on the alienation of football since World War Two, included in a *U203* reader (Waites *et al.* 1982) and discussed briefly in Chapter 8 below. Critcher is subtitled as a 'Sociologist of Football', and talks to camera from an empty football terrace, a technique designed to give his views first-hand authority, as we know from *U203* Programme 5 on realism (below).

The programme on the hundredth FA Cup Final (Programme 16) shows how the (unusual) live coverage is turned into a family occasion, linked to quiz shows and other popular television show 'specials', and to interviews with personalities and their families. The panel of experts appears to interpret the tactics for the occasional viewer and lend some 'colour' (often necessary given the very dull nature of football). The Cup Final is also a national spectacle, though, with an underlying unity emerging through the discourse – the presence of VIPs (Royalty on this occasion), the rituals of hymn-singing and mutual celebration. One might add, although the course team do not do so, television's careful attempt not to transmit to the viewers the vulgar abuse – often personal, rude, cruel, unsporting, unchristian, partisan, sexist and racist – emanating from the fans.

Even some of the OU programmes on drama reinforce the 'national unity' theme, while they are there, so to speak, most noticeably in the discussion of documentary and dramatic accounts of the 1926 General Strike (Programme 5). Television drama about the Strike was to assume a particular significance in some of the debates about realism and political television in *Screen*, as we shall see, and most of the programme deals with issues such as the positioning of the viewer and the privileging of claims to realism in the different popular television programmes analysed. However, Bennett's commentary also shows how the 'General Strike' episode of *Upstairs, Downstairs* constructs a discourse about the nation, allowing (rather strange) representatives of each side in the Strike to speak in a number of voices, but also taking care to position certain authority figures (the dominant males, of course) in the centre ('both visually and politically', Bennett points out very neatly). At the end of the episode, 'the nation' emerges strong and united, with Parliamentary politics, reason and common-sense vindicated, as the Bellamy character says.

In the Postscript to Block 2, Bennett and Donald also make a similar point in terms of British films of the 1930s.

CONCLUSION

These OU programmes offer interesting mixtures of themes which can be seen as an extension of the Hall *et al.* concerns, and, once more, a partial reconciliation with the debates in other areas (especially in *Screen*). However, this reconciliation tries quietly to privilege the gramscian over the Lacanian 'line', the next chapter argues. The programmes also address emerging tensions inside left-wing media analysis to which we shall return, centred on the problem of pleasure. As with Brunsdon and Morley, there is some acknowledgement that viewers have to find pleasure in viewing, and there is a detailed account given of its possible sources and sites in these programmes. Yet, true to the pursuit of 'serious' politics, pleasure is still subordinated to the ideological message, as it were: it is mistrusted, seen as the lure to ensnare the viewer while the text positions that person in ideology. This hierarchy was to be dissolved, as we shall see.

One last comment on the *U203* programmes. Although raising the issue of realism (on television and in the course readers), the programmes themselves follow a relentlessly 'academic realist' pedagogy. This uses clips and passages from popular television programmes, displays their inadequacies (e.g. critiques their claims to objectivity or naturalness, not always directly, but by arranging instructively contradictory or predictably similar sequences of clips, for example), and introduces the reader or viewer to an underlying 'truth' delivered by a more authoritative 'academic' discourse by way of commentary on the clips. This sort of criticism has been levelled before at OU 'case study' programmes (Thompson in Barrett *et al.* 1979), and at *It Ain't Half Racist, Mum*, as we have seen. The extraordinary detail of the Broadcast Notes (Open University 1984) illustrates the extent of this realist strategy. As later chapters will suggest, such realism is peculiarly overdetermined by the academic context of teaching and assessment: to raise one issue now, OU programmes often struggled to justify themselves, as an expensive element of the course production system, and had to follow particularly closely the conventions of 'effective communication' as a result (Harris 1987).

7

POSITIONING, PLEASURE, AND THE MEDIA AUDIENCE

INTRODUCTION: MANAGING 'SCREEN THEORY'

Rival approaches to gramscianism, like 'screen theory', do appear extensively in the Open University course *Popular Culture* (*U203*) (Open University 1982), apparently from the need for academic courses to offer the best of recent representative work in the area of film and television studies (see the Introduction to Bennett *et al.* 1981a). The *Study Guide* sent to students justifies the inclusion of this 'rather difficult' material on pedagogic grounds, to 'denaturalise' the naive realism of the common-sense views about the relation between reality, author, text and reader (Open University 1984: 16), and to break with the 'usual academic methods for studying literary and aesthetic objects' (*ibid*: 14). Thus, as we have seen before, tactical coalitions with rivals are pursued to dethrone existing conservative disciplines and approaches.

Any subsequent conflict is managed very much on gramscian ground, though, this time in terms of an old CCCS concern – the 'culturalist/structuralist' debate. Students are told that 'structuralism' is introduced as a 'broad categorical alternative to the concept of culturalism', but also that there is no 'clear-cut division' between 'experience, culturalism and Block 3 on the one hand, and "texts", structuralism and Block 4 on the other' (*ibid*: 14). The recommended approach, which shows that the authors of the *Study Guide* really know their audience, is to be selective, and to use the material as a 'sort of "toolbox" which will provide you with a range of approaches to the issue of pleasure in different cultural forms' (*ibid*: 16).

The work that appears is variable, in terms of its ability to offer a serious challenge to gramscianism. In one of the course readers (Bennett *et al.* 1981a), the early *Screen* 'realism debates' appear, with specific critiques of attempts at political 'critical realism' in films like *Culloden*, and a consideration of more 'Brechtian' alternatives like *The Cheviot, the Stag, and*

129

the Black, Black Oil. These critical pieces even help develop the emphasis on 'national discourses', since they feature 1970s versions of Scottish history as 'struggle'.

The Maccabe discussion of the classic realist text is more clearly based on 'positioning theory', perhaps, but even here, an element of space for 'struggle' is available (Maccabe in Bennett *et al.* 1981a). Neale and Mulvey offer a 'positioning' account, but Neale's work on genres is somewhat domesticated by Martin's commentary on the concept in Unit 13, *U203* which fails to develop the wider implications for the critique of the viewing subject. The first stage of the *Screen* realism debate, which deconstructed the realistic effect of the film itself, was acceptable to gramscians ('semiotics 1' as Hall called it – in Hall *et al.* 1980). Mulvey's famous piece on 'the gaze' (in Bennett *et al.* 1981a) is ambiguous too, in this respect, with its Lacanian implications not fully unfolded: it can look like a conventionally Freudian reading of pleasure. Despite its advocacy of the avant-garde along with Kristeva, Mulvey's piece also helps the cause of gramscianism since it helps to fix attention on sexism, which privileges 'serious politics' and serious struggle.

In the second course reader (Bennett *et al.* 1981b), the dice are even more loaded in quantitative terms, with the 'culturalist/structuralist' debate prestructured by an opening contribution from Hall, followed by selections from each approach. The 'structuralist' camp includes Coward and Ellis, but also Volosinov (!), and even Culler's and Barthes' contributions are far from 'pure'. A hefty section on Gramsci follows.

In the *U203* course units themselves, the theoretical debates (principally found in Block 4) cover ground with which we are already familiar. Gramscianism 'manages' screen theory (and other critiques) in the familiar ways: some examples follow.

Very briefly, in the Introduction to the Block, Martin charts the interests in language in 'structuralism' and addresses issues of the codes at work in text and context, including concepts of genre and narrative – both explained in some depth later. The work on narrative as decentring the author moves to the full horrors of what Hall called 'semiotics 2' (in his Critical Note in Hall *et al.* 1980), where the reader too is constituted or fully positioned by the text. Martin's Introduction ends by moving to 'post-structuralism' where positioning theory is denied as an adequate account of all the effects of the text. We have a rather rapid history of 'structuralism' as a result, and a managed one, which moves on to criticism almost before the reader has had a chance to try to understand the main points.

Unit 13 itself goes on to illustrate these points, mostly using them tactically, to counter 'common-sense' or 'obvious' interpretations, by reference to a range of popular texts including *Dad's Army, Jaws, Dallas,* and police fiction. Unit 14, by Bourne, offers a good summary of the same theoretical ground, and rehearses the use of the term 'interdiscourse' to deny that single texts position single readers, as we have seen Morley do already (Chapter 2). This Unit ends on a particularly relativist note, though, despite using advertisements as some unproblematic demonstration of how ideology works, and admits there can be no rational choice between different readings (*U203* Unit 14: 64).

The realism debate summarised in Unit 15, uses the notion of narrative to perform the slide from constructed author to positioned reader, as above, using Barthes' *S/Z* and Metz (so the real thing is summarised at last). However, Donald and Mercer also criticise Maccabe, demand more concrete analysis of readers and texts, and proffer Williams's view (on the realist novel this time) that realism is a contradictory form and thus a 'terrain for struggle'.

Units 16 and 17 consider pleasure. Middleton in Unit 16 tries out a number of analyses of popular music, including Adorno's, and, after working through critical theory, semiology and culturalist analysis (especially Hebdige's) concludes, as we have already suggested in Chapter 5, that music offers a source of pleasure that defies formal analysis. Barthes' concepts of *plaisir* and *jouissance* seem to offer promise. In Unit 17, after a splendid summary of Freud and Barthes on pleasure, and Lacan and Metz on language, film and positioning, Mercer (again) uses Volosinov this time to argue for a contradiction between the personal and the social nature of the sign, thereby arguing against a pleasurable recognition of oneself totally in the works of other people (a denial, in effect, of the fully positioned subject). Mercer's Unit does firmly introduce the importance of the notion of pleasure to any analysis of popular film or television, though. Both Mercer and Middleton offer readers open ends to their discussions too, although it would be a competent student reader indeed who was able to feel confident enough to think of alternatives.

Narrative closure of the course awaits, though, in the concluding comments by the main authors. Bennett has organised a last word for himself after the authors of Units 4, 7 and 8, as we shall see in the next chapter. Hall has a last word in his conclusions to Block 7 (*U203* Unit 28). The strategy follows a familiar course of demonstrating the non-natural nature of popular culture or the State, and then privileging a gramscian account instead, this time a Laclau-type notion of articulation again. En route, Hall replies briefly to Anderson's critique of the vagueness of the relation between civil society and State in Gramsci, and introduces the work on Fordism as an emerging alternative clarification. One of the case-studies in this Unit concerns the establishment of the BBC as a corporate institution, with Reith as an 'organic state intellectual' (Unit 28: 32), television as a licensed alternative helping to preserve balance, and the claim again that this structure can be 'traced through to the actual forms [on television] e.g. current affairs' (*ibid*: 36). In other words, despite all the

131

arguments that had gone before, gramscians offer us business as usual. The core gramscian arguments are seen as solid sensible ones, gloriously immune to any criticisms of an exotic nature that might have gone before.

HEGEMONY, POLICE SERIES, SITCOMS, JAMES BOND

The specific analyses of concrete popular television programmes and texts in *U203* break some new ground. Both Clarke and Woollacott extend the gramscian notions of hegemonic crisis and the imaginary resolution of tensions into analyses of works of fiction for the first time. Both use *Policing the Crisis* (Hall *et al.* 1978), and Clarke also refers to Hall's piece on the ideology effect (in Curran *et al.* 1977), as an organising theory of crisis and the articulation of a national discourse. Clarke's work on the television police series (in his Unit 22) fits very neatly, of course, and he traces different themes and images of policemen in crime series in terms of social settlements and contradictions, and the ideological work they produce. He shows the traces of changes in real police practices in dramatised forms: an increased social realism, or the change in image from the cop as representative of the community (*Dixon*) to the anomic hero of *The Sweeney*. There are complexities, of course, like those arising from certain contradictions in the narratives centred on 'anti-statism' themes and family life.

Woollacott tries out the sitcom as a similarly complex effect of television conventions, social crises, and ideological work. Sitcoms offer an 'unresolved tension' between stereotyped characters who are 'stuck with each other', she argues (*U203* Unit 23: 64). Some of these stereotypes are of social class (of 'roughs and respectables', for example) and of gender and race, which brings in 'serious politics'. Woollacott insists that these stereotypes are not the product of 'bias' however, but of the 'formal organisation of the look, and the way narratives work to produce identification' (*ibid*: 86). This work is designed to 'articulate, work upon, and attempt . . . to resolve contemporary ideological tensions' (*ibid*: 89). However, fictional forms, especially comedy, offer many possible sources of contradiction, providing difficulties for articulation, and thus guaranteeing the place, at least formally, of 'struggle'. Even at this stage, Woollacott and Clarke offer purely formal analyses of 'popularity' and audience reactions, and thus still leave us with the suspicion that these are *analysts'* encodings and decodings.

The jewel in the crown must be Bennett's and Woollacott's analysis of James Bond, tried out here (Unit 21), and subsequently developed into a book (Bennett and Woollacott 1987). Only a small illustration of the scope and sophistication of the pieces can be given here, of course. Let us discuss the course unit first.

Drawing in part upon Eco's work on 'the Bond formula', Bennett and

Woollacott argue that Bond films and novels realise and permutate a number of codes, largely to order and relate a number of diverse ideologies about sex, class, Empire and the Cold War. Bond has to deal with both a villain (the SMERSH model or the SPECTRE model, according to the state of the Cold War and the relations between Britain and the USA) and a woman, often an enigmatic one who is somehow initially 'out of place' (e.g. unconventional sexually). The resulting tensions and their intertwined resolution is the main source of pleasure for the viewer.

Bond offers an 'imaginary resolution' (again) of international politics as he uses English guile to overcome American money and Russian evil to win the Cold War or restore international order, and construct a new, modernised role for Britain after the decline of the Empire. The Freudian undertones of Bond's relationships to the Bond girls, the out-of-place female and to 'M' are revealed in the 'phallic code': using the ambiguity in Lacan between the actual phallus and 'the Phallus' as the key to the symbolic order, Bennett and Woollacott argue neatly that as Bond subdues the females with his actual phallus, so they submit (partly) to the Phallus and cease to be out of place sexually or politically.

The piece demonstrates the formal sources and sites of pleasure in the viewer, but is much less sure when it comes to the political significance of Bond. Of course, there still had to be a 'serious' political purpose to analysis in those days. Thus, there is some correspondence or 'homology' (!) between the events on the screen and real shifts in ideological tensions engendered by international diplomacy, or modernisation (Unit 25: 31, 32). Bond is even an imaginary resolution to a real crisis in Tory hegemony, and it was 'surely no accident' that the films were popular at the height of the Cold War (Unit 25: 9). Codes in films and ideologies are related, but it is a two-way relation and rather like the nested relation between dominant ideology and professional codes in Hall's 'encoding' piece (Hall *et al.* 1980). We do not know if the audience sees Bond films in this way, of course, or if they do have any detectable effect on sexual or political behaviour, but the movies are undoubtedly popular (so therefore there must be some effect?). Of course, Bennett and Woollacott notice the elements of parody in Bond, but do not pursue them further, let alone claim them as some guarantee of 'struggle' (indeed, there is very little mention of struggle).

U203 offered a new definition of popular culture, as we shall see, and shifted gramscian work on to the media, and on to popular television especially. Things have moved on quite a lot since, however, and this final section can only hint at some of the more recent struggles and, above all, the ways in which gramscians have attempted to keep up with them.

OUT OF *U203*, 1: THE TELEVISION AUDIENCE

It seems an obvious step to take to fill out the analyses of the text with some actual audience research to establish whether or not there are any detectable effects of films or television. Critics have often seen this as a particularly significant lack in gramscian work (and in 'screen theory' for that matter). Despite Morley's work, and leaving aside Hobson for the moment, few of the gramscians developed any concrete studies of the audience. Asking the actual audience what they think of programmes seems such an obvious way to fix the floating signifiers and ground analysis, to check the dangers of endless elegant but fanciful speculation about the significance of texts, that it is hard to see why it was not done in the work we have just reviewed.

To take Hall's work in Chapter 6, for instance, why was he not interested in seeing if audiences really did see the social world in 'corporate' or racist terms, or whether they actually used the phoney divisions and unities of the 'ideology effect'? Why specify the formal conditions only of decoding and not examine actual decodings by actual viewers? Surely, these and other urgent political matters could be settled by audience research – was *Panorama* more effective ideologically than *Nationwide* or *The Likely Lads?* Which one should socialists protest about first?

Of course, there are serious dilemmas faced by any investigator. There is the critique of empirical data like attitude surveys (one obvious existing method of empirical research). This sees 'attitudes' as but the phenomenal appearance of deeper constituting social forces (see Bennett's Unit 13, *DE353*, Open University 1977). However, there might be other ways to investigate audience responses, like ethnography, although that too has its problems for some gramscians, as *Resistance Through Rituals* showed (Hall and Jefferson 1976). Any empirical data, though, faces problems, at least for bourgeois sociologists and historians, from the sheer complexity of pinning down isolated media effects, choosing suitable categories, finding suitable samples, and establishing the causal paths between public opinion and media discourse (see Braham, *DE353* Units 14 and 15). Braham suggests that shifting to talk about long-term effects, unwitting bias, unconscious effects, non-empirical phenomena and the like offers an evasion rather than an answer. And of course, some empirical evidence has been smuggled in, in *Policing the Crisis* (Hall *et al.* 1978), say, as we have seen.

All this is irrelevant for those who believe that analysis should focus on texts and 'subject positions' in their own right, as a branch of literary studies, of course, but gramscians do not hold this view (or do not hold it strongly), although Bennett was to deploy a discourse theory argument to raise doubts about the existence of empirical subjects outside of any texts (Bennett 1980b). We have seen some of the attempts to find a middle way (to put it enthusiastically) between these dilemmas, and whatever their success in rescuing gramscianism, they should still be able to offer a powerful critique of any empiricist enthusiasms.

The problem is reduced a little for those uninterested in the serious political effect of texts. At least they are spared the interpretive dilemma faced in the early work of Hobson and Morley: both found that sectors of their audience were unengaged by the carefully detailed ideological discourses they had identified. Hobson's working-class housewives were dangerously exposed to all kinds of sexist discourse by Radio 1 disc jockeys – but they seem to have hardly bothered to listen (in Hall *et al.* 1980). Morley's sample were shown *Nationwide* at its insidious best, but one group at least remained largely silent and uninvolved when asked to comment. Was such indifference evidence that the omnipotence of the media had been overestimated, just as the old 'effect analysis' suspected (Braham's suspicion), or was this some new form of 'struggle' and 'Great Refusal' (Fiske's interpretation, as we shall see)?

Ethnographic studies

The impetus to restore ethnographic studies of the audience seems to have arisen from a number of developments, according to Kaplan (1987). The weakening of 'screen theory' was one factor, introduced by a debate about film and history (including the status of historical subjects). There were more general theoretical reservations emerging too (including some we have discussed, centred on 'interdiscourse' – see Moores 1990). Morley (in Seiter *et al.* 1989) also offers a useful account of this renewed interest in the audience.

Feminist writers played a particular part in this too, driven by a continued insistence on the importance of women's personal experience, arguments first rehearsed in that uneasy peace with their male colleagues that the women at CCCS had mentioned (Women's Study Group 1978). Feminist media theorists also had their own particular version of positioning theory to contend with in Mulvey's influential work, which seemed to subordinate women permanently under the control of the various male gazes (although there was the threat of disruption posed by the female 'narrative stopper'), and saw no redeeming merits in any popular film. A comprehensive discussion of Lacan, Mulvey and others can be found in the *Screen* special on 'difference' (Volume 28) – see especially Merck (1987).

As Geraghty (1991) indicates, the response in film studies involved the exploration of other types of address and female pleasure, in an attempt to reclaim the discredited Hollywood categories of women's film, like melodrama. As a brief indication of this sort of 'redemptive reading', 'female melodrama' was seen as centring and exploring structures of feeling and thus revaluing female abilities to read emotions. Romance often offered a kind of female triumph and utopia, as the wayward male heroes were softened and feminised (Geraghty 1991) – see also Brunsdon (in Seiter *et al.* 1989). Female desire and the possibility of a re-evaluation of fantasy as a position from which to read the film outside of its determining narrative also figure in several accounts – e.g. Stacey (1987).

Of course, there were plenty of patriarchal genres too, to balance these liberating effects. Even the most promising genres had their narrative closures, attempting to insert women viewers back into patriarchy – by showing the high costs of romance for women, for example. Nevertheless, the inclusion of melodramatic and romantic themes in soap operas helped feminist critics to see at least the potential of popular television too.

There was also the realisation that television might well have quite different forms from film. For Kaplan, at the most obvious level, it is clear that watching television takes place in quite different circumstances from the dream-like and dependent state of the engrossed film audience. Television is more mundane and real, and can be integrated into everyday life (see Silverstone *et al.* 1991). Hobson was one of the first analysts to notice this (but for radio), and to detect important kinds of viewer resistance and reintegration (her slight anxieties and puzzlement about how to square this with the gramscian trends dominant hitherto can be seen as characteristic of works of the break). Television viewers clearly can switch off, change channels, play their own pre-recorded material, or simply disattend. Television also offers a range of forms of address too, which can vary from one programme to another (Silverstone *et al.* 1991). Indeed, Fiske argues that television must work hard positively to attract the attention of the viewer (in Seiter *et al.* 1989). These options are not so available to the film viewer, and they serve as a serious source of resistance to the spell of the narrative and of the gaze.

Fiske (1987) locates a deeper source of resistance in the television viewer who is a privileged sort of consumer because they do not have to be disciplined by the price mechanism in terms of their specific choices. The diversity of television output is another bonus, and Fiske insists that this diversity is not circumstantial but commercially necessary (with some reservations). The uncertainties of the market, the insecurities of the producers, and the real power of the consumers have also combined to produce a characteristically participatory ('producerly') text for television, seen best in the sketchy and unfinished nature of the characters in the soap opera, which can be inscribed with personal meanings by a wide range of audiences.

A number of ethnographic studies seemed to show the considerable competence of the television viewer to do precisely this sort of inscription. The audiences for various soaps, for example, were able to use the material to develop acutely personal meanings, ironic and subversive readings, even something approaching deconstructivist meanings. The work of Ang, Hobson, or Gledhill are described in the summaries cited above: Buckingham's study showed even the allegedly vulnerable adolescent audience displayed a grasp of the technical, contractual or artistic reasons for particular developments in *Eastenders* (Buckingham 1987). Both he and Geraghty detail the competence of the viewer in appreciating the shifting genres deployed in the modern British soap (light entertainment, melodrama, romance, documentary realism). As a quick example – (female) viewers' talk about the characters and stories between the programmes used to be seen as a sign of being unable to disentangle fiction and reality, but Geraghty sees it as a skilled 'balancing act' between engagement and distance (Geraghty 1991: 23). One might see this as a popular version of the use of the 'historical present' in literary criticism (and in some commentaries on Gramsci, who 'teaches us lessons' even though he has been dead for over 40 years!).

Fiske (1989a) details studies of subversive (and vulgar) appropriations of advertisements by schoolchildren, similarly sophisticated readings and uses of Madonna videos (and other texts) by young females (and by Madonna herself), and the skilled reversal of the narrative resolutions which reassert white dominance in *Miami Vice*. The last example shows one way to subvert the ideological closures at the denouements of fantasies and romances mentioned above: you switch off (literally or metaphorically) when a bit comes on you do not like. Of course, *Miami Vice* is a convenient example to make Fiske's case, since it barely features narrative at all (Grossberg 1987).

Audience competence: a celebration?

Fiske sees these developments in relentlessly optimistic, and thus asymmetric, terms, as part of the celebration of pleasure we will discuss in more detail in the next chapter, and as part of a continuing and widespread struggle to deny the hegemonic attempt to impose safe and falsely universalised meanings through television. His concrete studies of the pleasures to be had extend to those in watching television news being constructed as stories develop – pleasure in access to the process of representation as his earlier piece put it (in Seiter *et al.* 1989). In some ways, Fiske echoes the discussion of the role of the presenters and anchorpersons in the pieces on news and current affairs we have discussed earlier – but it is also with his discussion of television news that Fiske comes finally to break with this centred reading, in the pursuit of these pleasures of access. There is far more going on in the programme than just the articulation of a dominant ideology through the professional codes of the broadcasters, he is compelled to notice. Other discourses are being deployed to 'discipline' the events and create stories, as in the 'power/knowledge' couplets in

Foucault (Fiske 1989a). This sort of analysis implies precisely the earlier criticisms of CCCS work as embracing a 'transparent' unproblematic construction of news, which we have seen in the previous chapter.

Kaplan (1987) is not so optimistic as Fiske, seeing popular television, and MTV in particular, as highly contradictory. There is a danger, for example, that ecstatic consuming of the endless flux of rock videos will only deliver viewers further into the hands of the entertainment industry, as they see even more frantic consumption as the only way to restore a 'split subjectivity'. And, drawing still further on Jameson's critique of postmodernist aesthetics, Kaplan emphasises the tendency for MTV to 'flatten out' all its materials, even those which might be potentially critical.

The same sense of tension runs throughout Geraghty's works on soaps too. For her, they are both a space and a ghetto, valuing female skills but defining them in a highly conventional manner, and soaps are still a low-status area of television. The focus on the personal does set limits in introducing public issues. Finally, soaps may be changing as pressures increase to widen the audience and move away from a reliance upon women.

Liebes' and Katz's study of the international *Dallas* audience notes the different kinds of oppositional readings among their sample, but rather than just celebrate them, they point to the limits of each major type. Thus 'moral opposition' to the worlds of *Dallas* also credits the programme with some importance, an 'ideological critique' is often a mere inversion, an 'aesthetic critique' lets ideology 'slip by', and a 'playful critique' remains just that, and may 'fail to bring one back to earth' (Seiter *et al.* 1989: 218–19).

Methodological issues

Modern writings return to another old issue – a methodological one – in asking whether the ironic readers which analysts have found were typical, or even very numerous. Buckingham (1991) raises an important issue when he shows some of the difficulties in interpreting the responses of young children to television. The familiar issue of 'interviewer bias' is raised (and see Silverstone *et al.* 1991 in the same issue) via Buckingham's awareness that his presence might have prompted the critical remarks the children made. Buckingham extends that point by suggesting that the children were using a number of discursive strategies and repertoires in discussing television, some of which were energised by the group discussion itself. So, for example, programmes were rated first highly then poorly when an unpopular child declared an interest. Anti-racist sentiments were expressed both to criticise a programme and to demonstrate sincerity and a sense of tactfulness to other children present.

These repertoires were not just produced 'externally' by social class (offered as a rebuke to Morley's study of the *Nationwide* audience) but were developed within the group, as when 'each individual contribution builds upon the last'. Buckingham seems to have discovered what might be called a local and emergent 'reading formation' at work behind the apparently individual or sociological subjects in the discussion (see below). He has also discovered that television can become a 'hypertext' or a 'pretext' for more general discourses, for talking about oneself, politics, relationships and so on. Morley and Silverstone have found the same practice of viewers' inserting what they see on television into the 'perambulatory rhetorics of everyday life' in deCerteau's phrase (Morley and Silverstone 1990: 48). Students also do this, it will be suggested, in the perambulatory rhetorics of their assignments.

Buckingham has also awakened the old anxieties about empiricism in ethnographic studies too. One might ask whether the subjects in Morley and Silverstone (1990) are empirical subjects, somehow untrammelled by texts, and whether studies of households as the key site of interpretation (with neighbourhoods, the economic and the wider cultures displaced as determinants) can be justified by the simple empirical observation that people physically watch television in households. A similar point is made against the influential deCerteau as we shall see (Frow 1991).

Does the ironic or 'discursive' reading really belong to the empirical viewer, so to speak, or might it too have been supplied by television itself, in programmes like *Soap*, perhaps, or *Monty Python*, or *Moonlighting*, or *MTV*, or even *The Monkees* (see Gostree 1988)? Grossberg refers to (US) television's 'in-difference', its increased use of irony and repetition in offering viewers comments on and references to its own productions, its self-mockery in programmes like the ones cited above (which he sees as one effect described by terms like 'postmodernism'). This irony is also combined with other features like 'wild realism' and 'heterodoxy . . . Otherness rather than difference' (Grossberg 1987: 37). Things have advanced so far, for Grossberg, that it is time to abandon the emphasis on the representational functions of television altogether (a development arising elsewhere too).

Grossberg's interest is in the emotional tone and excesses of television, where 'every image is equally open to affective investment because everything is a media event, a style, a pose' (*ibid*: 44). Grossberg argues that this development will free the subjectivity of viewers again to roam unfixed by narratives or representations, in an 'affective democracy'. We shall examine the idea of 'nomadic subjectivity' in the next chapter, but if Grossberg is right, there is little sense in trying to study the audience as an 'anchoring moment in a sea of signification' (Brunsdon in Seiter *et al.* 1989). Morley argues instead that there are (empirical) clusters of meaning and response in practice, whatever the polysemic possibilities (in Seiter *et al.* 1989).

However, these textual excesses need not be permanent, and both Kaplan and Grossberg point to the persistence of what looks like old-fashioned ideology even in postmodernist television – in the conventional representations of faces and subjects, and in the banality of the words in rock videos for Kaplan, and in the persistence of modernisms, social reality and power for Grossberg drawing upon, of all things, Hall on 'articulations'. Goodwin (1991) also argues that although the cultural distinctions may have collapsed (in rock music), following postmodernism, it does not follow that distinctions based on cultural capital have also disappeared among the audience.

Goodwin also shows how *MTV* has incorporated and absorbed postmodernist aesthetics into a mere category – 'pomo' – really a mere synonym for 'progressive rock', 'art rock' or 'College radio'. Conventional television may not be far behind in this turn towards the domesticated again. Whatever the actual future pattern, these opposing trends show the tremendous flexibility of modern television as it patrols the contradictory demands for diversity and 'readerly' texts. Such flexibility threatens one-sided analyses like Fiske's above. Has Fiske pointed to a permanent contradiction between viewer and producer, for example, or are we merely in an unusual conjuncture, or in one of those phases of looseness and renewal as in the music business? (A fuller discussion of Fiske follows in the next chapter.)

For that matter, what part do modern writings on television, in the popular press, in fanzines, or even in Media Studies courses play in the provision of viewer competence and cultural capital? Would there still be semiotic warfare without gramscians telling us that that is what we are doing when we doze off in front of the *Nine O'Clock News*?

Audience studies: the future

Fiske's line seems to have triumphed, though, and it is now possible for gramscians to welcome ethnographic studies that show considerable audience resistance and refusal, forgetting their old doubts, both methodological and political. There is also a turn away from the interest in the unconscious level of meanings, of course, both in the audience and in the analyst (see Walkerdine in Formations 1987). All the optimistic studies are suitable for the new times, the open advocacy of pleasure in viewing television, the abandonment of the old respectable fears of the 'plug-in drug'. Unfortunately, some of those respectable fears emanated from gramscian analyses of the hegemonic tendencies of television sitcoms or racist comedy, as we have shown, and new times gramscians have had to keep quiet about their own part in the 'earnestness' of the past, and blame the 'old left' or 'screen theory'.

The final irony is that the new studies are acceptable only in so far as they can be claimed for the new kinds of struggle, which renders analysis just as asymmetrically as the old notion of hegemonic discourse did. In the absence of very much research, the analyst is tempted to construct an account, based on her viewing habits and competencies, says Frow (1991).

There is one interesting piece which offers a novel approach – Philo (1990) rounds off his work on television news with an interesting attempt to establish whether audiences do reproduce news coverage. He invites members of the public (rather strange groups of members of the public in fact), to examine some photographs and construct their own news stories. These amateur efforts can then be compared to the professional news stories: Philo's own preliminary work suggested some close matches.

The work reveals, according to Philo, just what messages do come through, despite the polysemic possibilities in theory, and he argues that this ideological effect is still the issue (against advocates of the non-representational effects of television like Silverstone, or the celebrations of diversity of use in Fiske, both of which are virtually indifferent as to the content of the television programme). Of course, this study tends to depend on empirical subjects acting as a test bed for the reception of effects from just news, and from a concern for 'serious politics'. Nevertheless, the Glasgow Univesity Media Group's kit has become available for teachers of media studies, and will doubtless be used to perform very similar work in the future.

With some exceptions, already audience research in cultural studies has become rather repetitive too, and so ethnographic studies even lack 'surprise'. They seem condemned to repeat the discovery of 'semiotic struggle' just as much as the old non-empirical studies did. There are attempts to go beyond gramscianism, of course. Morley and Silverstone (1990) focus on the way television paces and regulates time and space for viewers, both day to day (as in Hobson's insight in Hall *et al.* 1980), and over the year. Although it is possible to harness these analyses to vaguely critical ends, in the 'left-wing functionalist' manner we have described earlier (that is by seeing social integration as a bad thing), it seems to be Giddens who lends the project authority, not Gramsci.

In this sense, Donald's critical review (1990) of Fiske's *Television Culture* was right when he said that we still do not know what television is. We need an account of the cultural production of television, rather than an endless repetition of textual readings and audience research. Donald couples his critique to the fashionable, and not entirely altruistic pressure to develop 'practical' courses in media studies (see Stafford in Buckingham 1990 for an account which fills in more of the micropolitics, and Aronowitz in Giroux *et al.* 1989 for a possible radical appropriation of the new interest in technical skills). However, the last development to be studied, offers a less 'apostatic' way to conceive of the missing element of cultural production.

OUT OF *U203*, 2: BOND, BENNETT AND WOOLLACOTT

Bennett's and Woollacott's book (1987), written after the demise of *U203*, and after many of the sea-changes in media theory outlined above, develops the substantive analyses of Bond much more fully, and marks the development of media studies away from the old 'political' interests. We now have a major focus on pleasure, and a split with the old readings 'centred' on the main condensations of 'serious politics' in class, gender and race.

Bond and Beyond achieves and signals this split through focusing especially upon 'context' in a cultural rather than a political sense. The context of the Bond films reveals for the writers and producers the inter-laced effects of both cultural resources (for example, the Fleming novels, other literary sources including adventure comics and detective fiction), and production conventions. These combine in producing different emphases in specific Bond films and in accounting for the remarkable 'mobility' of Bond as a hero.

Bennett and Woollacott stress inter-textuality (with a hyphen) ('the ways in which the relations between texts are socially organised within the objective disposition of a reading formation' *ibid*: 86), rather than mere intertextuality (without a hyphen) ('a set of signifying relations that is alleged to be manifest within a text, the product of the permutation of texts it deploys' *ibid*: 86). This helps dethrone the idea of 'the text itself' as the proper object of cultural analysis, and it also moves us beyond positioning theory since the reader as well as the writer has a variety of texts to inform their reading. This implies a focus on the audience as constituting the Bond phenomena, again in the formal sense, rather than as a result of any empirical work. The readings provided by the audience determine the meanings of the text, despite, as it were, the author's own sources of meaning: 'Intertextualities . . .are the product of specific socially organised inter-textualities' (original emphasis) (*ibid*: 86) (that is, multiple meanings are activated not by the internal allusions and quotes in the film, introduced by the author, but by the different competencies brought by the viewer which help recognise these allusions).

This seems to be an improvement on the usual notions of 'inter-discourse' or the Volosinov option, but it still fails to bring us much closer to actual audiences. At least we now have segmented audiences (rather than just social classes) – males; females (the popularity of Bond films with females leads the authors to rework some of the themes in Mulvey – Bennett and Woollacott 1987: 211–20); the assumed audiences of Fleming, Broccoli, and other members of the production team; intellectuals; members of different social classes; and people of different nationalities. Each of these will bring a reading competency based on their possession of different textual 'regimes' and themes – e.g. women bring to Bond films materials from 'codes of romance'. The final component of a 'reading formation' is the 'institutional practices which bear on the formation of reading competencies' (*ibid*: 248), so reading competencies are not left floating or abstract, with no organisational base. Little is done to develop this insight, but it is a useful one for studies of the student audience, as we shall see.

The authors use the notion of a 'textual shifter' to try to resolve the old issue of whether subject positions are the same as real concrete subjects. The textual shifter is a kind of 'advance organiser', film publicity like a poster, say, which both organises expectations and the 'signifying currency of Bond' (*ibid*: 248). They 'produce texts for readers and readers for texts' (*ibid*: 249). Finally, the issue of privileged reading is discussed, and again a middle position taken: there is no way to ground a privileged reading, certainly not by some naive reference to 'the text itself'. Yet there is no anarchy either – social conditions set limits to possible readings, and so do politics.

The connection with the old projects on hegemony remains as tenuous and cautious as before. There is still only the 'clearly no accident' relation (*ibid*: 280) (not further specified) between crises in hegemony and the emergence of particular themes in fiction like law and order, national identity, Cold War, male domination. Popular fiction is a more flexible region for new articulating principles in hegemonic discourses to be tried out, than, say news or serious television, and here the authors refer back to *Policing the Crisis* (*ibid*: 279). Yet it is also more autonomous in another sense – the films cannot be read any longer in terms of a hierarchy of determinations, as in the familiar metaphor of the nesting of codes between professional producers, dominant ideologies, and underlying social crises (i.e. precisely as Policing . . . tries to do). Bennett and Woollacott have a number of criticisms to make of that approach, referring to their own case-study on Bond done for the OU (which I have not traced, possibly one for *DE353*), and specifically rejecting the 'tinge' of false consciousness readings there (*ibid*: 188). They point to the difficulty in explaining the actual production process implicit in such attempts to 'read [Bond films] as a fictional working over of contemporary ideologies' (*ibid*: 183).

Bennett and Woollacott prefer the term 'conditions of production' instead of determinations (*ibid*: 188), and they mean the process by which the production team incorporate all sorts of diverse intertextual elements, including some 'ideological projects', into a specific 'filmic form'. The analysis which ensues suggest that the Bond production team tried to undermine, if anything, many of the existing nationalistic and sexist elements. The source of these elements is still in doubt, though – although the nearer we get to what might be called 'low class' fiction, or publicity material and advertising, perhaps, the more clearly appears a blatantly propagandist source.

The ideological codes mentioned in Unit 25 (see above) are still present in *Bond and Beyond*, though. The films still interpellate and locate people in ideology. But it requires certain reading formations, to see Bond in a particular light in the first place, to be so interpellated. The sinister messages in Bond about Empire and the adventures of the phallus are now located at the intersection of producers and readers: they are the meanings of the film for 'the male reader of the 1960s' (*ibid*: 141) who brings with him all his particular intertextual competencies and orientations.

This is a sophisticated formulation to hold together a claim that Bond is ideological and to avoid the problems of determinist readings. There are of course still questions to be asked. Does this level of sophistication apply to all films, including those less developed and less intertextual than Bond – are there some primary ideological texts which appear in a less 'worked on' and less rich form? Are there any reasons for stopping at the level of abstraction expressed in 'the male viewer of the 1960s', or could we expect an infinite number of fractionated or even individual interpellations too? (A paper by Feuer which suggests that the concept of 'reading formation' simply endlessly defers the problem of meaning like this is discussed briefly in Morley's contribution to Seiter *et al.* 1989). Is there a characteristic (ex-)Open University academics' reading formation, and are Bennett and Woollacott simply offering it to us: what makes their reading of Bond authoritative?

The authors seem to answer the last two questions at least by commending to us a particular politics, using a formulation first tried out in Bennett's Unit 13 in *DE353* – we should consider the political use of readings, engage in a struggle to make readings, and above all, reclaim popular texts for marxism. We are to do this in a form Fiske uses too, one suitable for the new times: 'the development of critical strategies which may engage with popular reading without hectoring the reader as a subject whose tastes need to be reformed' (Bennett and Woollacott 1987: 268). There is no support for the 'authentic voice' of the reader here as in more populist views of the audience (see Brunsdon in Seiter *et al.* 1989).

Again, the floating nature of the Bond signifier allows it to be detached from other ideological practices and thus to be more easily manipulated. Bennett and Woollacott offer a marvellous 'alternative scenario for Bond's future development, a kind of identity kit from which a Bond for the left might be assembled' (*ibid*: 283) (first published, inevitably, in *Marxism Today* in fact). 'An ideal Bond for the 1980s would try to unionise espionage workers, campaign for gay rights in the Secret Service, encourage Miss Moneypenny to leave M and set up an abortion clinic' (*ibid*: 284). Unfortunately, as their Postscript reveals, the next, and so far the last, Bond film remixed the ideological formula yet again to produce a film in which 'Bond's sexuality, like his Englishness, is little more than a damp squib' (*ibid*: 292), while contriving at the same time to remain 'deeply misogynist' (*ibid*: 293). Professional Bond-manipulators seem to have won out over well-intentioned amateurs yet again, alas.

CONCLUSION

Despite their flaws, recent developments out of the original gramscian readings of the media have improved greatly upon the partisan, pre-determined and repetitive 'discoveries' of endless hegemonic articulations. A detailed attention to really popular texts and 'normal' audiences, and an initiative where feminists took a lead (probably the only group within CCCS or the Popular Culture Group able to look beyond Gramsci and escape the heavy hand of gramscianism), has dethroned the orthodoxy, drawing upon methods which developed a little symmetry and a genuine openness to exploration at last. The results have been of great interest for, and applicability to, a wide range of the concerns of this book, beyond the issues of 'the media' specifically, in education, recreation and politics.

As suggested in my Introduction, Bennett's and Woollacott's work seems to have a great potential for grasping academic texts, their production and reception, and we will return to this idea in the last chapter. One of the abiding curiosities is that in the midst of the great developments and debates about the media, the gramscians never gave us their insiders' account – for they, above all, were *in* the mass media, in publishing, in making television programmes both for the Open University and for the public television services.

Analysts like Geraghty, Hobson, Fiske, Bennett and Woollacott have been tactful about their own and their colleagues' earlier work, but there is no doubt now that the hegemonic reading remains as an option, even if a preferred [*sic*] 'right-on' one. Jensen (a former fan) refers rather doubtfully to Gramsci's concept of hegemony as 'suggesting how a road paved with discursive polysemy and audience pleasures may terminate in a state of social domination', but suggests a range of other works to revitalise cultural studies (1990). Gramscian 'articulations' are now only 'surely not accidental', and interest in them largely optional or residual. The origin of gramscian analysis is no longer simply assumed to be a natural starting point but is dispersed in particular reading formations, even if these are still largely unresearched. Its relevance (and its style) are a political liability, given what is suspected of the audience's tactics in the new non-ideological hedonistic times. Its characteristic themes can now be grasped as a rhetoric, perambulating through a number of other discourses and projects.

Because of the strange boundaries between academic specialisms, the decidedly gramscian 'articulation' reading can persist in some relatively unevenly developed regions, as we shall see in the chapter on politics, but it has been exhausted in this crucial area, despite every effort. Gramsci remains now as a token presence, on the frontispiece of *Bond and Beyond*, and one wonders how long it must have taken a diligent researcher to find that particular quote!

8

LEISURE, PLEASURE, SPORT AND TOURISM

INTRODUCTION: CONSTRUCTING THE FIELD

The material to be reviewed in this chapter is held together rather tenuously by particular combinations of largely academic determinants. In the 1970s and 1980s, a number of studies began to cohere into a new field or specialism, 'leisure studies', 'tourism' or even 'recreation studies'. Some newer pieces were written by CCCS alumni or cultural studies fellow travellers, and, in accordance with what must now look like a familiar pattern, they had to insert themselves into spaces contested by rivals. CCCS members struggled with the Sociology and English Faculties at Birmingham University, as we have seen. Gramscian media studies flourished initially as one strand of an Open University course launched jointly between Social Sciences and Education, *Mass Communication and Society* (*DE353*) (Open University 1977). Gramscian leisure studies began in sections of the OU course *Popular Culture* (*U203*) (Open University 1982). *U203* arose from some adroit manoeuvring by Bennett too (Bennett 1980a), and a fuller discussion can be found in Chapter 10. Later still, after *U203*, gramscian work faced a new struggle to win a place in 'leisure studies', finding itself having to 'break' anew with sociology, history, recreation management and market research, as Clarke's and Critcher's (1985) well-known book reveals. Tomlinson (1989) gives a similar account.

Leisure studies and sports studies still are rather loosely bounded areas, and are still traversed by conflicting approaches. Gramscianism is but one perspective on offer here, and it is by no means the dominant one, although there have been substantial publications and a considerable presence at the Leisure Studies Association conferences and in the LSA journal. Right from the start, though, leisure studies was open to considerable diversity, and rivalry, from sociological approaches (functionalist, Weberian and interactionist – see Deem 1986), different critical perspectives including those from Barthes and Bourdieu (see John

147

Hargreaves in Jennifer Hargreaves 1982), and later Elias and Simmel (see Rojek 1989). The teaching profession, leisure managers and Government researchers were also elements to be considered, not least for the finances they deployed. Gramscian analysis had to situate itself in this contested field, and this explains the shape of some of the general introductory texts.

For example, Clarke and Critcher spend a good deal of time establishing their claims by refuting the work of Parker and Roberts, critiquing official statistics on the familiar methodologial grounds we have seen before (they reflect phenomenal rather than real levels of analysis, they are abstracted from the real differences and conflicts, and so on), and disputing the official views of the coming of the 'leisure society' (a big theme in Britain in the mid-1980s). What emerges, as might be predicted, is an emphasis on 'struggle' to explain both the apparent diversity of lesiure practices and their continued capacity to reproduce divisions based on class, race and gender.

The underlying emphasis on reproduction (described simply as a 'marxist' perspective) helps stave off the 'value-neutral' approaches of Parker with his attempt to explain patterns empirically, as the result of a combination of a number of separate empirical factors (like 'orientations', 'skills'). Clarke and Critcher want to offer a familiar notion of the social totality to stave off this sort of 'functionalist' approach, and to point to the underlying determinants of class and gender.

Roberts is more difficult, since his work contains an explicit discussion of the 'class domination model', which he rejects on similar grounds to those of Braham in media studies discussed earlier (see Chapter 6) – the model fails to account adequately for complexity, despite its attempts to find ideology and struggles over legitimation everywhere. Clarke and Critcher deal with this objection by suggesting that such complexity conceals a structuring, and, in the end, 'simply dissent from a model . . . which explains social life as the aggregated and individual choices made within social networks, somehow shaped by the interplay of free-flowing variables' (Clarke and Critcher 1985: 42). We can see a rerun of Critcher's CCCS work (Clarke *et al.* 1979) on breaking with bourgeois sociological studies of working-class community as a matter of interlocking variables, often with 'family' as the dominant one.

However, leisure is a difficult field to define, since it is empirically complex and covers a wide range of phenomena (everything that people do in their spare time for some writers, everything that expresses non-work values for others and so on – see Roberts, cited in Deem 1986). The close link between work and leisure in the way the very concept of leisure is defined enables gramscian analysis to get a foothold in the struggle, by arguing that leisure is determined (in some cautious way) by the economic, but at a price. For one thing, the bourgeois definitions of leisure as merely and uniformly 'non-work' include far too much material for gramscian analysis to handle. It has become conventional, for example, following a discovery of the patterns of women's non-paid work, to include gender as a more or less separate focus to further grasp activities like watching television (among other things). Other problems await too, as we shall see.

Gender has been connected with class in several ways, as we have seen in Chapter 5 above. Arguments in leisure studies range from Clarke's and Critcher's use of feminist analysis to help make their general case for the structuring of leisure against individualistic, pluralistic or empiricist analysis, to a more integrated approach in Hargreaves (1986), where gender and class intersect in particular fragmentations, accommodations and alliances, rather in the fashion of Willis's work (1977). Hargreaves says that some non-competitive recreations enable bourgeois men and women to form alliances at the expense of working-class men, for example, while working-class leisure tends to offer male class solidarity but also a hostility to working-class women. Hargreaves offers a classic account of 'elaborated gramscianism' to overcome other types of complexity, as we shall see.

This debate between empirical complexity and underlying forces was to continue to dog the gramscian project and to reappear in debates with historians and figurationalists. The outcome of the debate will have repercussions for feminist work too, although it is less well developed there. But Deem also tries to argue for the structuring of apparent complexity in an exactly analogous way, this time to show the underlying structuring significance of gender instead of class/gender, much as in McRobbie's settling of accounts with subcultures (in Bennett *et al.* 1981b). Later debates displace the issue slightly, as we shall see, by considering consumerism as a site of struggle: here, the issues concern the relative freedom of the consumer to choose and to subvert politically the cultural hegemonic tendencies of capital.

THE DEBATE WITH THE HISTORIANS

A substantial effort was devoted in the heyday of CCCS to offer historical accounts of popular leisure pursuits of the past, to show the rich 'lived experience' of the British working class, and to illustrate the principles of hegemonic struggle in the field of leisure and popular culture. Historical analysis would offer a political lesson, to deny the common views of the British proletariat as conservative, or uncivilised (as Johnson's or Brehoney's pieces on popular education did in Chapter 3). Historical analysis would also denaturalise existing practices like the patterning of leisure by gender or social class.

Inevitably, this involved a theoretical struggle as well, with those historians who held different views. Johnson's account of 'proper history' (in Clarke *et al.* 1979) has been mentioned briefly in Chapter 1, and he comments upon a number of approaches to the study of working-class culture. There has been a good deal of bourgeois history, of course, focusing on the 'great men' [sic], or offering some evolutionary account of progress. Some of the more sympathetic histories attracted Johnson's attention, though. They involved the study of social institutions, for example, or tended to reduce culture to a 'representation' of economic changes. Both of these approaches fail to connect with culture as 'lived experience', as complexly determined by political, economic and ideological/cultural levels. Hence the need for Johnson to 'retrace [a] path out of Hobsbawm . . . and into an encounter with Gramsci' (Clarke *et al.* 1979: 62).

The struggle between 'culturalists' and 'structuralists' lay in the way in 1979, however (a version of the more general struggle with Althusser and with structuralism). Johnson deals with the Althusserians in his own account of this struggle in a familiar way: 'hegemony is in effect Althusserian reproduction but . . . without the functionalism . . . the normal state . . . is a state of massive disjunctions and unevenness' (Clarke *et al.* 1979: 233).

CCCS work

The approach can be seen in a number of concrete studies of leisure pursuits. Blanch describes attempts to police working-class leisure 1890–1918 (in Clarke *et al.* 1979) by fostering the emergence of respectable organisations like the Boy Scouts or the Boys' Brigade to effect an 'attempted resocialisation'. Blanch argues that the effects of these initiatives were uneven, and that they met with resistance, especially from the 'rough' working class, yet they were effective in forging nationalism. This is one of the few accounts of nationalism in the entire opus, in fact, revealing perhaps the most glaring omission in gramscian conceptions of popular culture (see also Hobsbawm's critique in Hall and Jacques 1983)

Wild's study of recreation in Rochdale 1900–40 (Clarke *et al.* 1979) details the interpenetration of capitalism into the existing networks of recreation. The struggles against this interpenetration are charted, and the final colonisation of those 'popular' (in the sense of 'from below') recreational activities by commercialised forms. The analysis ends with the triumph of the dance-hall and the cinema, replacing the pub, music hall and chapel. Introducing a major critical theme, Wild notes that these new forms required only a 'limited commitment and an esentially casual usage' (*ibid*: 159), instead of the old tightly woven links of membership of the older forms.

One of the last CCCS specials supplied a more general theory of crisis and its management in an historical account of the British State and its social policy (Langan and Schwartz 1985). Briefly, and as one could guess from earlier work reviewed, this saw the State involved in a series of regulatory policies, expressed in a 'proliferation of discourses', ranging from coercion to winning consent. Some of its policies involved what might be called disciplining the masses via various moral campaigns about prostitutes or unfit mothers. Others attempted to achieve a 'passive revolution' (a concept in Gramsci that had failed to be worked in very well, according to Hall's 1985 reply to Jessop), imposing a settlement from above, via extensions of the franchise and social democratic reforms, to forestall a threat from below. Many of these themes were to return in a popular form in the Open University course *Popular Culture (U203)*.

Rebellious structuralists and historians in *U203*

In one of the course readers for *U203* (Bennett *et al.* 1981b) Hall returns to the culturalist/structuralist issue, and constructs a kind of inner history of CCCS in the process. Williams and Thompson play for the culturalist side. Despite their good works in introducing notions of culture as lived experience, both are susceptible to the (Althusserian) critique that they conceive of the social formation in too simple a way, as an 'expressive totality', with the cultural level as the dominant one. Althusser's project is summarised on behalf of the 'structuralists', and he is accused of the usual sin of functionalism, put in the slightly unusual terms of a then current critique: Althusser and Balibar offer us a picture of the social formation as a 'combinatory', a structure composed of variations of the same 'eternal' basic components.

That ideology was seen as a mere 'representation', rather than as a signifying system in its own right is also noted, linking in notions we have discussed elsewhere (in Chapter 6 on media via Mepham and Chapter 7 on the contradictions of screen theory). Hall is alert to the dangers that discourse theory will run away with him, however, and he cautions against both 'pure' semiology and the work of Foucault. It will come as no surprise to any readers who have followed this story in other chapters that Hall's answer is 'enriched gramscianism', a theory of 'articulation' via Gramsci and Laclau. Such an approach will permit an attention to the specificity and unity of discourses, to the rival insights of seeing work as both culture and ideology, to the complex relations between the economic and the social. Enriched gramscianism incorporates all the concerns of the other approaches and improves upon them, naturally.

The tendency to 'have the last word', noted in Chapters 3 and 6, is also marked in the discussion of some of the concrete historical studies in *U203*. The course studies popular cultural activities in a number of periods and formats – music halls, and sports in Victorian Britain, holidays, popular films of the 1930s, and the emergence of public radio and TV broadcasting (all in Blocks 2 and 3 of the course).

The *Supplementary Material* for the course (Open University 1984) reveals that a number of debates and disputes among historians are developed during the course of these sections, concerning the extent to which hegemony was achieved in particular periods, what were the most efficacious means of achieving it (areas of activity where the classes semed to join together in alliances or accommodations), and where the most resistance came from (where classes remained distinctive or actively in conflict). I am not competent to join in the debate as an historian, although it is possible to make some general methodological points. As before, the main interest is in how gramscianism is maintained as a superior system to rival approaches in these debates.

It has already been suggested that gramscian concepts run the risk of depending for their effect on being 'asymmetric' and evasive. In one sort of asymmetry, selected examples can be used to carry the burden of the argument, and, in another sort, the concrete analysis can be pre-structured by the search for privileged concepts (like 'struggle'). Given the weight of gramscian writings, it is impossible to claim a kind of theoretical innocence in undertaking historical empirical work, of course – certainly by the time Hall came to write his historical review in Unit 28, both the theoretical and the substantive themes had been tried out many times before (in some of the pieces we reviewed in the previous chapter, for example). The gramscians give us few clues about how they are using empirical data anyway – as an illustration of the themes? as a partisan review designed to persuade us for some ulterior theoretical or political reason? As marxists, they certainly could not see data as empiricists do, as somehow convincing in its own right, as self-evident: indeed, in other works (Clarke and Critcher above, for example, or Hebdige, reviewed in Chapter 3) they scorn the use of empirical data.

As for evasiveness, the arguments involving various surface-depth metaphors run the risk of being circular and self-confirming. In skilled hands, any activity which looks as if it reveals choice, or autonomy, or political innocence, for example, is liable to be reinterpreted by some underlying articulation to show that its very autonomy is a source of its usefulness in hegemonic unity. Hegemonic cultures can reveal traces of dominant and subordinate cultures, united by either alliance or struggle, either in some sort of temporary equilibrium or in an immanent state of disequilibrium: pretty well everything can be explained by the term hegemony, therefore, especially when combined with various asymmetries, including one characteristic of history – hindsight.

These issues lie at the heart of the dispute with the historians in *U203*. In Unit 4 of the course, Golby and Purdue discuss the emergence of an urban popular culture in Britain. They point to trends which are pretty much agreed by all the parties and describe the changing patterns of work and leisure following industrialisation and the emergence of class divisions in the modern sense. A complex picture emerges of marked class divisions in some areas of social life (e.g. in drinking behaviour, in town districts, in the popular radical press), but a good deal of confusion among the ruling classes, and some cross-class alliances (e.g. among the respectable working class and in religious behaviour). There were attempts to control recreation deliberately, via campaigns for 'rational recreation' – that is, organised, rule-governed, orderly recreation instead of the old raucous carnivals, drunkenness, blood sports and fairs for example. We need only add to this account the emergence of commercialised recreation, as in the Wild article above, and mentioned especially by Cunningham (in Waites *et al.* 1982), to list all the ingredients of the debates which followed.

If the elements of popular culture in Victorian Britain are agreed, Golby and Purdue dissent from the gramscian 'preferred reading' of these elements. Hegemony is too one-sided an account, they argue, still privileged by marxism, still economic determinist despite its sophistication, still based on a 'prior concern with the failure of the working class to fulfil a given role' (*U203* Unit 4: 34). The concept of hegemony serves oddly to explain a non-event, and a non-appearance, and this predisposes gramscians to look for class determinants instead of, or behind, patterns of consent between the classes, to devalue what the classes had in common – liberal politics, religion, an interest in respectability as a 'realisation of the sheer brutality of much of contemporary life . . . and a corresponding desire to assert one's distance from it' (Unit 4: 38). Finally, urbanism as much as social class, as well as these ideational elements, formed the various 'cultural publics' in the period, and that goes for the publics formed by bourgeois and aristocratic classes as well.

Aldgate too, in his history of British cinema, seems happier working with the term 'consensus' rather than hegemony, as a description of the ideological effect of the films of the period (illustrated in accompanying Open University television programmes). In a curious passage, he feels obliged to suggest that 'as Tony Bennett tells us, a high degree of consensus is characteristic of a period in which a "condition of hegemony" obtains. . .[so]. . .one must assume that the forms and institutions of the mainstream British cinema had a hegemonic role to fulfil' (Unit 7: 11) – a lukewarm endorsement if ever there was one.

Bennett and Donald wrote a Postscript (Block 2) to put their case, and began by arguing for readings of history rather than the 'chimera of real history'. They argue for their 'reading' in a persuasive way – hegemony is not a condition to be tested for but a process (Block 2: 80). Hegemony need not be found in every area, so the case-study of the cinema, even if adverse, does not threaten the whole theory. Further, consensus is a necessary but not a sufficient cause for the establishment of hegemony. Finally, hegemony can be 'passive' as well as 'expansive' (as in Mouffe's notion of enrichment). As we also know, hegemony can include periods of dissent too.

Certain periods of history like the 1930s can be ones where hegemony is still being reconstructed, after a period of class dominance (which is not the same as hegemony since it lacks the element of moral authority). This is revealed in the culture of the period as an imaginary realisation of unity, a sign of absent leadership (*ibid*: 81).

Films in particular cannot be easily interpreted, 'they are not transparent, although their ideological power depends on their ability to create a sense of being realistic' – thus the films of the 1930s do not reflect consensus but produce 'an imaginary resolution of it, "under the sign of an encompassing humanity"' (*ibid*: 82). The films themselves must be grasped in their context – we must see how the penetration of British cinema by Hollywood silenced radical documentary makers, for example. The notion of a diversity of 'struggles' instead of a simple concern with an audience ends this Postscript – struggles in institutions, between Britain and America, between bureaucrats and entrepreneurs, conservatives and marxist intellectuals.

Doubtless, all these points are well-founded, but the decision to deploy them here, against a critical assessment of the concept of hegemony, implies a largely tactical status for the arguments. Such objections do not seem to have been made to prevent gramscians from doing empirical history, for example.

Readers are invited to interrogate these arguments for themselves, in best OU pedagogic style, to see if gramscians think empirical evidence is crucial to their argument or not (given the requirements to 'read' it, context it and so on), and if so, how one might use it systematically. The in-text questions for OU students that spring to my mind after reading these passages are:

Is any kind of concrete historical research suspect, or just 'bourgeois' versions? What defines a 'bourgeois' version?

Can gramscian readings ever be (a) falsified, (b) modified, (c) developed by concrete historical research?

Depending on your answers to the first question above – why *is* there any empirical historical research in gramscian writings? Why not just offer the 'readings'?

Sport, power, culture, society, ideology – oh and hegemony

The puzzles continue in John Hargreaves' influential book on sport (Hargreaves 1986). Rather as in the ground-clearing operations we have discussed earlier, the terrain of sport had been claimed for marxist analysis by writers like Whannel (1983), who had pointed to the ways in which capital interpenetrated sport via processes of commercialisation, sponsorship and Cold War politics. Whannel had gone on to show how deeply media coverage had constructed sport as a spectacle (to use an argument mentioned in the previous chapter – Whannel had been a consultant in the making of the relevant *U203* television programmes). Media coverage had drastically affected the structures of competitions and even the rules. US football is the clearest example, but athletics competitions, showjumping, Sumo wrestling and tennis could all serve to make this point. Some sports which even then had resisted these changes had paid the price of loss of popularity (Whannel 1986).

After noting the possible models available for the study of sport (in Hargreaves 1982), Hargreaves develops a gramscian analysis in his later work. Hall's Foreword picks up the issue of historical study by arguing that the topic of sport 'makes little sense' without an historical framework, but that this framework is also a 'context in which serious theoretical issues can be posed'. 'The relationship betwen sport and hegemony . . . is organic to the treatment, not merely parachuted into place', Hall adds (Hargreaves 1986: xi). Again, then, it is not at all clear whether the data are used primarily to illustrate the 'extended conception of power', whether the conception somehow grows out of the history, or whether both are informed by some political, or, in my view, pedagogic project.

Hargreaves develops a résumé of the themes already established above (State intervention, moral concern over male working-class youth, attempts to coerce and divert in 'rational' forms) in his treatment of historical frameworks and contexts. Again, everything fits into the scheme of class fragmentation and class alliance as moments in the establishment of hegemony. Combinations of class and gender are particularly significant as women join recreational activites to cement class solidarities and so on, as above. As an example of the detail in some of the analyses, Hargreaves suggests that attempts to codify popular sports can help to turn even football matches into moral demonstrations, as players are sent off in front of a working-class audience much more commonly than in rugby, with its predominantly middle-class audience (Hargreaves 1986: 84). Special football matches are also venues for the 'theatre of the great', where royalty or senior politicians show their abilities to command loyalty.

Hargreaves claims sport for popular culture not leisure, and further selects from the sports he will consider to make his case, so he is able to deploy 'enriched gramscianism', with its interest in articulating discourses. He also employs a Foucaldian interest in 'disciplinary technologies' (or discourses), designed to produce 'normal' persons, and control deviant ones.

These technologies enable him to describe the hegemonic mechanisms in the alliances we have mentioned, as sectors of the working class or women demand access to sports only to fall under various disciplinary technologies. These technologies include the 'athleticist technology', where the athletic body comes to symbolise the ideal bourgeois male form, and the ideal citizen and representative of the nation. Interestingly, the media and the school (public schools in the Victorian period, and State schools via various health and hygiene movements, and Physical Education syllabi) are sites for the deployment of this technology too.

These specific technologies are all 'implicated' in the overall struggle for hegemony, though, in the old sense. One hegemonic strategy is to elaborate and extend the power network, for example. Part of this elaboration involves subjecting women and black people to the disciplinary technologies. Of course, a case could easily be made for the old, the poor, the unfit, the ugly, the overweight, the ill-dressed, and the sexually unattractive also being disciplined in this way. As before, the list of subjects for hegemonic discipline is almost endless in principle, but cut short by some notion of 'class domination' or 'serious politics' involving the big three 'condensations' of class, race and gender.

Consumerism above all offers the most articulated combination of such technologies as, for example, the fitness craze exposes the subject to the 'athleticist-fitness, medical-pharmaceutical, nutritionist-culinary, and beautician-sartorial' discourse (*ibid*: 135). The focus on universal themes (eating, health, etc), and the concentration on the young, sexy, healthy, energetic body makes consumerist sport particularly insidious too.

Hargreaves is no fan of consumerism, it is clear. The disciplinary technologies draw on the unequal distribution of cultural and economic power – hence the absence of any socialist policies in sport or leisure. Of course, gramscianism is not gramscianism without resistance and struggle, and for Hargreaves there have been struggles and still will be: consumer capitalism cannot deliver on its promises to offer, say, both proper sport and commercialisation in sport, or to hold out the promise of sport for all while continuing to deny inner cities adequate resources. Here, Hargreaves mentions specifically Habermas's work on 'legitimacy deficits' (*ibid*: 221–2). Oddly, Habermas's main work is not developed, however, presumably because the unspoken ban on critical theory remains (see Chapter 9 for a brief summary of Habermas on legitimation crisis): as a result, history may not have been 'parachuted in', but the concept of 'legitimation crisis' has been, and in the nick of time to ground 'struggle'. As we will see below, deCerteau offers another way to insert struggle into Foucault, and thus to help gramscianise him at last.

Hargreaves' work is substantive, at least, and a move on from the ground-clearing interventions. He does consider the effects on the participating subjects in sport rather than just exposing the inadequacies of other approaches. Nevertheless, there is a good deal of unevenness here. Hargreaves reads the activities in the old manner, as texts with a centred reading. Media studies moved on from that position, as the last chapter showed. There is no attempt here to consider audience competencies or inter-textual 'reading formations' which might investigate how the participants themselves saw sport or recreation when they played or watched. Without such investigations, difficult as they are, the old problems return – are these elegant analyses of the hegemonic implications of keep-fit, or the Scout Movement, merely the results of the analyst's reading, rather than being 'really there'?

In a terse critique, Haywood (Mangan and Small 1986) also returns to the issues of audience and complexity. Hargreaves fails to grasp the specificity of sport, Haywood argues, in his concern to apply the gramscian formula. For the participants, sport can be egalitarian, an alternative to, or critical of, the existing social arrangements, Haywood suggests. The participants' enjoyment can be organised along a number of dimensions, and a fundamental reason for the near-universal appeal of sport lies in the challenge offered to the individual. The diversity of meaning in sport requires a diversity of (sociological) methods, not the 'ideological cage' of gramscianism. The asymmetric nature of Hargreaves' analysis makes it hard to deal with these points.

What actually happens between the symptomatic readings of discourses as hegemonic, and the development of the actual political positions of the oppressed is really anyone's guess, in Hargreaves' work and in a good deal of gramscian analysis. The gap between critical reading and assumed political positions is filled in by a species of what used to be called the illicit argument *post hoc ergo propter hoc*: so, for example, we can see that working-class conservatism did develop after consumerist recreation, so the latter must have been responsible for the former. Any bourgeois sociologist knows that this is a dubious argument, since, for example, some third variable might be causing both consumerist recreation and conservatism.

This is no mere academic point – gramscians surely need to know if *sport and recreation* have a specific effect, and if so how strong it is, compared to, say, work practices, tourism, or popular television, if they are to consider their political priorities. As a concerned parent, should I withdraw my son first from Boy Scouts or football matches, or would Hargreaves recommend a withdrawal from all sport and recreation, just to be on the safe side? Have I become sceptical about gramscianism because I have been swimming too much, and thus fallen under the spell of a disciplinary technology? Are there any sports that are ideologically sound?

There are still no studies that I was able to trace that deal with the audience directly. There are studies of the modalities of spectatorship in sport, like Guttmann's (1986). This shows the complexities of possible audience pleasures in viewing sporting activites, but Guttmann is content to list possibilites rather than test particular hypotheses. When he does discuss marxist accounts, it seems to be American work using a rather strange 'alienation' variety of 'critical theory' that is discussed, not the 'interpellation of subject positions' approach. However, Guttmann's anecdotes and speculations match Hargreaves' in fact, and Guttmann too sees sports as offering spectators an 'irresistible urge to allegorize the sports contest and to feel that collective identity is somehow represented by [the players]' (Guttmann 1986: 182), although he would not necesarily see the big three as the only or major collectivities available in America.

Tourism

I am even less of a specialist here, so I can offer only a brief review of work that looks as if it might fit the theme of this book. I have condemned exactly this sort of practice as 'asymmetric' in others, I have just realised. Two major pieces show the possibilities.

Hewison is not a gramscian or a semiotician, in so far as it is possible to tell from his books, but he is clearly an informed critic, and, with the aid of a few specific concepts and a parachute for them, he could become a full gramscian should he so desire. His book on the heritage industry (Hewison 1987) offers a familiar account of Britain's decline, for example, and focuses upon a particular discourse as symptomatic – not Thatcherism but 'heritage'. In the heritage industry we find 'symbols of national understanding', only conveyed in a misleading way, in a 'picturesque aesthetic' (Hewison 1987: 91), or via 'historic inventions' (*ibid*: 95). The reconstruction of the past is ideologically inflected, a gramscianised Hewison might argue, most spectacularly in the way it depicts black people as absent, as an alien minority, (or as imported exotics, a possibility for the tourist industry to which Urry 1990 points).

Mostly, though, it is social class which is depicted ideologically (to gramscianise again) – the myth of the past is inflected in the cult of the country house, for example, so that the private ownership of large houses is linked to national prestige. Meanwhile, the working classes are absent or romanticised in a style Hewison describes as 'modernised past, and antiqued present' (*ibid*: 132). Class lurks behind the scenes too, as Hewison reveals the commercial and political interests in the heritage industry. Ideology appears as an absent presence throughout, demonstrated best, perhaps, in the constant references to the past as a constructed reality. Ideology is present as a concept in the excellent chapter on industrial museums which spring up exactly as the old real industries are being destroyed, as a kind of ironic mockery of the lives of the work force.

The past is appropriated by capital as a floating signifier and used to soften the public image of British Nuclear Fuels, or sell popular varieties of brown bread (Hewison is at his most theoretical here, discussing postmodernism as an aesthetic of fragments and surfaces driven by the cultural market). Nostalgia is the emotional equivalent of pastiche, he argues, which jams together elements from different times, out of context, and acts as an emotional 'sedative'. Such pastiche suggests that history is over, and this limits action for the future – there is a similar critique of David Lynch's treatments of the past, incidentally, by Denzin (1988).

Powerful as the critique is, it is limited by its isolation from other work. The critique of the phoney realism of the heritage industry could have been extended via the *Screen* debate (see Chapter 7) to consider the effects on the positioned subject, for example. Hewison sees hope only in 'critical realism' and thus seems to imply that there is a real past which ought to be described – it would be easy to dismiss that claim, of course. He himself seems nostalgic for it, and there are echoes of the work of Williams or Hoggart. Urry takes up some of these criticisms, and rebukes Hewison for leaving out sources of resistance to the heritage industry (including what Urry calls the post-tourist response, which is, as we shall see, to engage mockingly with the discourse).

However, Hewison's work can be read as speaking for and on behalf of the people who do resent the way the heritage industry transforms their towns and their past, usually via some arrogant alliance of global finance capital and petit bourgeois cultural capital. In my own home town, Portsmouth, which has been drastically 'heritagised', there was a protest movement against the trend to fill the docks with old 'historical' ships while the real ones departed, symbolised by people wearing T-shirts saying 'Portsmouth Ratepayers – Throw Back the Mary Rose'. (The *Mary Rose* was an old ship salvaged at enormous expense from Portsmouth Harbour.)

In my view, Hewison is on to something which is potentially very useful to those who would wish to construct a new popular-democratic discourse about Britain and its history, and his work seems to offer an example of what can be achieved without gramscian concepts privileging the route through every analysis. One problem is that only this generation of people will have experienced this form of colonisation of their history and will have some immediate recollection of a different past – unless the heritage industry is a permanent installation ready to transform the 1990s in due course as well.

Urry's work on the 'tourist gaze' (Urry 1990) deploys a Foucaldian approach rather like Hargreaves', but without the gramscian last word, and he suggests that tour companies try to discipline the gaze of the tourist, via a discourse about the places to be visited, in order to deliver that essential customer pleasure. The struggles by some tourists to escape these gazes show some interesting paradoxes – the lonely attempt to extract personal meaning (via the 'romantic gaze'), or to search for the 'authentic' culture one is visiting, have already been incorporated by the industry, for example.

Struggles by the workers in the tourist industry can take a specific form, given the peculiar nature of the activity: since the companies want the tourists to be happy and relaxed while they consume, it becomes possible for employees to fight a subtle 'war of smiles', to take industrial action by not smiling (Urry 1990: 70)!

Urry analyses a number of pleasures in tourism, concluding that a search for the 'extraordinary', defined against changing definitions of 'the ordinary', is the main source. As he points out, this pursuit can include the enjoyment of parodying the official discourses.

In his discussion of postmodernism and its impact, Urry offers an investigation of the sociological origins of the main promoters of postmodernist ethics, via Bourdieu. These 'new petit-bourgeois' have developed a distinctive type of tourism, including a return to visiting the countryside, and are evolving into the 'post-tourist', as they enjoy the pleasures of what Hebdige calls the 'second degree' (see Chapter 5), shifting between the different gazes, playing with both the 'high culture' significance and the 'pleasure principle' immediacy of their holiday destinations.

In this way, social class (and gender, generation and ethnicity) structure the available gazes. Different social groups, for Bourdieu, have access to different classificatory systems, based on different cultural capitals, circulating in different 'cultural economies'. This work has been criticised as being too sociologistic again, as we saw with the brief discussion of Morley's use of the Bourdieu-like term 'repertoires', and Urry's work lacks any detailed account of the possible interpretive effects of 'reading formations' rather than sociological groups. Nevertheless, Bourdieu might help us later in explaining the sociological orgins of gramscianism, as we shall see.

Finally, Urry's work is useful for showing the 'collapse of internal divisions' between, or the 'implosion' of, the hitherto separate areas of tourism, leisure, media and education – it becomes hard to separate out the seeker of the extraordinary who watches travel or wildlife programmes on television from the actual visitor who will see an equally mediated view via an equally organized gaze, for example. Again, the growth of 'edu-entertainment' in museums and heritage centres (and the growing numbers of pedagogues anxious to use this material in 'projects') implodes two more areas. There must be even more confusion and anxious micropoliticking among academics in 'leisure studies' and other fields, these days, as the boundaries around their specialisms look more and more fragile.

The companies, and other providers, also commission research to see what it is that the tourist has perceived. This provides some fixity in the flux, again, although Tomlinson suggests that the market is becoming highly unstable and volatile (Tomlinson 1990). There is some academic research in this area too. Of course, the context and organising frameworks are different, and they touch the interpellation issue only obliquely if at all. Nevertheless, Botterill's (1989) work offers a chance to do something like Philo's experiments (see Chapter 7), using, perhaps, tourists' own photographs as the basis for a story which might reveal how and whether the subject position constructed by the tour companies was or was not accepted by the customers.

We know from the media work that there would still be problems with the empirical status of the customers and their non-textual sources of resistance (if any): is the critique of the artificiality of package tourism merely an effect of other discourses of 'authenticity' promoted by rival companies, or by travel writers, for example? The effects of the researcher's discourse, the unconscious levels of meaning, and the fantasies of the participants would all be relevant. And the significance of all this for hegemonic discourse would still have to be established, of course, if the field were to be reclaimed for gramscianism.

Indeed, even Bennett, who developed the notion of a reading formation, as we saw in the previous chapter, offers only the barest sketch of how the audience (in this case visitors to Blackpool) might be able to exploit the splits in the town's overall 'narrative' (in Bennett *et al.* 1986), and Fiske, who has done more than most to extend the implications of the work on the audience in TV to studies of leisure (as we shall see), has done little more than suggest possibilities by analogy. In the field of tourism too, we seem to be left with critical symptomatic readings by experts, and some market research by providers, without knowing what the customers themselves really make of it.

There is a recent attempt to construct a critical audience for tourism, though, by trying to form and lead an embryonic 'new social movement' based on an organisation called Tourism Concern (Botterill 1991). This move is seen as requiring the classic 'break' with existing academic approaches to tourism, a new methodology of participation, and a new intent to develop activism and critical interventions on behalf of the victims of the tourist industry. The first stage in the struggle, to establish a new academic course in 'Tourism with Social Responsibility', at my very own college, has been won. Whether the movement will be able to transfer out of the academy into real politics, despite all the contradictions and dilemmas attached to such 'expressive radicalism', is less certain, as Botterill acknowledges.

CHRIS ROJEK AND OTHER *ENFANTS TERRIBLES*

There has been a particularly strong reaction to gramscian claims to be in possession of exclusive rights to the field of leisure among a groups of analysts located in Leicester or Glasgow, and one of the most prominent figures here has been Rojek. Since the struggle with marxists has sometimes stolen a leaf from the gramscian book and claimed to be a generational one, Rojek in particular currently enjoys a reputation as an *enfant terrible*.

Rojek develops a familiar critique of marxist work in this field as ultimately reductionist, wanting to privilege 'the economic' as the ultimate determinant, and wanting to use the old marxist terms to come to grips with what he sees as a fundamentally changed society. The critique has been mounted in Rojek (1985), for example. Rojek suggests that marxist work can be over-formalist rather than concrete, and it seems to incorporate the same dubious definitions, of leisure as 'free time', as were rebuked in the claims to have made a 'break'.

Rojek considers 'figurational sociology' as an alternative explanation to the historical patterns in leisure (in Rojek 1985). Again, there is surprisingly little disagreement about the events themselves – in many ways, Rojek (in Rojek 1989) reads exactly like Hargreaves (1986) in his account of rational recreation especially, for example. But whereas Hargreaves wants to deploy elaborated gramscianism to tie the developments to an underlying hegemonic project, Rojek would simply see a complex pattern of emergent alliances and developments with no centred determination by class, important though social class might be as one factor. For the reader interested in the substance, the theoretical issues hardly make a difference: for Hargreaves, the elaboration of power is so elaborate that one hardly notices (nor cares, perhaps) when the allegedly central framework for the whole discussion is revealed.

Figurational sociology draws on the work of Elias to argue that social life can be grasped as a series of configurations, 'structure[s] of mutually oriented and dependent people' (Rojek 1985: 158) which often cross class boundaries and also feature multiple centres of power rather than some subtle domination by capital. A number of summaries (Dunning in Rojek 1989, Mennell 1985, Rojek 1985) explain the approach. There is an underlying mechanism of social change – a social–psychological tendency towards the disciplining of emotions and the development of consideration for others in one's personal conduct, the regulation of spontaneity, what Elias calls the trend to 'civilisation'. This latter is an unfortunate term since it has undertones of moral evaluation and moral progress, although enthusiasts like Dunning insist that the term has a technical meaning only in Elias – see his piece in Rojek (1989). Apart from anything else, this concern with underlying psychic patterns of restraint help deny that leisure is 'free time' at all – the activities in question express an 'historically specific affect economy of balances and restraints' (Rojek 1985: 164).

The approach enables a complex analysis of a range of recreational phenomena. Purely to illustrate the method, we can examine work on football hooliganism and eating. The substantive analyses are important only as illustrations, and there is no intention to simply commend figurational analysis. However, it is important to demonstrate that gramscian analysis is not the only form available. Of course, figurational sociology has its problems too, analogous ones to those of gramscianism or any other account that has to manage specific and general levels of analysis.

Dunning et al. (1986), for example, uses figurational analysis to explain the strange 'segmental' nature of the alliances that form up to fight at football matches. These have more than just a class determinant – indeed, both rivals and their victims are often from the same working-class groups. Young used a similar argument against the view that street criminals were vanguards of the proletariat, as we saw in Chapter 4. The fans form shifting and emergent alliances – supporters of southern teams will fight among themselves but unite against northern teams, and all English fans will sometimes unite against foreign fans. This phase of the argument serves to qualify marxist analysis like Critcher's (in Clarke *et al.* 1979) which stresses class struggle and alienation among fans induced by the commercialisation and capitalisation of the game (see Wagg (1984) for a fuller account of marxist approaches).

Dunning also uses the civilisation theme to modernise a common view that some sort of deprivation lies at the heart of football hooliganism. In Dunning's case it is exclusion from the mainstream of social life which consigns the fans to a relative isolation from civilising forces, but the general theory can only be deployed speculatively.

Mennell (1985) reviews a number of different approaches to the study of food preparation and eating, including 'structuralist' ones. One such structuralist analysis, incidentally, appeared in *U203*, where James (in Waites *et al.* 1982) considered the meaning of the habit of children in eating junk food. She concluded that the children's delight in such food was a deviant inversion of official parental food values, and as such displayed an element of semiotic struggle. Mennell acknowledges that structuralist analysis (including some done by Douglas, Barthes and Bourdieu) shows the cultural and aesthetic elements in eating, but is reductive of complexity and process. Elias's work restores such complexity and emergence in the social and personal development of tastes. In this process, the economic clearly has a role, in terms of both forces of production in the food industry, and in the ways in which social classes use food as codes to differentiate themselves. But nations, individuals, psychological factors, and the emergence of professional cookery also combine in complex ways to explain the 'civilising of appetite'.

As one small example of what is a long and complex analysis, Mennell traces one development in the modern English diet from an early break with medieval cookery in Renaissance Italy, which spread to the nobles of France in the seventeenth and eighteenth centuries, then to the French bourgeoisie where it underwent further development as a result of an early concern with good health as one way of distinguishing refined tastes from vulgar, and eventually formed one strand in the development of modern eating disorders like anorexia (Mennell 1985: 32–8). Fascinating as the account is, it is impossible to decide if events 'really did' take that course, or if Mennell is using figurationalism as one resource in his 'reading formation' to construct a skilled narrative which itself connects the events. We are left with the problem – are there any rational grounds upon which to choose a figurationalist approach, this time, rather than another?

In his later work, Rojek seems to have developed other approaches too, and his essays on modernism draw upon a number of writers to show the conflicts at the heart of concepts of leisure, and the emergence of distinctively modern forms. Other essays in the collection (Rojek 1989) raise important points for gramscianism more directly. There are clear demonstrations of alternative perspectives, including figurationalism, but there is also a sustained attack on some of the assumptions in gramscian work (often, Clarke and Critcher are the specific targets). These criticisms put into doubt the whole claim to have made a break with the other approaches in the field: at the heart of radical marxist work lie some very conventional definitions of leisure and work.

Moorhouse argues, for example, that there is an assumption that work is always alienating and miserable, producing a definition of leisure, shared by bourgeois writers, as a compensation for work, however illusory. The discovery of female unpaid domestic labour modifies the work–leisure split a little, but at the expense of taking over the view that all unpaid domestic labour is alienating work too. Bishop and Hoggett also criticise the near-universal work–leisure split by arguing for the analysis of a number of kinds of activities that look like both – as in the 'informal economy', the unrecognised economy, the black economy, the communal economy and the household economy. Their discussion of the last category raises implications for feminist work too (of the kind often found in gramscian work), in at least two directions: they recognise that men do unpaid domestic labour too, and they argue that such labour can be, in certain circumstances, not only fulfilling but anti-capitalist, since it exists, like all the other versions, outside of the realm of exchange-value.

Moorhouse, and Bishop and Hoggett, also suggest a need for ethnographic studies to examine what participants actually do feel as they work and engage in leisure (early in his piece, Moorhouse innocently commends the work of Parkin to think out possible audience decodings!). Of course, this is not easily accomplished, given the serious reservations about ethnographic work developed in the last chapter, but without it, a good deal of licence can be taken by marxist writers, as we have seen, and the analyses can lean towards 'asymmetry'. Moorhouse specifically mentions the tendency of Clarke and Critcher to select suitable examples (e.g. street culture rather than commercialised culture when they want to talk of resistance), or to place undue emphasis on the hooligan football fan. Generally, the concrete work still needs to be done: 'consumerism . . . hegemony and the like merely indicate where detailed analysis might begin and by no means represent analyses in themselves' (Rojek 1989: 31).

Moorhouse recommends the specific use of Weberian concepts like status groups and lifestyle to rethink the distinctions between employment and non-employment. The rest of the Rojek (1989) collection also offers a number of new directions – into Freudian analysis of the subjective moments of pleasure and fun in consumerism, for example, with the use of the promising term 'leisurework' to describe how wishes are attached subjectively to objects (Ferguson's chapter). Simmel on modernism and the city, Elias, and Foucault (in his own right rather than used to elaborate gramscianism) all appear too. Gramscianism appears, via the work of Jennifer Hargreaves on the specifically gendered aspects of elaborated gramscianism, reworking the themes and territory of John Hargreaves summarised above. This seems to me to gramscianism's proper place, as one option rather than the only option, as in modern media work.

The suggestions made in Rojek (1989) are not far from the conclusions of gramscians in other fields – the need for concrete studies of the audience is granted in analyses of the media, the attempt to link Freud into a theory of pleasure is well-known to CCCS and *U203* theorists, and the need for a complex history accepted. The Rojek collection produced a rather astringent review by Tomlinson (1990), but this may owe as much to the issues of academic rivalry as to serious theoretical disagreements. Gramscians seem particularly defensive in lesiure studies, though. In many ways, the real break for gramscian leisure studies was to come in the shape of the new attention to consumerism and unofficial leisure.

THE TACTICAL CONSUMER

The old leisure studies field included academics and planners, it has been argued, and there are clear advantages in accepting some of the definitions of the latter groups as items on the agenda for research. Planners have the resources to launch initiatives (and support conferences), and their leisure centres, exhibitions, games and tourist developments provide a ready-made source of objects for the analysts to consider. Providers and analysts could enjoy a rather cosy division of labour in the common interest in city pedestrianisation schemes or new tourist facilities: analysis could still be critical, but it would also provide some dignity (and even a kind of market research) for local planners.

Further, there is a party political issue here, since the Thatcher Government launched a vigorous campaign to privatise leisure provision, if only by starving the initiatives of local authorities of funds. Local authorities' provision could be seen as about the only way to move towards the longed-for socialist lesiure policy, and it becomes as important to defend it as to defend any other local expenditure on the community.

Inevitably, support for such policies involved some compromises, since there must be a degree of imposition of choice, a prioritisation of approved forms of leisure, an unavoidable echo of 'rational recreation' or even 'muscular Christianity' – why finance student versions of the Olympic Games and not more skateboarding facilities (to quote a recent controversy)? Should the version of 'serious politics' offered by Labour

Party councils always be supported? Is there not an inevitable élitism, a quiet assertion of bourgeois values still in the attempts to get leisure off the streets and under supervision (to paraphrase Clarke and Critcher 1985), even if it is now to be done in socialist pleasure palaces?

Work like that of Fiske (1989a, 1989b) threatens that alliance between socialist researchers and socialist local authorities, since it breaks with 'serious' leisure altogether, and refuses to condemn 'vulgar' or commercialised forms of consumerism. There is an almost total inversion of the critical stance towards consumerism found in Clarke and Critcher or Hargreaves (or early MacRobbie for that matter), and a new celebration of the joys and empowerments to be found in private, unofficial, even rather scandalous and unorganised consumption.

The relation of the new interests to marxism, especially to gramscianism, is confusing in this work. Fiske uses a common technique of apologising for his own work, and offering both the analyses and comments on them. In various introductions, and in concluding sections to chapters (in 1989a, for example), one can see a last despairing effort to square his work with the marxist tradition. Politically, Fiske's heart lies with Gramsci and with socialist politics conceived in terms of counter-hegemonic blocs and popular alliances: his head, however, seems elsewhere.

In the concrete analyses, the work is far away, certainly, from early gramscian orthodoxy, and the chapter on news (Fiske 1989a) finally and quietly abandons the gramscian problematic. This and other discoveries from work on the television audience (reviewed in the last chapter) lead to a new perspective on the consumer of leisure.

Popular culture is now about winning a space for progressive rather than radical or counter-hegemonic definitions. The careful attempts to trace back cultures to an underlying cycle of settlement and crisis are no longer necessary: the authors Fiske quotes are permitted to say this, of course, although it is the essential message of bourgeois sociology as well.

Fiske's work is driven and inspired by Barthes, as was Hebdige's, but Barthes at a later stage, the Barthes that reveals his 'move away from his early party political phase to one in which the concept of pleasure takes over from the concept of ideology . . . acompanied by his concern with the body of the reader' (1989a: 62). The shift to the focus on the body has already been noted in Hargreaves' work above – see also Mercer for a brief history of this move (in Bennett *et al.* 1986). Finally, Fiske draws heavily upon the work of deCerteau, who sets out to establish the sites of resistance to the power apparatuses outlined in Foucault.

The seeking of semiotic pleasure becomes the central form of resistance, the appropriation of signifiers the substance of politics, linguistic practice the archetype of all subjective and cultural practice. Since the linguistic now includes every activity, from shopping to fantasising to playing video games, and since language is always open to subversive enunciations, Fiske finds semiotic struggle everywhere: in wearing jeans, in shopping malls, on the beach, in the video games arcade, among Madonna fans, in rock videos, in country and western music, professional wrestling on TV, females wrestling in Jell-O, and in popular programmes like game shows and quizzes on (Australian, US and British) television.

This linguistic imperialism perpetuates the old activist vision of a culturally resisting populace doing proto-politics even when they shop or go surfing, denying the hated 'mass culture thesis', and rescuing the people from the accusation of being 'cultural dopes'. Dominant ideology theories can be resisted too, since no one would submit to dominant ideology for long if it gave them no pleasure: the search for pleasure, including the pleasures of letting the body play with the signifiers, in the 'semiotic brothels of the machine age' – the video game arcades, for example (Fiske 1989a: 93).

There is a constant attempt to resist the claims of high culture to distinctiveness in the course of this account – video games players are as creative and as constrained as are 'authors', for example, since, on the one hand, the 'lack of narrative authority in the games . . . works to evacuate the author, and into that space the player inserts himself' (*ibid*: 89), while, equally, 'our postromantic culture still ascribes to the author a degree of power and determination that is both false and widely believed in' (*ibid*: 90). Talking up one activity, and talking down another, enables them to meet in the middle in some kind of populist equality. Or again fantasy (of the kind enagaged in, apparently, by female viewers of Madonna videos) is as equally powerful a mode of representation as 'the more public representations of language and the media' (*ibid*: 124).

Fantasy is also politics, or at least proto-politics since it 'can stimulate politically progressive and positive fantasies . . . [which] . . . may well chime with other traces of feminine power in the viewer's subjectivity, and may, eventually, in some cases, translate into political action' (*ibid*: 124–5). This is one reason for claiming Madonna as on the correct side too, and there are several quoted examples from ethnographic studies of TV audiences where female viewers have claimed to have felt more confident, assertive or insightful as a result of having watched *Dallas*, or *Cagney and Lacey* (see Fiske 1989b: 189–90, for example).

The 'political' itself is transformed via the old 1960s and feminist insight that 'the personal is the political', or 'the interior is the political' (Fiske 1989a: 124), and in these interior personal struggles self-empowerment is won, forming a kind of reservoir of progressive feelings which might one day feed radical politics as in the escalation of consciousness depicted above. In this sense, Fiske claims that 'economic power is both underpinned and exceeded by semiotic power' (*ibid*: 9–10). This is the old idealism, of course. Fiske (1989b) describes several ways in which this escalation might happen – via crisis (but this is unlikely now), by the emergence of 'new social movements' based on 'nomadic subjectivities' (of which more later), but above all by the development of a suitably 'producerly' socialist rhetoric, aided by the critic who can 'assist in the socialisation of the interior . . . help the personal to be generalised outward' (*ibid*: 190).

Such escalation is unusual, though. Like deCerteau, Fiske sees the main forms of resistance as 'poaching, tricking, speaking, reading, strolling, shopping, desiring' (see Frow 1991). Subversive politics works with what has been provided, within the indeterminacies necessarily included in attempts to regulate space and time, a politics of transgression, of 'getting along' rather than openly challenging. Although this kind of work is widely admired, it seems very like the early insights in the studies of resistance in the education system, in Willis (1977) or Gintis and Bowles (1980).

Willis has returned to the fray in his recent ethnographic work on young people and their 'symbolic creativity' (Willis 1990). The same sort of uncritically populist material is presented as in Fiske. Everyone is their own artist or semiotician, and meaning can be found everywhere. We are invited to admire the ways in which young people make their own cultures from what is provided, and Willis tries to persuade us to blur the distinctions between high art and popular artistry, and between production and consumption, more or less as Fiske does.

Willis argues that common culture reveals a 'grounded aesthetic', and he uses brief examples from interviews to illustrate what he means. As an example, a young woman's comments on a soap opera reveal for Willis a 'grounded fictive aesthetic which can separate and recombine representation and reality' (*ibid*: 33). Whether or not we would have noticed that without the 'textual shifters' (see Chapter 7) in Willis's commentary is uncertain, however. We have here the usual problem with ethnographic data and whether it is intended to merely confirm and illustrate, as opposed to test or generate, the theoretical commentary.

At the risk of appearing élitist or pessimistic, the whole tone of the Willis piece confirms for me the dangers of an over-partisan, over-anxious analysis. The author(s) are desperate to make their point, but succeed only in raising suspicion about the validity of the findings. The learned and 'educated' commentaries around the rather commonplace quotes look very much like the 'morale boosting' that is so familiar to anyone who has heard public relations spokespersons, politicians, advertisers, or other persuaders and spin doctors talking up their product. The book reminds me particularly of those 'curriculum mongers' who defended 'vocational' training schemes for unqualified youth on the grounds that they would offer wonderful skills like 'being able to work cooperatively in a team, to interact with mechanical equipment, and to perform an agricultural operation' – i.e. they would be trained to mow the lawn.

I am not criticising the young unemployed, but the analysts who patronise them by this sort of argument. Only a very cloistered bourgeois (writer? reader? local politician?) could be so 'surprised' that the young unemployed are still able to speak articulately and criticise soap operas. Such people cannot have talked to 'ordinary people' lately, or even watched any televison documentaries on unemployment. Of course, the piece is designed to be partisan, to appeal for funds for community arts (Willis's earlier contribution, in Giroux *et al.* 1989, is even clearer about this).

Despite the solemn warnings about the need to take these skills seriously if we want to build socialism upon them, Willis has found out almost nothing about the political views of these young people directly (and nor does Fiske): once again, the respondents provide the innocent data, and the analysts provide the politics for them. Despite Willis's perceptive rejection of the term 'hegemony' (in the Afterword here – and he expressed reservations in a footnote in *Learning to Labour*), he is not very far here from the mainstream of gramscian cultural politics.

Reducing everything to the level of semiotic struggle and resistance also blurs other distinctions. Methodologically, the whole breathtaking opus depends upon substantial generalisations about the populace and its motives and competencies, based on slender resources like some Madonna fans' letters, or some overheard remarks on surfing or shopping. Fiske confesses that he does not know if these generalisations are sustainable, but then empirical study is impossible anyway, he argues, given the fleeting and polycentric nature of popular resistance. Willis also apologises for his data, and then argues that 'even one example shows the theoretical space for our argument' (Willis 1990: 135).

Fiske is really in business to offer readings concerned to demonstrate the processes at work in the scattered fragmentary examples he chooses, and thus, by extension, at work everywhere. He still uses empirical evidence, however, in a rather rhetorical way. The chapter on television game shows (Fiske 1989b) seems to assume that viewing figures simply demonstrate a widespread audience participation (Fiske knows this is dubious with viewing figures for news), and he elides the studio audience's (artificially?) exuberant endorsement of the shopping skills of the contestants with the reactions of the public audience watching at home.

Often, Fiske himself is his own evidence, as a participant in and analyst of television viewing, video games, tourism in Chicago, or news broadcasts. His task as a critic of news is identified as a task for the popular audience too, and his refined reactions and those of the typical audience are often blurred, and differences denied: 'I am. . .misusing their resources for my pleasure. . .And in this I believe I am typical of the people in general' (1989b: 178–9).

This sort of 'fluidity of the pronouns' (usually, it is a fluid 'we') is found in some feminist readings of the TV audience, and, says Brunsdon (in

Seiter *et al.* 1989: 124), involves a broader tactic to ground the analysis, and fix the flux of meaning in an authentic 'I'. The phenomenon can be seen as a postmodernist implosion of the internal divisions between the author/researcher's voice and the respondent's. Or it could be seen, following Bourdieu, as an 'aristocratic' disdain for mere empirical confirmations of the professor's reading.

DeCerteau's work has been criticised recently too. Using arguments which look strikingly similar to those deployed in the debates on media, Frow (1991) suggests that deCerteau has too monolithic a view of ruling power (just like the problem with 'preferred readings' in Chapter 6), and there are methodological doubts about the empirical independence of these raiders, poachers and flâneurs. Frow suspects that these unofficial activites are structured, more systematic than they look, and 'coded' or text-like. We have long known, of course, that the 'principle of rebellion is the same as that of conformity' (Durkheim 1953), and we have seen arguments in earlier chapters which suggest that opposition from 'subject positions' can be seen as effects of texts. Willis does not seem to have questioned whether the comment on soap operas he makes so much of (Willis 1990: 33) might have come from the 'soaps' column of the *Sun.*

In a re-enactment of the dream of the radical intellectual to meet the public on equal ground mentioned by Johnson (in Clarke *et al.* 1979), Fiske speaks as a kind of people's ventriloquist's dummy (to semiotically appropriate a phrase). His unity as a subject, embodied in the authorial voice, somehow guarantees theirs. Politically, he, like Willis, urges us to embrace the people's semiotic causes and leave behind our élitism and pessimism in a gesture of political solidarity with the people. With an eye to the real audience, in academic life, Fiske covers his theoretical back with Barthes, Baudrillard, deCerteau and Foucault, and Willis juggles with homologies, 'integral circuitings' and dialectics.

Of course, it is still a highly refined and cultivated populism that is on offer, designed to raise the morale of the radical petit bourgeois. We hear only about the semiotic struggles of the politically correct. There is no analysis of the interplay between nature and culture in popular bloodsports, nothing on the blissful potential re-entry into nature and *jouissant* loss of self as the pitbulls clash, or the terriers seize the foxcub. At least Willis is ethnographer enough still to notice, rather reluctantly, what he thinks of as excessive alcohol consumption, and fighting in pubs.

We still have an asymmetric methodology, working backwards from approved and self-evidently popular activities to some underlying semiotic struggle, and tautology is never far away. Nor is 'moral nihilism' as in the piece where shoplifting is 'not just a guerilla raid upon the storeowners themselves but upon the power bloc in general: parents, teachers, security guards, the legal sytem' (Fiske 1989b: 39). This is ultra-leftism, or possibly the lofty disdain of those who are above mere 'trade'.

In the new leisure studies, all commodities are now cultural, 'purified into their signifiers', and figure in the new politics as purely cultural. Whereas the old marxism neglected the use-value side of the commodity, there is now almost no reference to the exchange side, save for an acknowledgement that most popular culture 'makes do' with previously provided commodities. Of course, not all people can consume the goods or take part in the rituals of the Australian version of *Blind Date* – but then there is vicarious participation since 'the characters on television are embodiments of ideological values not iconic representations of real people' (Fiske 1989a: 144).

Given the broad scope of semiotic guerrilla warfare, it is almost impossible not to participate somewhere: any normal individual, like Fiske or Willis, will have to negotiate 'contradictions' in media messages, Madonna videos, or the clash between scientific and popular accounts of events if they so much as glance at a copy of *Weekly World News* (*Sunday Sport* seems to be the British equivalent). This is apparently the evidence for continued agency and the failure of interpellation, this pragmatism and tricksterism and joy in punning is the new source of 'rebellious subjectivity'. The 'scally' (a 'Liverpool lad' living on his wits, stealing, conning and cheating his way as he goes off to support his football team, often at the expense of foreign shopkeepers or his family) is the new cultural hero.

The 'new times' theorists also celebrate the new consumerism and stress its political potential, of course. Nava (1991) points to a range of consumerist techniques, ranging from the boycott or green consumerism ('implicitly socialist') to the terrorist raid (spraying cyanide on US grapes), and argues that these have been more effective than strikes and picketing. Shopping offers a 'new and very immediate democratic process: voting about the environment can take place on a daily basis' (*ibid*: 168). However, she also fails to mention any consumer pathologies – the (possibly apocryphal) 'shopaholic', the youths who mug passers-by for their new trainers, the schoolchildren who suffer abuse from their 'style fascist' playmates because they are not wearing the latest bumbags. Presumably she feels herself capable of coping with consumerism, supported, perhaps, by some consumer guides and those networks of knowledge that help suppport the 'connoisseur consumer' (as Tomlinson 1990 calls them), and again, via the figure of the slippery pronoun, perhaps she assumes such cultural capital is shared.

It is also likely that Nava has underestimated the capacity of the market to counter consumer boycotts or preferences, to simply replace US grapes with South African ones, or to take over the term 'green' as a marketing term (not everyone agrees that green politics are implicitly socialist for that matter, of course – see Sylvan 1985). For every consumer preference that forces a retreat by capital, another extends it – Simmonds (in Tomlinson 1990) argues that one effect of political vegetarianism, for example, is to bring African peasant farmers into the cash-crop economy as the demand for mange-tout grows. Tomlinson's piece also concludes with a reminder of the flexibility of the market – any system that can give you 'individualised' coaching as you work out on a weights machine can incorporate most forms of personal needs.

Sivanandan (1990) has made many similar points in criticism of the socialist populism in the 'new times' as we have seen already – 'Thatcherism in drag' as he calls it. It seems fitting to cite one of his best retorts in summary of the semiotic politics of consumption: now we know why the poor in London sleep in cardboard boxes – because cardboard boxes are a wonderful way to signify poverty!

CONCLUSION

Of course, the analysts are writing for a different market altogether – the student of cultural studies. The student audience requires the equivalent of *The Face* to provide them with the cultural capital to cope with a range of things they feel they should be caring about, but without the desire [*sic*] to embrace the theoretical or political obligations of 'earnest' approaches like marxism.

Pieces like Fiske's are ideal for the student raider or cruiser, with their essay-type format, their high levels of repetition and redundancy, and their concreteness. They are designed for the second-generation scholarship person who is now secure enough to be able to play with the signifiers, as the economically secure or the relatively sexually liberated always have (Bourdieu 1984).

These books offer an agreeable style – irony and parody for those in the know, a comforting familiarity for the more naive. There is a fashionable and reassuring relativism in the comments about the end of the university and the scorn for 'education' and its grand narratives, and a deep compromise at the same time with 'preaching' and 'mastery'. Above all, there is cultural capital, perhaps, for those students (or lecturers) who wish to justify their scepticism towards the authority of the old 'earnest' order, just as the 1968 generation drew upon situationist and surrealist slogans. Consumerism and 'postmodernism' hurts 'the earnest' most of all, and acts as the terrain for oppositional meanings and as a resource for micropolitical strategy.

Bourdieu (1984) argues that the aesthetics of high culture were always defined against the popular, and Fiske is right to suggest that a celebration of disorder and populist taste are ways in which the popular fights back. But it is more likely to be used as a tactic by the student (or by the 'new petit bourgeois' member of the British Communist Party) not by the (adult) proletariat. At a guess, when this sort of material is presented on a course or in a textbook, as agreeable sound bites or summaries, it does nothing to

172

undermine the sentimental or opportunist politics of this audience, but is nicely affirmative.

Those politics are facilitated by the empty signifier of the 'nomadic subjectivities' or the transformed gramsican 'moving equilibrium', (or the 'new social movements'). This terrain is empty and always rentable. It looks like any good cause can occupy it – Band Aid and Comic Relief, green politics, feminisms, CND or END, even, with a little skill, Animal Liberation, any local protest movement, any 'political' cultural fashion, anything. The next chapter considers this charge in more depth.

9

GRAMSCIAN POLITICS

INTRODUCTION

Political considerations have appeared throughout the other chapters too, of course, since an interest in political outcomes is deeply linked to the theoretical projects in gramscianism, right from the very first consideration of Gramsci's work as a 'philosophy of praxis'. This term urges us to develop socialist politics, but it also serves a theoretical function to provide a limit or 'fix' to relativism: given that all accounts are historically constructed, what makes marxism valid is its suitability for the politics of the time.

Politics serve to unify the social formation and avoid the dangers of merely theoretical solutions, and this marks Gramsci's superiority over Althusser, as we saw claimed in Chapter 1. The search for the mechanisms of this political unity guides the analysis of a number of popular cultural forms. It lies behind the work on encoding, decoding and preferred readings, and energises the work on news, current affairs, and fascism. After a long and complex analysis of the sources of meaning in James Bond movies, for example, Bennett and Woollacott (1987) declare that the only fixity is that one should select readings which have political significance.

Hall is even more explicit, in his discussion of the 'national popular' (in Samuel 1981), insisting that the notion of political struggle should define the very term popular culture (as opposed to, say, a focus on the content of the activity). Later, he rejects a version of postmodernism on the grounds of its political implications, and prioritises the need to incorporate a sense of struggle over the dynamics and impetus of 'theoretical logic' in his account of his differences with 'post-marxisms' (Grossberg 1986). Although less explicitly, a number of gramscian pieces seem to have followed this attempt to stabilise definitions of the proper scope and conduct of radical enquiry by using a politics to interview theoretical candidates. Hall concludes his piece in Samuel with a comment which was to be cited at the beginning of Clarke's and Critcher's book – that popular culture is one site 'where socialism might be constructed. Otherwise, to tell you the truth I don't give a damn about it' (Hall in Samuel 1981: 239).

Yet this can accord too much influence to the political moment. There are clear theoretical impulses in the work too (and what I have called academic ones). What vision of politics was it, for example, that led the Media Group at Birmingham to spend a whole year coming to grips with 'screen theory', or that led to all those efforts to clear the ground in other fields? These efforts can be seen as 'political', of course, but in a rather localised and specific sense. It would be interesting to hear of a defence of these efforts as an urgent priority in the construction of socialism. There seems to be a complex interrelation (what else?) between what might be called 'macro' socialist politics conceived on a national or international scale, 'micro' politics where one struggles in whatever space one finds oneself in to expand one's freedom of action, and specifically academic politics which feature in the accounts of the development of the perspectives of cultural studies.

GRAMSCI'S LEGACY

We have noted the difficulties in reading Gramsci in Chapter 1. Gramsci's specific political activities seem to have ranged from a strong interest in activist work in 'factory councils' to a sustained attempt to think out a suitable role for an Italian Communist Party, and to guide its relations to other parties and movements in Italy and in what was then the Soviet Union. Even in Italy in the inter-war period, Gramsci's politics failed. Attempts to turn the proletariat from its traditional syndicalism towards bolshevism during the 'red weeks' of the 1920s failed (Clark 1977), and there was no popular front or any other alliance to resist fascism. Even sustained attempts to validate Gramsci as a forebear of Eurocommunism look less impressive now that the Italian Eurocommunist moment of the 1970s is past.

Of course, a very different political context existed in Britain for the reception of Gramsci's ideas. All the difficulties for socialist politics had been identified in the early articles by Anderson and Nairn (Anderson *et al.* 1965) – a conservative and corporatist working class, an anti-intellectual Labourist socialist party, a tiny Communist Party, inadequate theoretical resources to begin to analyse British capitalism or to understand its crisis. That diagnosis was criticised by Johnson (in Hall *et al.* 1980), who pointed to the strangely abstract nature of classes in the analysis: they appeared as collective subjects with 'ascribed' wills which ignored concrete struggles. As we have seen though, for the gramscians, those struggles were located in the past or in the 'alternative proletariats' of youth, black people, and women, and took place largely outside of party politics.

There was some continuing working-class industrial militancy in the

1970s, based on the traditional British reserves of syndicalism and unionism rather than any theory – Willis (1977) and, later, Hall *et al.* (1978), in their different ways, told us about the notorious mistrust of theory among the working classes. The respectable working class in particular was particularly prone to recognise themselves in the dominant ideology (a tendency going back some years), and this was confirmed by the string of Thatcherite successes at the polls from the end of the 1970s.

Perry Anderson had predicted difficulties arising from certain ambiguities in the writings of Gramsci on the key concepts of hegemony, State and civil society. The 'east–west' model in particular, it will be recalled, suggested that civil society was the main bulwark of capitalism in the west, with an oddly 'neutral' view of the State. It is easy to see that the task for socialist politics in Britain would come to look like an almost exclusive focus on cultural politics.

This can be combined with Coward's comment that cultural studies always displayed a certain historicist politics itself, with its reading of history as the inevitable clash of capital and labour in a series of crises, and with each combatant somehow directly represented by the main British political parties. The Labour Party became more attractive as the Thatcherite revolution unfolded, and as the agenda was set more and more firmly to the right: as the Welfare State was rolled back, elegant marxist criticisms of it seemed indulgent as well as outdated. If the British 'people' or 'masses' did not appear fixed in the Labour Party, it was difficult to materialise them anywhere else on the political scene, except as an absent presence (Hall in Samuel 1981) or as somehow articulated to those visible struggles by youth, black people, or women and, later, the 'new social movements'.

Cultural politics took on a peculiar pedagogic turn in British gramscian-ism too. Gramsci had emphasised the positive role of intellectuals, of course, especially 'organic ones'. Williams in particular retained a life-long interest in adult education as a means of contacting the working class on relatively equal terms, he had thought. The events of 1968 had radicalised a number of the senior gramscians including Bennett (1980a), and student revolt is carefully analysed in Hall *et al.* (1978). Hall describes his intention at the Birmingham Centre as producing organic intellectuals too, in his section of the Introduction (in Hall *et al.* 1980). Cultural politics converged with educational politics in this policy, and there are echoes of the old 1960s policy of the university as a 'red base' in the support for the 'Communist University of London'. Even the Open University was once seen as offering knowledge somehow unmediated by bourgeois cultural power (see Harris 1987).

We will discuss these particular pedagogic determinants in the final chapter. For now, given these academic and cultural contexts, it is hardly suprising that much political activity involved academic analysis, a grams-cian version of Althusserian 'struggle in theory'. We have seen some of the attempts to reveal the hidden political dimensions and struggles in curricula, in youth styles, and in leisure pursuits. The project to understand 'Thatcherism' directed attention to political discourses in a more explicit sense.

THATCHERISM, LIBERALISM, FASCISM

The main thesis in *Policing the Crisis* (Hall *et al.* 1978) has been reviewed earlier. Rooted in the early CCCS 'mugging project', the book developed the idea that particular definitions of crime, and specific concerns of the police and the authorities were transformed into a more general symbolic discourse about Englishness, permissiveness, and industrial militancy, ending in a turn to a more authoritarian 'law and order' society in the late 1970s. The media played a key role in this, coding or articulating together themes from official sources and populist sentiment, while acting within their professional obligations. The official discourse coalesced around core images in ideologies of crime and images of society – respectability, discipline, the problems of the city, the turn to law as a solution to political crisis.

The discourse is more tightly integrated following media activities like 'convergence', where two or more separate activities are joined – as in 'student hooliganism' (Hall *et al.* 1978: 223), and feelings are amplified by 'signification spirals'. These media activities serve as a substitute for argument, and offer a kind of populist account of both the economic decline of Britain, and the increasing difficulties of any recognised political party to arrest this decline (and the options are reviewed in Chapters 8 and 9). The book ends with a return to the issues raised by 'mugging' specifically, but the overall apparatus of explanation was to serve to grasp the phenomenon of the continued success of 'Thatcherism'.

Thus many of the salient points about economic decline and political impasse are also found in the collection of writings from *Marxism Today* in Hall and Jacques (1983). Thatcherism constructs a new discourse to gain support in its move to the right-wing 'social market' option to end the impasse in economic policy (by defeating the Trade Unions and reinvigorating capital-led regeneration). This discourse obviously resonates favourably with (some of) the representatives of capital, but it also responds to genuine popular political grievances among the petite bourgeoisie and the skilled working class (who have long played a decisive role in general elections in Britain).

Some of these grievances first have to be disarticulated from left-wing social democratic discourse. The most spectacular examples are probably those of women's rights – see Gardiner (in Hall and Jacques 1983) – but there are also widespread hearty dislikes of the bureaucratic aspects of nationalised industries and Trade Union abuses of power. Others are reactivated and taken from previously marginal political discourses like those of the far right (especially racist themes). Still others belong to the past, especially the liberal tradition of political economy, and these energise the intellectual wing of Thatcherism, the economists, philosophers and journalists who supported the turn to a 'free market' or to 'individual liberty'. These and other elements are rearticulated into a new and appealing, even if inconsistent, series of doctrines – as Hall suggests, for example, the doctrine that liberty and equality must depend on strong authority (*The 'Little Caesars' of Social Democracy* in Hall and Jacques 1983), permitting both a free market and a strong State.

This discursive nimbleness was to be demonstrated as the 1980s developed, utilising the symbolic possibilities of the Falklands War, for example. The war was used to reverse the deep unpopularity of the first Thatcher term. The sight of the naval armada and the 'historic' regiments, the sense of national emergency, the promise of an end to decades of national humiliation after the end of Empire, all touched deep roots of national pride and gained massive support (Hobsbawm estimates about 80 per cent of the population were in favour of the war – in Hall and Jacques 1983). Mrs Thatcher was even able to unite her own party by appealing to the old 'One Nation' traditionalists, Gamble argues (*ibid*). Hobsbawm insists that this patriotism was genuinely felt by the British people, that it was not just manufactured by the media, and that it can sometimes be 'progressive': on this occasion, though, it led to a second term for Mrs Thatcher.

This analysis set the agenda, more or less, for attempts to understand Thatcherism and to construct a socialist alternative, a new popular-democratic alliance and discourse. In these discussions, a number of alternatives are reviewed, including a revitalised Labour Party, regrouped around the Labour Left and less dependent upon Trade Unions, offering new socialist policies on a range of matters from disarmament to socialist leisure. Coalitions and popular fronts were advocated, centred on Labour or the Communist Party, or even on an alliance with the Social Democratic Party (especially when that party once looked likely to be able to defeat the Tories in a general election in 1981).

In these discussions, Hall tends to lean towards the new extra-Parliamentary alliance as the new base for Labour, and he expresses serious doubts about the SDP, as we shall see. Behind both these judgements lies his belief that Thatcherism has not solved the underlying economic crisis and that it can never finally capture the terrain completely and achieve full hegemony. These views will be discussed below.

The left grouping centred on the journal *Marxism Today* offered a range of analyses and policies, therefore, including some on the economic strategy of Thatcherism and on a likely left response (see Bleaney in Hall and Jacques 1983), but Hall's specific contributions have been accused of an overemphasis on ideology.

Hall, Jessop and Thatcherism

In a famous series of articles in *New Left Review,* Jessop *et al.* argued that Hall's treatment of the discourses of Thatcherism failed to grasp the real economic shifts and social reconstructions the Thatcher project was able to make, at least after its initial hesitancy. The first article in the exchange (Jessop *et al.* 1984) pointed out the confusions in the definitions of the State in *Policing the Crisis* which we have noticed before (Chapter 5), and went on to suggest no less than ten possible meanings for the key term 'authoritarian populism' (AP) in the work – as a new ideological field, as a Conservative electoral strategy, as a new accumulation strategy and so on. Now that Mrs Thatcher has gone, we might also add the possibility that AP was a personal strategy too. There is a reminder here of the oversimple views of 'preferred readings' too, of course. Further reminders of old methodological problems emerged in Jessop *et al.*'s suggestion that the unifying nature of AP came from Hall's abstractions rather than from any real unity in the Tory Party.

The economic is also insufficiently explored, including the crucial shift to finance capital away from manufacturing, the tensions and struggles this induces, and the effects it has. Jessop *et al.* use a model of 'two nations' to describe the polarising effects on British society: the better-off 'nation', clustered around the new growth points, have definitely benefited under Thatcher, and it is perfectly rational for them to support her, at least in the short term. On the one hand, these economic and social changes, as much as the ideological discourse, enable Thatcherism to maintain sufficent electoral power. On the other, these strategies too face fundamental dilemmas and leave a space for alternative socialist economic and political restructuring. Jessop *et al.* go on to develop these points in several more articles (1985, 1987, 1990). Hall (1988) offers a further collection of essays on Thatcherism.

The writers in the collection in Hall and Jacques (1983) do address the economic issues more fully, in fact, and Jessop and his colleagues were also to give ground finally and admit that ideology was important, especially as Thatcherism seemed able to go on and on without a serious ideological challenge. Leys (1990), one of the writers cited in the debate, also endorses Hall's emphasis on ideology rather than on political economy as central to Thatcher's hold on power. Hall's (1985) reply to the Jessop *et al.* onslaught has been cited elsewhere (in Chapter 1).

Thatcherism and legitimation crisis

Jessop *et al.* accuse Hall of neglecting the contradictions in Thatcherism at the political level too, and their discussion invites comparison with another powerful approach to neo-conservatism in the work of Habermas (1976) and Offe (1985). This work is too complex to summarise in any detail here, but, very basically, both writers had pointed to the serious systemic and social contradictions in advanced capitalism arising from the need for the State to perform contradictory tasks: to act as the representative of universal interests on the one hand, while prioritising the sectional needs of capital on the other. In its welfare state form, contradictions arise from having to manage the economic system to permit continuing accumulation, while administering a set of welfare institutions which operated on quite different principles (need instead of profit, use values instead of exchange values).

These tensions had left social democracy in a crisis-prone condition, and Habermas (1976) in particular went on to develop a theory of structured crisis and escalation: economic crises became displaced on to the political level as the market failed to solve them, actions by the State became increasingly partisan as capital had to be rescued, and so the State lost its universality and entered a legitimation crisis. Finally, a motivation crisis is likely as the State attempts to control and manipulate social life itself to prevent the economic crisis from deepening. Increasingly, social institutions (like the education system or the media) are subject to 'systematically distorted communication' or other 'strategic communications', and while these might work in the short term, they fail in the long term to offer a suitable basis for the genuine reproduction of social life, and people withdraw their support from them.

The whole model is closely connected to Habermas's work on language and its role in social and political life (see McCarthy's Introduction to Habermas 1976), and, apart from other insights, this helps gain some sort of purchase on the vexed issue of what an 'ideological' discourse actually is. Briefly, the key lies in terms of its strategic intent rather than its content. The work is not without its difficulties, of course, but it avoids the need to do an inventory of good and bad themes in a particular discourse. Habermas and Offe are also far more systematic in identifying, discussing and clarifying the different aspects of system and social crisis (see Offe 1974, for example).

The neo-conservative turn in Britain, Germany and the USA can be seen as the latest response to these crises: rolling back the State is one solution to the problems of the over-extended and thus contradictory welfare state of social democracy, for example (see Bernstein 1985, Chapter 3). The appeal to a free market represents a desire to avoid legitimation crisis by apparently disengaging from the economy. The return to traditional values represents a new initiative at the cultural level to stave off motivation crisis and to revitalise initiative and enterprise. This last element in the policy often takes the form of an attack on intellectuals as responsible for the moral decline. Habermas uses this anti-intellectualism to link into a discussion of the conservative elements of postmodern aesthetics, which also denies the enlightenment potential of 'intellectual' arts (Bernstein 1985: 90f) and approves of capitalist modernization.

These approaches are viable and influential, but they appear only as traces in gramscian analysis. What would make them uncongenial to British gramscians in the late 1970s, perhaps, is that they offer no easy options for traditional party politics. Habermas (1979) argued that one option (the move towards a decentralised and 'more supple' kind of left-wing party) would weaken its ability to unify at the national level, while another (celebrations of more anarchic forms of protest) would risk deepening the dangers of fascism, which has always specialised in the 'mobilisation of affective forces in a crisis'. 'Serious politics' is difficult for a left-wing party searching for a broader popular base, but non-rational and uncritically populist politics runs the risk of fighting on a terrain already well-colonised by fascism (or, possibly, in Britain, the Social Democratic Party).

Fascism

Gramscians were remarkably slow to analyse fascism, in fact, despite the overwhelming victory of Mussolini in the contest for the hearts and minds of the Italian people in Gramsci's time. Again, one can compare the extensive work done in 'critical theory', including Adorno on fascist propaganda (in Arato and Gebhardt 1978). The *Prison Notebooks* contain little of direct interest to any analyst of fascism either.

Mercer's analysis of Italian fascism (in Donald and Hall 1986) uses Laclau on articulation (Laclau heavily structures the whole collection in this Open University reader) to advance an apparently novel thesis that Mussolini had organised popular support. Fascist 'systems of narration' found in party press articles disarticulated old ideas and rearticulated them in a fascist discourse. Mussolini himself organised a 'gigantic semiotic' to stylise and symbolise the key themes of the nation and its organic links, and its connections with the citizen as 'producer'.

Again, a certain semiotic nimbleness is detectable, Mercer argues, as the audience changed from proletarians to petits bourgeois, and as various 'radical, jacobin and popular positions' were connected into a power bloc. Mercer is particularly interested in the fascist system of organised leisure, the 'dopolavoro', and he commends it for socialist attention (in Bennett *et al.* 1986). Inevitably, sources of resistance are discussed and even Mussolini had little success in the end in articulating women to his cause. Mercer almost suggests that the female guerrillas, who, he tells us, were more numerous in Italy than anywhere else, were responsible for Mussolini's downfall, although surely the Allied invasion must have had some effect.

We can detect the political interests in Mercer's reading formation with particular clarity. This is a centred reading of the texts of Italian fascism, again, with the audience appearing as positioned. De Grazia's account of the 'dopolavoro' (also in Donald and Hall 1986) argues, by contrast, that the organisation was never very effective, in fact, in politicising the Italian people. An echo of Habermas's motivation crisis attends this analysis – the organisation was too bureaucratic really to attend to people's needs, and its over-organised structure induced a passivity and lack of real support. The 'dopolavoro', for de Grazia, tried too hard, and it is to be hoped that socialists, in their discussions of leisure policy, have learned that lesson too.

Liberalism

Donald and Hall (1986) contains a piece by Hall on liberalism, also using Laclau, and still following the formula of identifying diversities and unities in the discourse, and how they condense into themes. These themes are articulated to classes via an homology (of all things) between patterns in political thought and political and economic relationships (*ibid*: 51) so that certain property rights can be asumed as universal (in the work of Locke, for example).

Different social classes are articulated to different elements in liberalism, in fact, as the struggle between Paine and Burke reveals, and Hall offers a history of transformations as liberal themes develop into modern political philosophies, including Thatcherism (*ibid*: 67). Thus liberalism does not represent the bourgeoisie directly, but it does help articulate a conception of bourgeois society.

The whole analysis is open to exactly the same sorts of objections as in the Jessop *et al.* debate, and to those discussed earlier. It is about discourses, or ideologies, almost entirely. It assumes these discourses must have a real political effect, since they are homologous in some way to the (attributed) positions of (real) people. This looks very close to a 'dominant ideology' reading in its conceptions of the mechanisms of ideology transmission, despite Hall's protests about the term, and despite the apparent complexity introduced by articulations. Asymmetry in the analysis is inevitable since the whole thing is a 'post hoc' reconstruction, and, one feels, the 'articulation' motif is one that must and will be discovered almost before the analysis starts. Thatcherism, fascism, liberalism – all alike are merely grist to the enriched gramscian mill. Possession of the sacred concepts will deliver knowledge of any major political creed, it seems. It is not just the work on Thatcherism that lies open to sustained critique like Kelly's:

How has he [Hall] come by these penetrating insights into popular attitudes?. . .Hall [prefers]. . .to rely upon his imagination to conjure up images of the Thatcherite supporter, and to grant him[self] direct and privileged access to people's 'needs, experiences, aspirations, pleasures, and desires' without the aid of method and evidence. . .the essays [in Hall 1988] are oblivious to any alternative interpretations; indifferent to methods of analysing the influence of ideology; almost entirely devoid of empirical evidence; and punctuated by sectarian attacks on caricatures and parodies of Marxist thinking.

(Kelly 1988)

NEW TIMES IN OLD BOTTLES

Hall and Jacques (1989) describe the launch of the 'new times' project as arising, typically, from a seminar, hosted by *Marxism Today*. The project is probably familiar, as it is still current and well-known through the pages of the journal. Briefly, it was an attempt to go beyond the analyses of Thatcherism, to develop some socialist alternatives at the level of actual politics. The Labour Left had failed to heed the warnings in Hall and Jacques (1983) or Hall (1988), and had done little to resist Thatcherism or to seize any new initiatives in the rearticulation of a national-democratic discourse. Indeed, in Hall and Jacques (1989), the continued success of Mrs Thatcher at the polls had been blamed largely on this lack of initiative, and the swing back to the old ground of traditional Labourism. One can sympathise with this analysis, but as usual, the issues are opened up only to be immediately snugly filled with gramscianism.

The Jessop and Gamble emphases on political economy had also been taken on board, and there was a new way to bring back the economic – post-fordism. As argued before (Chapter 2), this concept arose from work done on the new ways of analysing and regulating capitalism via the flow of finance, and the ways this had affected manufacturing industry. It also proved particularly acceptable, perhaps, since Gramsci had written about Fordism (in the *Prison Notebooks*), and the social and cultural changes that were likely to follow the introduction of 'Fordist' mass production, and rationally managed industrial enterprises into modern Italy.

New production methods after Fordism would decentralise and render more flexible manufacturing industry, and work conditions would change again. Industry would respond more quickly to the market (using new methods of stock control made possible by computerising stock flows), mass production would be replaced by small-scale dispersed production – and so on (see Murray in Hall and Jacques 1989). These changes had been hijacked by Thatcherism so far, and had been bent to the service of capital, in encouraging the growth of large supermarkets at the expense of local shops, for example (Murray *ibid*).

But the changes were not coterminous with Thatcherism, were not inherently on the side of capital. Countervailing powers – like the Greater London Council's Enterprise Board – could also make the benefits of flexible manufacturing available to the workforce, could encourage new ways of working, and new levels of skill. The Board could demonstrate cooperation in computerised stock control and marketing for the benefit of small businesses, for example, argued Murray.

Finally, these developments would also bring changes in social and cultural life. This would place cultural studies and cultural politics back into a new prominence and extend a new lease of life to gramscianism again. In this sense the 'new times' started to look rather old and familiar even before it had got off the ground.

The same political solutions were on offer in fact – new constituencies of strugglers, especially women, ethnic minorities and Greens – would be recruited to a new version of the democratic front alliances developed in a British version of Eurocommunism or as a left-wing Charter 88 (a petition for written human rights in Britain). These groups offered apparently universal, or at least very widespread, common interests against Thatcherism – interests in the environment, in equal rights for the oppressed, in vague demands for a greater participation in social life and in the politics of identity 'across the globe' (for Hall in Hall and Jacques 1989: 129).

Social class was no longer the main axis of politics, since it had been decomposed. Of course, the periphery of workers outside of the new flexible industries would still be out of work (or rather in and out of work) – but they could be recompensed with redistributive policies (Murray *ibid*). The trends towards post-fordism and its tendencies to split the workforce like this were inevitable, Murray assured us, and it was a question of having to go along with the trend and make the most of the changes.

It was clear that one major group of sceptics were the 'traditional left', the Labour right and the 'tankies' in the Communist Party. The promised struggle often turned out to be a struggle with former allies and fellow members, and led to splits and expulsions in the Party as well as what sounds like very acrimonious debate (Samuel 1987). The political ideas were hardly new, with the possible exception of the concept of post-fordism. There is now a new enthusiasm for the European Community as a means of restraining international capital. Meanwhile, Hebdige ('After the Masses') is still advocating socialist articulations, strengthened possibly by the new forms of flexible market research (!), and Thatcherism is still being understood in terms of the old authoritarian populism model ('Manifesto for the New Times'), both in Hall and Jacques (1989).

Throughout there is a tone of 'there is no alternative' to these analyses, and rather unstated claims to be able to represent the new realities of capitalism – but old hands at cultural studies will suspect that post-fordism is really a discourse or ideology as well. In an interesting excursus into the stir caused by post-fordism in distance education, Edwards (1991) argues exactly this for the claims of decentralisers hoping to use the concept to urge reform upon the British and Australian distance universities. Post-fordism to Edwards looks exactly like postmodernism does to leftist critics – a scare tactic directed tactically against opponents, and a device designed to ensure a market for the threatened cultural capital of the advocates.

Hebdige's piece uses some of the arguments of the postmodernists precisely in this way, to frighten the old guard of the left (if any were still reading *Marxism Today* by then) about the inadequacies of the old meta-narratives and the implosion of the social, and he then smoothly introduces the new 'narratives of emancipation' and the new social movements (fashioned out of the pop music audience) as if these were somehow exempt from the critiques he outlined before. Although this piece is written in a popular pedagogic way, there must surely be few readers who are still so unaware of the postmodernist sketch of the crisis of all values as to be persuaded by this appeal.

In any case, even if there are any takers for the seductively simple 'fixing' of the flux of discourses in economic changes under post-fordism, further readings in the collection provide doubts, as we shall see shortly: the collection still cannot make up its mind if it is a mass political project, or another more limited academic debate about gramscian concepts.

Hall is still an academic, of course, and he feels it necessary to air some doubts about post-fordism, so he and Jacques publish two critical essays in the collection as well. Post-fordism is not an orthodoxy, Hall assures readers, merely a position in a debate (although this does not seem to be quite accurate as a description of 'new times', certainly as far as the Communist Party is concerned, given the rows, splits and expulsions that ensued). At one stage in his discussion of the meaning of 'new times', Hall even seems unsure that post-fordism exists (Hall and Jacques 1989: 128), although we have already discussed this sort of apparent self-doubt as rhetoric, as an academic strategy to preserve balance while quietly privileging an analysis. The very cautious nature of most of the piece can be read in this way too. after the usual quick reviews of Marx, Althusser (and, for the first time fairly positively, Adorno and Habermas), Gramsci's essay on Fordism is commended to us, and the hero of the piece is not hard to find, of course – 'few better. . .confidence to address the problems . . . comprehensiveness and range' (*ibid*: 125).

Hall feels on safer ground when attacking the 'organised Left' and is far less cautious, but we all know they lie outside the pale of accepted positions and so can be treated in an unbalanced way (just as news and current affairs television programmes do). One consequence of rebuking the old left is to lead to an agreement at last with post-marxist formulations (Foucault rather than Laclau and Mouffe) on discourses as constituting political positions: 'Perhaps there isn't . . . one "power game" at all, more a network of strategies and powers and their articulations – and thus a politics which is always positional' (*ibid*: 130). This is what we have called the American usage of 'articulation', the fully postmodern form (see Chapter 2). Hall sustains this view in his subsequent discussion of gender and ethnicity as political positionings: ethnicity is now 'all those points of attachment which give the individual some sense of "place" and "position" in the world', and although Hall is not specific, it seems that ethnic identity must be discursive rather than 'something permanent, fixed or essential' (*ibid*: 133).

Insights like these must have come as a disappointment to all those who had spent so much time trying to show how the network did reflect one game after all – not only the old left, but gramscians like Hargreaves, or Hall himself. In his interview with Grossberg some three years before, for example, Hall had argued that Foucault's work really required a 'formation of discourses' (Grossberg 1986: 48) before it could develop an adequate politics. He was also unready then to embrace Laclau and Mouffe either, arguing that the social totality was not an open field, but was structured by 'determining lines of force of material relations' (*ibid*: 57).

Perhaps Hall has changed his mind. Perhaps the accounts are subtly consistent, holding both ends of a chain provided by a need to close with the detail of power in modern societies and yet still to bend the twig to gramscian theory. Perhaps one of the accounts is rhetorical again: maybe the networks can be grounded in something outside the text or not according to whether one is doing academic politics or party politics.

Criticisms of the new times

Some of the criticisms that are published in Hall and Jacques (1989) are rather friendly, in fact, at least as far as Rustin is concerned. It can be acknowledged without too much damage that the progress towards post-fordism is uneven, and that other modes of production will still exist, for example, and the rediscovery of the periphery of the labour force is not fatal either. What is still curious, though, is that this periphery is not to be the main target for the articulations and cultural politics: Mrs Thatcher sees the disciplining class effects of the new technology, so it is 'paradoxical that . . . [only] the theorists of the left have become so critical of class-based . . . political strategy on their own side' (*ibid*: 310–11).

However, Rustin has more acute criticisms to make too, raising all the old doubts about a purely cultural politics being unable or unwilling to take on capital: 'A disposition to methodological idealism – a preference for the level of culture over structure – has always been latent in neo-Gramscian thinking' (*ibid*: 317). Worse still, this version of cultural politics is identified as an ideology, the 'universalising of sectional interests' (*ibid*: 312). These sectional interests are those of the new intelligentsia – '"flexible specialists" such as researchers, communicators, information professionals and designers' (*ibid*: 311). This kind of analysis echoes a famous debate on the new left in the USA, as we shall see.

Why no party of the peripheral? The answer seems to lie in the inadequacies of Keynesianism and its old policies of State regulation of the economy. No longer can a national government inject funds to maintain full employment, most of the writers argue, especially since there are international flows of finance outside the control of national governments: Aglietta (1982) is clear and helpful here. Labour's Alternative Economic Strategy, that looked so promising in 1983, seems to have been abandoned as the Labour Left itself waned after Thatcher's third election victory. The 'new times' writers seemed to have argued their way into an impasse like the one suggested by Jessop, and like the one that informed the 'new realism' and later the economic pragmatism of the newly respectable Labour Party. Any future politics had to live with the reality of considerable levels of unemployment.

Hirst suggests that this impasse is largely the result of the post-fordist paradigm itself, though. The paradigm exaggerates t!.. role of capitalism in modernising production because of its residual economic determinism, and then takes Thatcherism at its word as a radical modernising force. Rustin (1989) and Sivandan (1990), in their different ways, make this point too. Real economic growth has come, Hirst argues, from the deployment of a technique he calls 'flexible specialisation', often introduced at the regional level and with local State support to provide the necesary infrastructure. This technique does not thrive in Thatcherism, hence the dismissal of the claims to economic miracles. Jessop *et al.* (1987) agree, suggesting that the Thatcherite strategy to modernise British industry by opening the country to international finance capital also destroys local and regional manufacturing. Flexible specialisation requires the political strengthening of regional planners, not a revived cultural politics – Hirst argues that flexible specialisation can be found in culturally conservative countries like Japan, for example.

Why does 'new times' socialism seek a constituency in the new metropolitan service class (with new social movements led by it)? Hebdige (in Hall and Jacques 1989) might offer us a clue here again. He had been disdainful before of the politics of rioting, and had lost interest in youth since the death of punk – perhaps the peripheral workforce or the respectable working class offered less potential for a satisfyingly cultural politics too? The Anti-Nazi League or Band Aid still retain his approval: aesthetics seem to guide politics here. Perhaps it is the old asymmetry again that thinks of the policy first then seeks the constituency afterwards? Or perhaps it is the old error of the intellectual – assuming (or wishing) that his own common-sense perceptions represent the obvious and natural world-view to be placed at the centre of all analysis and policy, much as Bentham did according to Marx (1954: 571).

The view that postmodernism, even in its post-fordist form, is the 'spontaneous philosophy' of the left-wing academic sector of the 'new petite bourgeoisie' as it strives to locate itself politically and culturally between Establishment politics above and 'vulgar politics' below has been tried out briefly already (in Chapter 8).

Certainly it is interesting to note the monopoly of communications professionals among the contributors to 'new times' analysis, and the thrust of the collections is still largely academic – explaining, analysing, gathering facts, discussing theories. With few exceptions (Murray is one), it is not at all clear what 'new times' theorists actually do, politically, apart from writing and trying to establish some sort of theoretical ground and academic leadership of the sorts of struggles they see as promising ones. Yet whether the women's movement(s) need such leadership, or the Greens, or the ethnic minorities is in some doubt – again, members of those movements are not always very welcoming – see Davis in Bridges and Brunt (1981), or Sivanandan (1990). To put a methodological issue raised earlier (about the role of analysts' meanings) in political terms, it is not at all clear who needs who politically.

Of course, perhaps some leadership will be needed to unite all these separate factions and struggles into one popular front counter-hegemonic force. The objective basis for such unity would be the universal oppression from capital, especially if the State is seen to be closely allied with it, as in 'stamocap' theories at the heart of some Eurocommunist movements (Jessop 1982) – but capital has shown itself able to divide the protestors pretty well in the past by policies of concession. Anyway, the 'new times' project is optimistic about the State, even if ambivalent about whether to vote Labour or Communist.

The political capacities of 'single issue' pressure groups like the Campaign for Nuclear Disarmament or the Greens have always been limited in the past, and old divisions have come to the fore when it came to general political issues, or even general elections. And there are genuine divisions among the constituencies of the struggling, as Sivanandan (1990) points out. For him, the Greens focus far too much on the affluence of the west rather than the poverty of the Third World, and peace movements are obsessed with nuclear wars rather than the typical local conventional wars of global capitalism. The politics of the personal can also lead to misleading abstractions: the enemy of 'women' is 'men', the enemy of 'blacks' is 'whites', and so on.

Consumer power

The turn to consumerism has been noted before in earlier chapters, and it has become a major theme in the reconstructed politics of the left in Britain. Leadbetter is perhaps the most prominent example among the 'new times' writers, and his piece in Hall and Jacques (1989) is most revealing. Leadbetter's 'new socialist individualism' looks very much like the old British liberalism analysed by Hall, summarised above (in Donald and Hall 1986). The familiar Millian anxieties about the capacity of the 'free market' to produce inequality and social division is at the heart of the analysis, and some form of State regulation, or countervailing powers to be developed among the weak, is the solution.

Leadbetter leaves out altogether other elements of Mill's analysis, though, as does Hall, especially the arguments about this regulation being based on real but long-term individual interests. Without this dimension, social regulation still looks irrational, and individuals are offered no reasons for not just trying their luck to make gains at the expense of others, short-term, 'in their own interests'. There is none of the subtlety of Mill on the dangers of 'tyrannous majorities' as a support for rights for minorities, merely faint echoes of the arguments for a Bill of Universal Rights in Britain advanced by Charter 88. Even Hall and Held are only a little more explicit in their very similar piece on citizenship (Hall and Jacques 1989).

Policies like a minimum income are justified as a hallmark of a civilised society, rather than as representing a genuine interest of all citizens in the rights of the poor. This kind of sentimental or humanist identification with the poor extends to the enthusiasm for aid to the Third World, according to Sivanandan (1990). Welcome as they may be short term, there are serious doubts about the possibility of building a long-term politics on such waves of sympathy unless arguments soon develop to persuade the enthusiasts that it is in their real political interests to support equality.

Yet this is precisely the area of 'serious politics' that the 'new times' socialists are so reserved about. There is still no programme of political education, no strategy to recapture the ground on the issue of rational interest rather than irrational pleasure. If there is a conflict between such a policy and immediate electoral appeal, 'new times' theorists seem to have opted for the latter, although this is to assume that the message is directed to the masses in the first place (see below). Both Hall and Hebdige advocate an appeal to 'imaginary communities' instead of to real interests. Presumably arising from a desire not to contradict Labour Party policies, Leadbetter advocates a 'responsible', even a decentralised, but still a conventional British State. More daringly, but only just, Hall and Held urge Labour to rethink its opposition to Charter 88.

Leadbetter also advocates the moral regulation of excessive individualism, in a passage that looks like an attempt to reinvent Durkheim's (1950) critique of liberalism (*ibid*: 144). Again, though, there is no attempt to argue the long-term benefits or social functions of such moral reintegration, no real discussion of its complex relations to individualism. There is no commitment to a redistribution of inherited wealth or a new principle of social stratification either: Durkheim is well to the left of the 'new timers'.

Leadbetter's (or Mort's) escalation scenario is naive in this sense too. They hope that consumer rights and consumer power will radicalise people and get them to raise their demands (echoes of de Tocqueville here?), perhaps even to the level of beginning to demand rights to own capital. These demands are quite different in kind, however, since the latter, unless it is going to be a version of Thatcherite 'property-owning democracy', could constitute a threat to the whole system of private property and would thus be resisted. It would require as a preliminary at least a version of one of the policies of the Labour Left in its heyday – Cutler *et al.*'s (1978) proposal to change the law to weaken the link between ownership of a majority of voting shares and the legal rights of control over a company, for example.

In the advocacy of consumerism, the 'new times' project is seen at its weakest theoretically. It offers a position that regresses to a point before the work of Durkheim and Mill, let alone Althusser and Marx. It seems that in their demoralised flight from serious politics, the Labour Party and the British Communist Party discourage the reading not only of marxism but even of bourgeois sociology and the radical bits of British liberalism. We have a regression to replace a break!

The only option left seem to be to rely on the power of the 'new times' discourse itself uniting people, as in Hall's article (or Mort's), and again, this is typical of American work like Kipnis (Maccabe 1986) or Giroux and Simon (Giroux *et al.* 1989). Thus Hall diagnoses Thatcherism's appeal, finally, as an ideology that 'invites us to think about politics in images. It is addressed to our collective fantasies, to Britain as an imagined community . . . while the Left forlornly tries to drag the conversation round to "our policies"' (Hall 1987: 19). The old charge of reading hegemony as 'dominant ideology' is only just rescued by some cautious admonitions not to forget the economic nucleus, and above all, as usual, by insisting upon the need for a new struggle in cultural politics. This vision is still overwhelmingly about securing a vote for socialism, and it arises from a new populist way of '[speaking] in words that belong to [voters] as late 20th century ordinary folk'. The view of 'ordinary folk' as incapable of any sustained political thought of their own is very revealing.

Designer gramscianism

The 'jailed Sardinian' (Hall 1987) is still taken as a justification for this project, as if 'ordinary folk' still needed some respectable academic theorist to validate their concerns. Really, of course, Hall is probably addressing new service-class radicals about the need to address 'ordinary folk' – there is no record I could find of what he actually says to 'ordinary folk' when he addresses them directly. Largely, though, Gramsci now exists as a kind of source for handy and stylish quotes, phrases or metaphors with which to embellish the project: Brunt likes his phrase 'whalebone in a corset' for example (Brunt in Hall and Jacques 1989). Geras seems to have been prescient in his account of how Gramsci's name was to function discursively in 'post-marxist' politics (see Chapter 2). Gramsci's concrete politics must be suppresed of course, since there is no major Communist Party in Britain, and no sympathy among gramscians for any attempt to contact proletarian 'organic intellectuals' via factory agitation.

There is no attempt to provide 'folk' with new words, not even via adult education, nor to critique the old words, or revitalise the latent linguistic powers in 'ordinary speech' to question the 'validity claims' of current politics. This is a 'second order' politics, which involves waiting for 'ordinary folks' to do the best they can to think out 'their' positions and then 'leading' or 'articulating' these concerns, or at least the progressive and acceptable ones. This is precisely what conventional politicians do too, of course, with none of the traditonal left concerns for rational or democratic discussions, or any attempt to develop adequate theories of social change. As we have noted before, the new cultural politics seems to propose an amateur or, probably worse, an academic effort as a counter to professional politicians' ones.

If an alliance with conventional parties is the intention (as in the *Manifesto* in Hall and Jacques 1989), conventional political discourse has to be fundamentally preserved, of course, even though some of its 'surface features' can be modernised. After learning lessons from Gramsci (fewer and fewer as the years go by, it seems), the 'new times' project looked as if it would like to act rather like a left-wing version of the Social Democratic Party (who did not seem to have read Gramsci at all). The SDP also had borrowed policies, operated with a dubiously fluid and opportunist constituency, but possessed a certain discursive power to articulate disillusion with the old politics.

Hall argued in his account of the 'little Caesars' of the SDP (Hall and Jacques 1983) that this meant a short-term solution to the crisis of capitalism by abandoning serious politics altogether, and trying to cobble together an alliance purely for electoral purposes, yet this now seems to be the goal of the left. Apart from leading to the obvious question – if the left win, what then – it is worth pointing out, perhaps, that the SDP Alliance finally failed as the major parties decided to play the same game, only better.

CONCLUSION

There are no easy answers, of course, and no obvious alternative to gramscian politics on the left. Yet it is possible to assess the political project of 'new times' against an earlier debate about the new left in the USA (Walker 1979), given suitable cautions about the parallels, of course. At one level, the debate in question turned largely upon technical issues such as whether or not there was a new 'professional managerial class' in the USA of the late 1970s or not. There is no intention here to address this issue directly, or to launch an enquiry into the social class origins and present location of the gramscians, or of readers of *Marxism Today*, although the academic location of the writers reviewed here will be relevant, and will be discussed in the final chapter.

As the originators of the controversy in the USA (the Ehrenreichs) argue, though, the technical sociological issues of class location are less relevant than an assessment of the political strategy on offer by the American new left in 1979 (before the neo-conservative turn).

The US new left was almost entirely located in the (upper) middle class, most of the contributors to the debate agree. Working-class conservatism in the USA had been discussed against a background of current affluence and deskilling, and a recent past of historical reconstruction by the agents of modern capital. This had led to a three-way polarisation, the Ehrenreichs argued, between capital, labour and the professional-managerial class (PMC). Debate raged around whether the PMC was a class or a mere stratum, whether it was unified or internally incoherent, but for many of the contributors to the debate, there was agreement that the main role of the PMC was to control, regulate and hegemonise the US working class.

What makes the PMC unusual, though, is that it also sees itself in struggle with capital, as its professional skills and expertises come up against the 'irrational' constraints and narrow self-interests of capital. The US new left, especially its student new left wing, aligned itself with, and drew most of its support from, this crucial class/stratum, and the ambivalence of the class location affects the political strategy of the new left. On the one hand, the new left can be very critical of monopoly capital and its irrationality, instability and rapaciousness, and this makes it a major reservoir of radicalism. But on the other, the new left was unable ever to work very closely with the working class: barriers existed between them, based on crucial and highly visible economic, political and cultural differences. These contaminations from class origin, as they became more apparent after various non-PMC radical groups pointed them out (especially Black Power), led to an astonishing internal crisis of confidence among US new left (student) movements, and made them very vulnerable to a right-wing backlash

The book describes a number of fascinating and, to British eyes, strangely familiar policies developed by the new left. Some decided to work as 'radical professionals' in working-class communities. Others developed a 'new communist' policy of trying to submerge themselves in the proletariat, while expanding the notion of the proletariat to include everyone except monopoly capitalists, often drawing upon Braverman's deskilling thesis. Still others tried to build new alliances with other groups like feminists, ecologists, civil rights movements, sometimes as a self-styled vanguard or leadership of those movements. The Ehrenreichs and several other commentators are adamant that these strategies are doomed to failure unless the class differences, in every sense, between PMC new left and these other groups are acknowledged, researched and discussed. An assumed universalism of interest, combined with the unreflected class assumptions of PMC intellectuals, especially those about the philistinism, gross materialism and ignorance of the working-class, will end in new left isolation.

The most refreshing articles are those which illustrate the clash of cultural values between working-class and PMC individuals. Again and again, the patronising and élitist stances of PMC intellectuals are demonstrated, and the corresponding hostility and suspicion they arouse among the working-class activists. PMC intellectuals are aware of the dangers of patronising or showing contempt for women or black people – but class stereotypes die hard. Failing to learn from working-class activists, and apologetic and deferential towards black or female activists, PMC intellectuals find themselves increasingly looking inward, critiquing themselves, undermining their own positions, continually and obsessively reworking their own assumptions. Their real role, though, say the Ehrenreichs, should be to do what they are good at – to critique monopoly capital and its cultural institutions from within, to do something that looks rather like Young's exposé of bourgeois practices (see Chapter 5).

One yearns for such honesty and self-awareness among British new left intellectuals. The social-class origins of postmodernists are analysed, often pretty crudely – Hall's interview (Grossberg 1986) sneers at the declining influence of French intellectuals under Mitterrand, and sees post-modernism as some petulant and pessimistic response to redundancy. Other analysts, like Urry (1990), as we saw in Chapter 8, offer more subtle accounts of the connections between the mobility and flexibility of postmodernist aesthetics, and the cultural politics of a 'new petite bourgeoisie' who specialise in the ownership and effective investment of cultural capital: this group fights its cultural battles against the working class and traditional bourgeoisie by maintaining and trying to police a constant pressure for fashion and change in what might be termed personal culture. Goodwin (1991) also offers an excellent short summary of this view, and the work of Bourdieu, upon which it is based.

Gramscians seem to imagine they are somehow classless and immune from the quiet reproduction of their class's or stratum's values, although they must have read Rustin before including him in *New Times*. Every other group has 'homologies' between class and culture except themselves. Yet there are obvious values in their fierce and usually wholly abstract condemnations of British working-class conservatism, sexism and racism, their caricatures of the traditional left (often accompanied by a sympathetic and admiring account of the new right), their often patronising enthusiasm for (politically correct) proletarian pastimes, and their almost complete lack of interest in the respectable working class. Distant admiration for 'scallies' or shoplifters, or other intra-class predators is hardly helpful here either. Some accounts of recent events in the British Communist Party seem to reveal rather authoritarian or self-righteous petit bourgeois tendencies too (Samuel 1987).

This is not just an attempt to tease the gramscians with their class origins – after all, everyone knows that Marx was a bourgeois – but to raise doubts about the effectiveness of any radical policy that knows so little about the culture of important working-class groups. This is the really glaring absence of gramscian work, in my view. Without it, 'new times' theorists seem to have to talk to 'ordinary folk' in the same ways the bourgeois always have, in that combination of hectoring, lecturing, and the patronisingly 'kindly tone' that Taylor (alone in CCCS work) identified as characteristic (of the ways bourgeois talk to working-class women in this case) (Clarke *et al.* 1979).

The mode of address of gramscian intellectuals among the British left is more specific than an upper middle class or new petit bourgeois one in general, the next chapter argues. It is primarily an academic one. The attempt to write popular texts has clearly not broken with bourgeois conventions (Fiske 1989b has some interesting advice to give). To sympathetic academics among the readers, or to those who have been students, perhaps, the text might seem familiar, graspable, decipherable, involving and powerful. Those in the same culture can fill in the meanings and find pleasure in doing so. For any proletarian readers, though, far too much of 'new times' socialism must seem simply schoolmasterly.

10

CONCLUSION

GRAMSCIAN CLOSURES

In the course of this book, I have tried to discuss both the strengths and the weaknesses of gramscianism. In case the critical focus of the piece has been misunderstood, let me repeat that gramscian work has opened a number of areas to critical inspection in a novel and interesting way. It has been responsible for the emergence of a critical sociology of culture and for the politicisation of culture, and these developments have generated very successful academic programmes of research and course construction.

However, to summarise my reservations about the project, there are also a number of tendencies towards closure in gramscianism too. I still think of these tendencies in terms of work like Adorno and his attack on 'identity thinking' (see Rose 1978), or Habermas, and his work on the limitations of 'strategic communication' (see McCarthy 1984). The self-denying ordinance described in the Introduction means that I am not going to offer a lengthy account of these concepts here – but they do inform my critique. Very briefly, gramscianism for me is far too ready to close off its investigations of social reality, to make its concepts prematurely identical with elements of that reality in various ways. Gramscianism's writings are liable to premature closure by being too 'strategic' for me, as well – by letting a politics privilege analysis, both an explicit national politics, and a less explicit local academic politics. Such closures have benefits, but there are also considerable losses, as I hope I have demonstrated.

The notion of closure helps tie together a number of other critiques too. We saw some argument about the need to do ethnographic or other kinds of empirical research: in these debates, there is a sociological counter to gramscianism too. Sociology and other bourgeois disciplines could claim to have maintained a more open relationship to empirical evidence, in other words, to have allowed for 'surprise', or for historical evidence which did not fit neatly with the theory of the stages of crisis in British society. Of course, these critiques do not warrant a reintroduction of empiricism, but they do point to a rather manipulative approach to empirical research.

Other sociological approaches can be more open to the claims of theoretical rivals too, in my view, less concerned to make everything show the predominance of a particular author or hero, and less nervous about letting rival accounts have their say: I have mentioned, just as one obvious example, the massive and unacknowledged theoretical labours of Giddens, or the more open editorial line of *Theory, Culture and Society*. Feminism too, even the limted range of approaches described here, has shown itself to be more open and productive in several key areas, and, indeed, has come to the rescue of gramscianism and revitalised it.

An accusation of closedness can be detected behind some of the more spectacular postmodernist critiques of social science too. We have had rather to arrange a confrontation between postmodernism and gramscianism, via discussions of post-marxism really, but it is possible to detect privileged concepts (especially 'struggle') and a foundationalism in gramscian arguments about crisis tendencies and hegemony. Of course, postmodernist critiques are unstable and contagious, and have affected all radical social sciences. Gramscianism's response has been rather disappointing, though – to reduce the arguments to a mere ideology of French intellectuals, or to resort to 'nihilist' moral crusades to try to fix the drift of discourses by invoking forms of political correctness. Meanwhile, as with its encounters with other critical discourses, gramscianism has also tried a quiet rapprochement, with postmodernist aesthetics at least, seen best at the level of 'style'. In certain argumentational characteristics, British gramscianism now seems to have crossed the Atlantic and to have quietly adopted the postmodernist 'American' version of concepts like 'articulation'.

At the theoretical level, certain closures have been discussed using terms like 'asymmetry', or ambiguity. Particularly in relation to concrete work, the theoretical frameworks have been chronically likely to structure and to close down possible avenues of exploration – of normal youth, working-class respectables, women's leisure, the status position of teachers, the full range of factors affecting class consciousness. As the last example indicates, gramscianism was premature and involved in self-misunderstanding in its relations with bourgeois disciplines: sociology should have been thoroughly interrogated first, and revolutionary fantasies of 'breaking' resisted.

I think the work of writers like Cashmore (1987) on the everyday logics of racism and inequality are informative and useful. If the gramscians need to rediscover a theory of social class to mediate between capital and the individual, they could do worse than look at the work of the neo-Weberians on 'closure' (Parkin 1979, Murphy 1986, for example). It may be apostatical of me, but these studies seem to get much closer to lived experience than do the abstract speculations on the radical consumer or the *jouissance* of the surfer. The results may be harder to manage in terms of a grand theory – but radicals will have to learn that that is the sign of a good set of data. Of course, such openness to lived experience might also make cultural politics more complicated. Finally, letting 'ordinary people' speak, without leaping in to police their views, is something which very few academics are good at.

The academic subspecies of the petit bourgeois world-view appears in the overemphasis on ideology, say in the accounts of Thatcherism, several critics have suggested. More generally, the 'new times' project seems to be aimed at demoralising and deskilling the 'traditional left' far more than at restraining capital, and policies like the new consumerism depend upon the assumed universality of bourgeois cultural capital to exercise choice and resist the culture industry. The selection of approved 'new social movements' (nsms) can look uncomfortably close to the old middle-class radicalism too, and various proletarian nsms have been misunderstood and undervalued (see Tucker 1991).

Some work on proletarian popular culture or new social movements looks uncomfortably patronising and suspiciously enthusiastic – Willis (1990) is the best recent example, perhaps. The piece was written with an obvious political intent, and it seems rather naive to have thought that readers would not have noticed, and would have been swept along in the enthusiasm and fine writing until they found themselves agreeing, almost against their will, to fund community databases or support Charter 88. To repeat a quote I have used elsewhere: 'For the sake of political commitment, political reality is trivialised: which then reduces the political effect' (Adorno in Arato and Gebhardt 1978: 308).

There has long been a tradition of writers transforming local cultures in order to make them acceptable to national elites, and talking up mundane experiences to give them a lofty cultural significance. This kind of 'noble savage' approach to common culture can assuage the fears and guilt of those elites, and deepen their sentimental humanism. The process has been detected and rejected by black activists and by members of the women's movement: British proletarians are the last group in need of liberation from this well-meaning but patronising gaze.

The theoretical and the political intertwine and co-determine each other in gramscianism. Some examples of this have been given already in the previous chapter – political considerations are used to fix possible readings of films or of youth cultures. In the opposite direction, we discussed earlier the strange choice of priorities that led an apparently activist CCCS spending a whole year coming to grips with the esoterics of screen theory, or the ambiguities in *Policing the Crisis*, where it is not at all clear if the book is a theoretical debate with Althusserians looking for illustration, or an activist call to arms to defend black youth against a further drift into a law and order society. Hall's reply to Jessop *et al.* (1985) shows the intertwining very well, it was argued – his work on Thatcherism was simultaneously a scholarly footnote, a further demonstration of his personal expertise, and a desire to assist Labour to win the next general election.

The political and theoretical priorities in combination have produced a narrowing, a prespecified job description: a suitable theory must be capable of avoiding determinism and prioritising struggle; it must contain, or be capable of containing, a suitable linguistics; it must be flexible enough to license, as proper politics, the women's movement, black activism, and any other new social movements as may be announced by the management; it should be able to function in the absence of a strong Communist Party; it must have a conceptual network that appeals to academics and other intellectuals, and encourages research; it must be capable of being applied to an infinite range of specific circumstances; it must be fun to work with, with witty and well-written arguments, and intriguing neologisms. Gramsci was made to fit that job description, even if he had to be enriched or elaborated: Bakhtin, in his own right, rather than as a resource for gramscian linguistics, seems to be his most likely replacement – see Stam in Kaplan (1988) for early advocacy.

At the risk of being very unfair indeed, it could be suggested that all gramscianism's intertwining of theory and practice has produced is a theory that is too political and partisan to be credible, and a politics that is too theoretical to be popular and effective.

THE PRODUCTION CONTEXT

This section borrows an approach from Bennett and Woollacott (1987) to discuss the contexts as well as the texts of gramscianism. The works of the gramscians themselves remind us constantly that they take place in academic institutions, for example. Hebdige discovers from his students the appeal of the 'second degree'. Donald and Bennett, in their final Unit for *U203*, speculate about the likely reactions of the Open University readers who make up their audience. As with the scholarship boys who preceded them, modern gramscians encounter 'ordinary folk' mostly in academies.

The effects of the academic context in which gramscianism was developed are important therefore. There is no intention here to reduce gramscianism to an effect of the academic 'level' of determination, but it is important to explore that level and trace its impact. There is still a dearth of theory about the 'production contexts' of academic ideas, though, so much of what follows must be speculative and possibilitarian.

Social-class origins

There is some work reviewed in this book which speculates about the social origins of intellectuals like the gramscians. Hewison (1987), Urry (1990), or Featherstone (1991) all suggest that postmodernist aesthetics are closely connected to the new petite bourgeoisie, who possess only cultural capital, and who have a vested interest in rapidly shifting and unfixed intellectual fashions as a major means of valorising it. This work is suggestive, but may be too general, as we shall see.

There is some earlier work on the characteristics of the new intellectualised 'service class' too, in Gouldner (1979), or Dahrendorf (1979). The Ehrenreichs, for the US new left (Walker 1979), and Rustin (in Hall and Jacques 1989), for the 'new times' British socialists, suggest the same class or stratum has brought the same distinctive class position into cultural politics too, as they struggle to locate themselves between the relative fixities offered by capital and by the traditional left. The Ehrenreichs' thesis has been developed most fully in this account (in Chapter 9). However, this work can offer only a partial illumination of the whole production context, and there is a danger of sociologism if it is allowed as a self-sufficient account. In particular, the work minimises the effects of splits and strata within the academic 'professional managerial class' (PMC). There are more or less insecure, peripheral and inflexible members, for example.

There is the connected matter of social mobility too. Again, the studies of the founding scholarship boys like Williams or Hoggart detect a certain nostalgia for the old communities they left, and a desire to re-establish contact, on equal ground, with the members of their class of origin (see, for example, McIlroy 1991). The world of the socially mobile scholarship person has been underresearched, but there can be insecurity and failure to be fully accepted by the class of entry, as Hopper (1981) suggests.

This in turn can lead to a marginality and a critical distance from the political values of the PMC. The Ehrenreichs identify this insecurity at the centre of the US new left's susceptibility to a backlash from more established members of the PMC, and to their obsessive interest in 'oppression' (Walker 1979: 38). To replace the terms of psychological pathologies, gramscianism for this relatively marginal group can be seen as an ideology in the classic sense – an expression of their world-views and as a belief system which has the 'practico-social function' of uniting and remoralising them.

This sort of distance might be responsible for a number of more positive 'critical' effects too, from scepticism about the university, seen clearly in Williams (1976) or Thompson (1970), to a peculiar feeling of having a privileged position in matters of popular culture, suggested in Lovell's discussion of:

someone who is deeply implicated in and familiar with what is observed: someone who has left that life behind, yet with a considerable sense of loss in moving through the education system, and who therefore brings to. . .observation the knowledge of the insider combined with . . . distance.

(Lovell 1990: 370)

This privileged position might be responsible both for the slippery pronouns in some studies of popular culture, and the lofty and sweeping condemnations of allegedly popular politics in *Marxism Today*. It can also be seen, perhaps, in the claims made by some feminist and black activist writers that their closeness to the realities of struggle privilege their views. The ethnic and gender aspects of social mobility in this context are almost completely ignored, and badly in need of research. Doubtless a break needs to be made with the predominantly British concern with social mobility as a matter of movement between classes (socio-economic groups, classically), perhaps with more attention to work on status mobility.

Finally, as the Ehrenreichs' suggest, socially mobile intellectuals are also in a position to effect a major critique of their class of entry, a task which would constitute for me the most important new area for modern cultural studies. However, Goldthorpe (1980) found that most socially mobile men were assimilated, politically at least, into the service class, while Hopper (1981) found most of the resentments of the socially mobile were focused on those groups nearest to them.

The intellectual culture

For the aristocrats of intellectual labour, there are studies of the relatively independent culture of intellectual endeavour, as they do fundamental research and choose between competing theories, as in the old disputes between Popper, Kuhn, Lakatos, Feyerabend and others: Lakatos's summary (in Lakatos and Musgrave 1979) foreshadows much of what Lyotard (1986) was to describe as the dynamics of science (although, as we have seen in Chapter 2, some critics see Lyotard as more akin to Feyerabend's more anarchic view).

Scientists choose the one among competing 'research programmes' which explains all the past theories and yet which contains an 'excess', a potential for new growth, says Lakatos. The research programme secures both continuity and commitment on the part of scientists. These research programmes are 'relatively autonomous' of social, psychological and empirical determinants (Lakatos and Musgrave 1979: 137). It is the perception of potential future growth which makes the process of doing science relatively rational, although a lot of work is also devoted to rethinking and rationalisation after a choice has been made (see also Mulkay 1979).

There is a clear similarity with Lyotard who stresses the 'narrative strategies' science uses both to legitimate itself and to proceed at all: there will never be a 'pure' science without such strategies (Lyotard uses this argument against utopians like Habermas, as we have seen earlier). The 'performativity criterion' comes to dominate debates about the legitimacy of science, but only as a device to justify research to those who award grants (Lyotard 1986: 54). Nevertheless, legitimacy debates are now inherent and integral to science itself, and there are only narratives as answers – science becomes a story which science is bound to verify (Lyotard 1986: 60), requiring scientists to become adept at 'paralogy': 'making the known unknown, and then reorganising this unknown into an independent symbolic metasystem' (*ibid*: 100).

Unlike science, though, for Lyotard social science is less open, more connected to struggles for or against the existing social system. As a result, theory choice becomes much more politicised here, and gets more implicated with performativity or 'terroristic' struggles to defy critiques. This sort of point helps explain the entanglements with politics we have discussed above, including micropolitical struggles and rivalries between different 'schools', sometimes even conducted in terms like 'betrayal'. These struggles usually appear, though, as theoretical debates, often at a level designed to subordinate rival concepts and install them under one's own (see Burniston and Weedon in CCCS 1978). Theoretical labours can displace more obviously political ones in the process: thus do Centaurs become Centres.

Nevertheless, these accounts of the growth of science might well help us understand developments like those we have described for gramscianism at the level of research programmes and 'little narratives' rather than as dependent either upon some external social-class determinants, or upon some apparently 'pure' and unmotivated academic debate.

To take one obvious example, the metaphor of the 'break' with the old bourgeois disciplines can now be read as a choice of a research programme with excess, or as a classic parologic attempt to make the known unknown again. More generally, gramscianism's struggles with its rivals, described in Chapters 1 and 2, can be seen as 'little narratives' designed to come to some tactical agreements with other research programmes while preserving the thrust of one's own. Here, the glorious ambiguity and flexibility of gramscianism discussed above seems ideal for such strategies and tactics, and for securing commitment.

The institutional level

There is a more specific level of analysis in the production context still: the institutional level. There are insightful analyses of the politics of subject groupings or faculties and their connections with knowledge production (see, for example, Bourdieu 1988 or Becher 1989), and we have discussed briefly something of the astute awareness of these issues in the work of Hall at CCCS (in Hall *et al.* 1980), and Bennett at the Open University (1980a) in getting their Centre and courses established.

Bennett was aware that there was no real theoretical unity between the areas to be covered, for example, and that the course was only a 'teaching object', already seen in terms of its strategic possibilities. The Open University's 'U' courses were to be free-standing, not tied to any disciplinary structure or faculty, or any pattern of courses as required by the degree scheme. The initiative was supported by some, especially by Professor Kettle in English, to broaden the University's appeal, and to further encourage interdisciplinary work, but the University was still vague about the details of 'U' courses (and, indeed, the University's associate student scheme has largely replaced those courses). Bennett seems to have gathered a group of OU staff and some outside speakers (including Williams, Eagleton, Stedman-Jones, Johnson and Hall), put in a bid for a course on popular culture, and persuaded the various University committees to provide the resources.

When it came to detailed specifications of the content of the course, some options, based on existing sociological or historical accounts, were rejected. Bennett favoured a focus on a 'system of cultural and ideological relations', which would narrow the focus and provide a teaching object 'capable of sustaining a theoretically productive teaching strategy' (Bennett 1980a: 28) (the pedagogue's version of a Lakatos research programme, perhaps?). Enriched gramscianism was to structure the object and break away from a concern with the text in isolation from its cultural and ideological context. If one wanted to be conspiratorial, one might suggest that this sort of work sets an agenda pretty firmly for the contributions that were to follow from the actual course team. The real point is, however, that *U203* was always defined and developed in a pragmatic 'academic' manner.

Conventions of production

However, there are also determinants on the shape of pedagogic work itself. Just as the BBC or the film industry has its codes and conventions, so do academic institutions. The aristocrats of intellectual labour may be able to resist them, and often one can see a definite change of style as a writer gains professorial rank, but they become more and more apparent in the work of the less aristocratic (although doubtless there are struggles behind the scenes).

I have summarised some of the immediate determinants on the uniquely collective production of academic work at the Open University, for example, (and some of the struggles) (Harris 1987). Although Hall (in Hall *et al.* 1980) is right to indicate the strengths of collective production (the same ones as accrue to any Fordist division of labour really), there are disadvantages too, especially in the 'malicious egalitarianism' that tends to flatten out any radical, critical or highly individual contributions (see also Riley 1984).

I have also described some of the conventions of 'academic realism' (Harris 1987, Harris in Evans and King 1991). These include the ways in which academic arguments are presented as a series of accounts 'at the surface', allowed to display their flaws to the reader, while a privileged account is allowed to emerge as 'more real': as in Maccabe's classic piece (in Bennett *et al.* 1981a), the whole movement towards the privileged level is controlled by a characteristic range of pedagogic narratives.

There are other conventions too – to conceal the writer's work from the readers so as to encourage a sense of 'involvement', or to appear to maintain a certain 'balance' while quietly setting agendas. It has been suggested, once or twice, that these conventions explain the course of arguments in gramscian work better than some supposed agreed procedure of moving from empirical or specific analysis to some higher level of theory.

There are several possibilities which it would be interesting to pursue, some of them based upon a reading of the contributors to Giroux *et al.* (1989). Realist narratives can be maintained by the use of personal interventions and asides, disclosures and apologies (all of which tend to feature these days in gramscian work): far from breaking the spell of the authorial voice, these devices strengthen it by hiding the authorship of the other bits, and naturalising the 'academic' accounts.

OU materials are interesting in that they deploy a range of modes of address, including populist ventriloquism and direct address: readers are invited to contribute their views and then the author of the Unit goes on to anticipate and deal with them (often very skilfully, and with the aid of market research). This is what McLaren and Smith call 'parapersonal communication' (Giroux *et al.* 1989), and they see it as rather sinister. OU 'supplementary materials' even attempt to interpellate and incorporate deviant readers, who selectively neglect aspects of the argument, and focus on the assignments. These materials act as 'textual shifters' perhaps?

One could go on: case-studies offer a kind of illusory co-presence as do ethnographic examples in other texts. A certain playfulness or a sentimentality in the materials serves to bind the reader to the narrative in a 'marketing contract' (Aronowitz in Giroux *et al.* 1989: 185). Charismatic writers or speakers in education can appear as 'prime knowers' (McLaren and Smith again), offering puzzled readers a way through the materials, often with a piece of homespun wisdom or a simple slogan: 'Let's look to the streets, to the common culture' (Willis 1990: 150).

This last point illustrates a particular paradox for gramscian work on the media: it develops highly penetrating critiques of mass media, but remains silent about its own story and its own involvement in mass media, in publishing printed books, papers and journals, in broadcasting, in working at Britain's 'mass media university'. Gramscianism must have inner knowledge of the effects of media conventions, since authors have faced those conventions themselves when they have written OU Units or readers, or made television programmes. Doubtless they did so with 'good' intentions: narrative realism can be 'good' in some circumstances, but there is an interesting story to be told.

They know all about the problems of 'balance' from the inside, since OU courses have to be balanced. In the process of writing academic materials, they develop discourses offering 'convergences', articulations and dis-articulations, and absences and presences. Despite all their critical insight, they continue to support the conventions that all this production work must remain largely invisible, authoritative, impenetrable and 'readerly'.

THE AUDIENCE

I have suggested that the audience for much of the output of gramscian work is a student one. Far too much academic work, even that at the Open University, works on the assumption that this audience is uncritical, or that its typical readings can be predicted and somehow worked into the text and its pedagogic strategy. Yet audience reactions are at the heart of recent work on the mass media, and what might be called student coping strategies have been researched in education for years: we know that students resist our pedagogic strategies, 'raid' our texts, perform 'cut ups', and reassemble our carefully structured arguments to meet their own priorities. The meanings of any text are produced as much by the inter-textuality of the reader as by the intertextuality of the writer, as Bennett and Woollacott put it.

This sort of activity is known about at one level, yet ignored at another. Perhaps the best example of the acknowledgement is Fiske's Introduction to Chambers (1986): Fiske knows that even this postmodern text is going to be used by students to write essays. Nevertheless, the main effort still goes into writing the text, or preparing the OU course at the design end, or, presumably, in working at a suitably popular tone for an address at a political conference, or for an article in *Marxism Today*. It is simply hoped that the audience will be affected in a desired way.

The ways in which student readers especially can rearrange and subvert all this effort has been described in Harris (1987). There, I described students on a radical education course who had barely read it, or who had reformed its arguments into far less critical discourses of their own, or had read the carefully developed arguments as a series of 'recipes' in order to get through the assignments with as little effort as possible, while keeping their own 'spontaneous philosophy' intact. Early radical beliefs that the part-time Open University students would be able to take critical materials back into their everyday lives and use them there seem to have been the opposite of what actually happened. In an echo of the Adorno–Benjamin dispute, summarised so one-sidedly in *U203* as we saw, students seem to have had the radical potentials of the reproduction of academic knowledge, in the OU's version of a non-auratic form, cancelled by their everyday views. Other work on the OU student audience reveals other possibilities which parallel these, my earlier work shows.

Of course, the student audience is different from the 'normal' audience who might read Hebdige's account of youth cultures, or *Marxism Today*. Students are assessed, and this overdetermines their instrumentalism, for example. Staff too have an interest in making their materials assessable too, of course. Both sides are often left wondering whether there is anything outside the test. On the other hand, students are expected to adopt a much closer, more committed and disciplined reading than that of the casual reader, like the film audience, to be more vulnerable to the spell of the academic narrative and its positioning effect. If educational materials can be resisted so easily, what chance is there for any serious political effect to be exercised by popular journalism (except on the already committed)?

Nor are these effects confined to distance education, in my view (indeed, the classic work on the 'hidden curriculum' was done at conventional universities). The Introduction to this book alludes to my own practice and how my students use gramscian texts for their own purposes. Research students might be different, of course, but it would seem strange if all those who went through CCCS were committed 'organic intellectuals'.

There are no studies of the audience for gramscian writings, as far as I am aware, yet such studies seem overdue, and crucial to any claims of likely political effectiveness. The lack of reflexiveness of the gramscians in this matter is astonishing: Fiske celebrates the raider and the poacher in his books, yet has he considered the possibility that readers are also raiding his work, leaving out the difficult bits, cutting the sections where he tries to close their narratives, keeping their own views intact while merely pretending to conform? We have heard a good deal about the proletarian shopper – now it is time to investigate the proletarian reader.

BIBLIOGRAPHY

Adlam, D. (1979) 'The Case Against Capitalist Patriarchy', *m/f* 3.

Adorno, T. (1978) 'The Sociology of Knowledge and Its Consciousness', in A. Arato and E. Gebhardt (eds) *The Essential Frankfurt School Reader*, Oxford: Blackwell.

Adorno, T. and Horkheimer, M. (1979) *Dialectic of Enlightenment*, London: Verso.

Aglietta, M. (1982) 'World Capitalism in the Eighties', *New Left Review* 136: 5–42.

Allen, R. (ed.) (1987) Channels of Discourse, London: Methuen.

Althusser, L. (1966) *For Marx*, London: Penguin.

——(1971) *'Lenin and Philosophy' and Other Essays*, London: NLB.

Althusser, L. and Balibar, E. (1970) *Reading Capital*, London: NLB.

Alvarado, M. (1981) 'Television Studies and Pedagogy', *Screen Education* 38: 56–67.

Alvarado, M. and Ferguson, D. (1983) 'The Curriculum, Media Studies and Discursivity', *Screen* 24.

Alvarado, M. and Thompson, J. (eds) (1990) *The Media Reader*, London: British Film Institute.

Anderson, P. (1976) 'The Antinomies of Antonio Gramsci', *New Left Review* 100: 5–81.

——(1984) 'Modernity and Revolution', *New Left Review* 144: 96–113.

Anderson, P., Balogh, T., Blackburn, R., Coates, K., Crossman, R., Gorz, A., Nairn, T., Titmuss, R., Westergaard, J. and Williams, R. (1965) *Towards Socialism*, London: Collins.

Angus, I. and Jhally, S. (eds) (1989) *Cultural Politics in Contemporary America*, New York and London: Routledge.

Apple, M. (ed.) (1982) *Cultural and Economic Reproduction in Education*, London: Routledge and Kegan Paul.

Arato, A. and Gebhardt, E. (eds) (1978) *The Essential Frankfurt School Reader*, Oxford: Blackwell.

Arnot, M. and Weiner, G. (eds) (1987) *Gender and the Politics of Schooling*, London: Hutchinson.

Ball, S. (1987) *The Micropolitics of the School*, London: Methuen.

Ball, S. and Goodson, I. (eds) (1985) *Teachers' Lives and Careers*, London: Falmer Press.

Barrett, M., Corrigan, P., Kuhn, A. and Wolff, J. (eds) (1979) *Ideology and Cultural Production*, London: Croom Helm.

Barthes, R. (1973) *Mythologies*, London: Paladin.

Barton, L. and Walker, S. (eds) (1983) *Race, Class and Education*, London: Croom Helm.

Bates, I., Clarke, J., Cohen, P., Finn, D., Moore, R. and Willis, P. (1984) *Schooling for the Dole?*, London: Macmillan.

Baudrillard, J. (1988) *Selected Writings*, ed. M. Poster, Cambridge: Polity Press.

Bauman, Z. (1987) *Legislators and Interpreters*, Cambridge: Polity Press.

Becher, T. (1989) *Academic Tribes and Their Territories*, Society for Research into Higher Education and Open University Press.

Bell, R., Fowler, G. and Little, K. (eds) (1973) *Education in Great Britain and Ireland*, London: Routledge and Kegan Paul in association with the Open University Press.

Bennett, T. (1980a) 'Popular Culture: A "Teaching Object"', *Screen Education* 34: 17–30.

——(1980b) 'S. Clarke's "One-dimensional Marxism"', *Screen Education* 36: 119–30.

Bennett, T. and Woollacott, J. (1987) *Bond and Beyond: the Political Career of a Popular Hero*, London: Macmillan Education.

Bennett, T., Boyd-Bowman, S., Mercer, C. and Woollacott, J. (eds) (1981a) *Popular Television and Film*, London: BFI Publishing in association with the Open University Press.

Bennett, T., Martin, G., Mercer, C. and Woollacott, J. (1981b) *Culture, Ideology and Social Process*, London: Batsford Academic and Educational Ltd in association with the Open University Press.

Bennett, T., Mercer, C. and Woollacott, J. (1986) *Popular Culture and Social Relations*, Milton Keynes: Open University Press.

Berger, P. and Luckmann, T. (1966) *The Social Construction of Reality*, London: Penguin.

Berman, M. (1984) 'The Signs in the Streets: A Reply to Perry Anderson', *New Left Review* 144: 114–23.

Bernstein, R. (1985) (ed.) *Habermas and Modernity*, Oxford: Polity Press.

Botterill, T.D. (1989) 'Humanistic Tourism? Personal Constructions of a Tourist: Sam Visits Japan', *Leisure Studies* 8: 281–93.

——(1991) 'A New Social Movement: Tourism Concern, the First 2 Years', *Leisure Studies* 10: 203–17.

Bourdieu, P. (1984) *Distinction: A Social Critique of the Judgement of Taste*, trans. R. Nice, London: Routledge and Kegan Paul.

——(1988) *Homo Academicus*, trans. P. Collier, Oxford: Polity Press.

Bowles, S. and Gintis, H. (1976) *Schooling in Capitalist America*, London, Routledge and Kegan Paul.

Brake, M. (1985) *Comparative Youth Culture*, London: Routledge and Kegan Paul.

Bridges, G. and Brunt, R. (eds) (1981) *Silver Linings – Some Strategies for the Eighties*, London: Lawrence and Wishart.

Brown, R. (ed.) (1973) *Knowledge, Education and Cultural Change*, London: Tavistock.

Buckingham, D. (1987) *Public Secrets: 'Eastenders' and Its Audience*, London: British Film Institute Publications.

——(1991) 'What Are Words Worth? Interpreting Children's Talk About Television', *Cultural Studies* 5, 2: 228–44.

Buckingham, D. (ed.) (1990) *Watching Media Learning. Making Sense of Media Education*, Basingstoke: Falmer Press.

Bulmer, M. (ed.) (1975) *Working Class Images of Society*, London: Routledge and Kegan Paul.

Callinicos, A. (1985) 'Postmodernism, Post-Structuralism and Post-Marxism?', *Theory Culture and Society* 2, 3: 85–102.

Cashmore, E. (1987) *The Logic of Racism*, London: Allen and Unwin.

Centre for Contemporary Cultural Studies (CCCS) (1976) *Working Papers in*

Cultural Studies 9, Birmingham: CCCS, University of Birmingham, PO Box 363, Birmingham B15 2TP.
——(1978) *On Ideology*, London: Hutchinson.
——(1981) *Unpopular Education: Schooling and Social Democracy in England Since 1944*, London: Hutchinson.
——(1982) *The Empire Strikes Back: Race and Racism in 1970s Britain*, London: Hutchinson.
Chambers, I. (1985) *Urban Rhythms: Popular Music and Popular Culture*, London: Macmillan.
——(1986) *Popular Culture: The Metropolitan Experience*, London: Methuen.
Chen, K-H. (1987) 'The Masses and the Media: Baudrillard's Implosive Postmodernism', *Theory Culture and Society*, 4, 1: 71–88.
Clark, M. (1977) *Antonio Gramsci and the Revolution That Failed*, New Haven: Yale University Press.
Clarke, J. (1991) *New Times and Old Enemies: Essays on Cultural Studies and America*, London: HarperCollins Academic.
Clarke, J. and Critcher, C. (1985) *The Devil Makes Work: Leisure in Capitalist Britain*, London: Macmillan.
Clarke, J., Critcher, C. and Johnson, R. (eds) (1979) *Working Class Culture: Studies in History and Theory*, London: Hutchinson.
Clayman, S. (1990) 'From Talk to Text', *Media Culture and Society* 12: 79–103.
Clifford, J. (1983) 'On Ethnographic Authority', *Representations* 1, 2: 119–46.
Cohen, S. (1987) *Folk Devils and Moral Panics*, Oxford: Blackwell.
Cohen, S. and Young, J. (eds) (1973) *The Manufacture of News: Deviance, Social Problems and the Mass Media*, London: Constable.
Coward, R. (1977) 'Class, Culture and the Social Formation', *Screen* 18, 1: 75–105.
Crook, S. (1991) *Modernist Radicalism and Its Aftermath*, London: Routledge.
Cubitt, S. (1986) 'Cancelling Popular Culture', *Screen* 27: 90–3.
Curran, J., Gurevitch, M. and Woollacott, J. (eds) (1977) *Mass Communication and Society*, London: Edward Arnold in association with the Open University Press.
Cutler, A., Hinders, B., Hirst, P. and Hussain, A. (1978) *Marx's 'Capital' and Capitalism Today*, vol. 3, London: Routledge and Kegan Paul.
Dahrendorf, R. (1979) *Life Chances*, London: Weidenfeld and Nicolson.
Dale, R. (1989) *The State and Educational Policy*, Milton Keynes: Open University Press.
Dale, R., Esland, G. and MacDonald, M. (eds) (1976) *Schooling and Capitalism: A Sociological Reader*, London: Routledge and Kegan Paul in association with the Open University Press.
Dale, R., Esland, G., Fergusson, R. and MacDonald, M. (eds) (1981) *Education and the State, Vol. 1. Schooling and the National Interest*, Basingstone: Falmer Press.
Deem, R. (1986) *All Work and No Play*, Milton Keynes: Open University Press.
——(1988) *Work, Unemployment and Leisure*, London: Routledge.
Demaine, J. (1981) *Contemporary Theories in the Sociology of Education*, London: The Macmillan Press.
Denzin, N. (1988) '"Blue Velvet": Postmodern Contradictions', *Theory Culture and Society* 5, 2–3: 461–74.
Dews, P. (1984) 'Power and Subjectivity in Foucault', *New Left Review* 144: 72–95.
Donald, J. (1990) 'Review Article', *Screen* 31, 1: 113–18.
Donald, J. and Hall, S. (1986) *Politics and Ideology*, Milton Keynes: Open University Press.
Downes, D. and Rock, P. (1988) *Understanding Deviance*, 2nd edition, Oxford: Clarendon Press.

Downes, D. and Rock, P. (eds) (1979) *Deviant Interpretations*, Oxford: Oxford University Press.

Dunning, E., Murphy, P. and Williams, J. (1986) 'Spectator Violence at Football Matches: Towards a Sociological Explanation', *British Journal of Sociology* XXXVII, 2: 221–44.

Durkheim, E. (1950) *The Rules of the Sociological Method*, Illinois: Free Press of Glencoe.

——(1953) *Sociology and Philosophy*, Illinois: Free Press of Glencoe.

Eco, U. (1979) 'Can Television Teach?', *Screen Education* 31: 15–25.

Education Group II (1991) *Education Limited: Schooling and Training and the New Right Since 1979*, London: Unwin Hyman.

Edwards, R. (1991) 'The Inevitable Future? Post-Fordism and Open Learning', *Open Learning*, 6: 2.

Elliot, G. (1986) 'The Odyssey of Paul Hirst', *New Left Review* 159: 81–106.

Entwhistle, H. (1979) *Antonio Gramsci: Conservative Schooling for Radical Politics*, London: Routledge.

Evans, T. and King, B. (eds) (1991) *Beyond the Text: Contemporary Writing on Distance Education*, Geelong, Victoria, Australia: Deakin University Press.

Evans, T. and Nation, D. (eds) (forthcoming) *Critical Reflections on Distance Education II* (working title).

Fay, B. (1975) *Social Theory and Political Practice*, London: Allen and Unwin.

Featherstone, M. (1991) *Consumer Culture and Postmodernism*, London: Sage.

Fine, B., Kinsey, R., Lea, J., Picciotto, S. and Young, J. (eds) (1979) *Capitalism and the Rule of Law: From Deviancy to Marxism*, London: Hutchinson.

Fiske, J. (1987) *Television Culture*, London: Routledge.

——(1989a) *Reading the Popular*, London: Unwin Hyman.

——(1989b) *Understanding Popular Culture*, London: Unwin Hyman.

Forgacs, D. (1989) 'Gramsci and Marxism in Britain', *New Left Review* 176: 70–90.

Formations (ed.) (1987) *Formations of Fantasy*, London: Routledge and Kegan Paul.

Foster, H. (ed.) (1986) *Postmodern Culture*, London: Pluto Press.

Franklin, S., Lury, C. and Stacey, J. (eds) (1991) *Off-Centre: Feminism and Cultural Studies*, London: HarperCollins Academic.

Frith, S. (1988) *Music for Pleasure*, Cambridge: Polity Press.

Frow, J. (1991) 'M. deCerteau and the Practice of Representation', *Cultural Studies* 5, 1: 52–60.

Geraghty, C. (1991) *Women and Soap Operas*, Cambridge: Polity Press.

Geras, N. (1987) 'Post-Marxism?', *New Left Review* 163: 40–82.

——(1988) 'Ex-Marxism Without Substance', *New Left Review* 169: 34–62.

Giddens, A. (1973) *The Class Structure of the Advanced Societies*, London: Hutchinson.

Giddens, A. and Held, D. (eds) (1982) *Classes, Power and Conflict*, London: The Macmillan Press.

Gilroy, P. (1987) *There Ain't No Black in the Union Jack*, London: Hutchinson.

Gintis, H. and Bowles, S. (1980) 'Contradiction and Reproduction in Educational Theory', in L. Barton *et al.* (eds), *Schooling, Ideology and the Curriculum*, Barcombe: Falmer Press, 51–65.

Giroux, H., Simon, R. and contributors (1989) *Popular Culture, Schooling and Everyday Life*, Massachusetts: Bergin and Garvey Publishers Inc.

Golby, M., Greenwald, J. and West, R. (eds) (1975) *Curriculum Design*, London: Croom Helm.

Goldthorpe, J. (in collaboration with Llewellyn, C. and Payne, C.) (1980) *Social Mobility and Class Structure in Modern Britain*, Oxford: Clarendon Press.

Goodwin, A. (1991) 'Popular Music and Post-Modern Theory', *Cultural Studies* 5, 2: 174–203.

Gostree, L. (1988) '"The Monkees" and the Deconstruction of Television Realism', *Journal of Popular Film and Television* 16, 2: 50–60.

Gould, J. (1977) *Attack on Higher Education: Marxist and Radical Penetration*, a report of a study group of the Institute for the Study of Conflict, London.

Gouldner, A. (1979) *The Future of Intellectuals and the Rise of the New Class*, London: The Macmillan Press.

Grossberg, L. (1987) 'The In-Difference of Television', *Screen* 28, 2: 28–46.

Grossberg, L. (1991) *Cultural Studies Now and in the Future*, London: Routledge.

Grossberg, L. (ed.) (1986) 'On Postmodernism and Articulation: An Interview with Stuart Hall', *Journal of Communications Inquiry* 10, 2: 45–61.

Guttmann, A. (1986) *Sports Spectators*, New York: Columbia Press.

Habermas, J. (1976) *Legitimation Crisis*, London: Heinemann.

——(1979) 'Conservatism and Capitalist Crisis', *New Left Review* 115: 73–86.

Hall, S. (1985) 'Authoritarian Populism: A Reply to Jessop *et al.*', *New Left Review* 151: 115–25.

——(1987) 'Gramsci and Us', *Marxism Today* June: 16–21.

——(1988) *The Hard Road to Renewal: Thatcherism and the Crisis of the Left*, London: Verso.

——(1991) 'And Not a Shot Fired', *Marxism Today*, December: 8–16.

Hall, S. and Jacques, M. (eds) (1983) *The Politics of Thatcherism*, London: Lawrence and Wishart and *Marxism Today*.

——(1989) *New Times*, London: Lawrence and Wishart and *Marxism Today*.

Hall, S. and Jefferson, T. (eds) (1976) *Resistance Through Rituals*, London: Hutchinson.

Hall, S., Critcher, C., Jefferson, T., Clarke, J. and Roberts, B. (1978) *Policing the Crisis: Mugging, the State, and Law and Order*, London: Macmillan.

Hall, S., Hobson, D., Lowe, A. and Willis, P. (eds) (1980) *Culture Media and Language*, London: Hutchinson.

Halsey, A., Heath, A. and Ridge, J. (1980) *Origins and Destinations: Family Class and Education in Modern Britain*, Oxford: Clarendon Press.

Hammersley, M. and Woods, P. (eds) (1976) *The Process of Schooling: A Sociological Reader*, London: Routledge and Kegan Paul in association with the Open University Press.

Haralambos, M. (ed.) (1985) *Sociology: New Directions*, Ormskirk: Causeway Press.

Hargreaves, Jennifer (ed.) (1982) *Sport, Culture and Ideology*, London: Routledge and Kegan Paul.

Hargreaves, John (1986) *Sport, Power and Culture*, Cambridge: Polity Press.

Harris, D. (1987) *Openness and Closure in Distance Education*, Barcombe: Falmer Press.

Hebdige, D. (1979) *Subcultures – The Meaning of Style*, London: Methuen.

——(1988) *Hiding in the Light*, London: Comedia/Routledge.

Held, D. (1980) *Introduction to Critical Theory: Horkheimer to Habermas*, London: Hutchinson.

Hewison, R. (1987) *The Heritage Industry: Britain in a Climate of Decline*, London: Methuen.

Hindess, B. and Hirst, P. (1975) *Pre-Capitalist Modes of Production*, London: Macmillan.

Hirst, P. (1979) *On Law and Ideology*, London: Macmillan.

Holloway, J. and Picciotto, S. (1978) *State and Capital: A Marxist Debate*, London: Edward Arnold.

Hopper, E. (1981) *Social Mobility*, Oxford: Blackwell.

Hunt, A. (ed.) (1977) *Class and Class Structure*, London: Lawrence and Wishart.

Institutionalisation Group, The (1991) 'The Institutionalisation of Cultural

Studies', 'From Ur-Course to PCAS', *Magazine of Cultural Studies* 4: 16–18, 24–6.
Jacques, M. (1991) 'The Last Word', *Marxism Today*, December: 28–9.
Jensen, K. (1990) 'The Politics of Polysemy: Television News, Everyday Conscious-ness and Political Action', *Media Culture and Society* 12: 57–77.
Jessop, B. (1974) *Traditionalism, Conservatism and British Political Culture*, London: Allen and Unwin.
——(1982) *The Capitalist State*, Oxford: Martin Robertson.
Jessop, B., Bennett, K., Bromley, S. and Ling, T. (1984) 'Authoritarian Populism, Two Nations and Thatcherism', *New Left Review* 147: 32–60.
——(1985) 'Thatcherism and the Politics of Hegemony: A Reply to Stuart Hall', *New Left Review* 153: 87–101.
——(1987) 'Popular Capitalism, Flexible Accumulation and Left Strategy', *New Left Review* 165: 104–22.
Jessop, B., Bennett, K. and Bromley, S. (1990) 'Farewell to Thatcherism?', *New Left Review* 179: 81–102.
Julien, I. and Mercer, K. (1988) 'Introduction: De Margin and De Centre', *Screen* 29, 4: 2–12.
Kaplan, E. (1987) *Rocking Around the Clock*, London: Methuen.
Kaplan, E. (ed.) (1988) *Postmodernism and Its Discontents*, London: Verso.
Keddie, N. (ed.) (1973) *Tinker, Tailor. . .The Myth of Cultural Deprivation*, Harmondsworth: Penguin.
Kellner, D. (1987) 'Baudrillard, Semiurgy, and Death', *Theory Culture and Society* 4, 1: 125–44.
Kelly, J. (1988) 'Iron Lady in a Nanny's Uniform', *Times Higher Education Supplement* 9 December.
Kuhn, A. and Wolpe, A-M. (eds) (1978) *Feminism and Materialism*, London, Routledge and Kegan Paul.
Laclau, E. (1991) 'God Only Knows', *Marxism Today*, December: 56–9.
Laclau, E. and Mouffe, C. (1987) 'Post-Marxism Without Apologies', *New Left Review* 166: 79–106.
Lakatos, I. and Musgrave, F. (1979) *Criticism and the Growth of Knowledge*, Cambridge: Cambridge University Press.
Langan, M. and Schwartz, B. (eds) (1985) *Crises in the British State*, London: Hutchinson in association with the Centre for Contemporary Cultural Studies.
Lawn, M. and Grace, G. (eds) (1987) *Teachers: The Culture and Politics of Work*, London: Falmer Press.
Leys, C. (1990) 'Still a Question of Hegemony', *New Left Review* 181: 119–28.
Lovell, T. (1990) 'Landscapes and Stories in British Realism', *Screen* 31, 4: 357–76.
Lyotard, J-F. (1986) *The Post-Modern Condition: A Report on Knowledge*, Manchester: Manchester University Press.
Mabey, R. (ed.) (1967) *Class: A Symposium*, London: A. Blond Ltd.
Maccabe, C. (ed.) (1986) *High Theory, Low Culture*, Manchester: Manchester University Press.
McCarthy, T. (1984) *The Critical Theory of Jurgen Habermas*, Cambridge: Polity.
Macdonnell, D. (1986) *Theories of Discourse*, Oxford: Blackwell.
McIlroy, J. (1991) 'Border Country: Raymond Williams in Adult Education' pt. II, *Studies in the Education of Adults* 23, 1: 1–23.
McRobbie, A. (1991) 'Moving Cultural Studies on – Post-Modernism and Beyond', *Magazine of Cultural Studies* 4: 18–22.
McRobbie, A. and Nava, M. (eds) (1984) *Gender and Generation*, London: Macmillan.
Mangan, P. and Small, R. (eds) (1986) *Sport, Culture, Society – International, Historical and Sociological Perspectives*, London: E. and F.N. Spon Ltd.

211

Mannheim, K. (1972) *Ideology and Utopia*, trans. L. Wirth and E. Shils, London: Routledge and Kegan Paul.

Marcuse, H. (1964) *One-Dimensional Man*, London: Sphere Books.

Margolis, J. (1989) 'Postscript on Modernism and Post-Modernism, Both', *Theory Culture and Society* 6: 5–30.

Marsland, D. (1978) *Sociological Explanations in the Service of Youth*, Leicester: National Youth Bureau.

Marx, K. (1954) *Capital*, vol. 1, London: Lawrence and Wishart.

Marx, K. (1973) *Grundrisse*, London: Pelican.

Marx, K. and Engels, F. (1950) *Selected Works*, London: Lawrence and Wishart.

——(1974) *The German Ideology*, ed. C. Arthur, 2nd edition, London: Lawrence and Wishart.

Mennell, S. (1985) *All Manners of Food*, Oxford: Blackwell.

Mepham, J. and Ruben, D-H. (1979) *Issues in Marxist Philosophy*, vol. 3, Brighton: Harvester Press.

Mercer, N. (1988) *Language and Literacy from an Educational Perspective*, Milton Keynes: Open University Press.

Merck, M. (1987) 'Introduction – Difference and Its Discontents', *Screen* 28, 1: 2–10.

Moores, S. (1990) 'Texts, Readers and Contexts of Reading: Developments in the Study of Media Audiences', *Media Culture and Society* 12: 9–30.

Morgan, G. (1986) *Images of Organization*, London: Sage.

Morley, D. and Silverstone, R. (1990) 'Domestic Communication – Technologies and Meanings' *Media Culture and Society* 12: 31–56.

Mouzelis, N. (1988) 'Marxism or Post-Marxism?', *New Left Review* 167: 107–23.

Mulkay, M. (1979) *Science and the Sociology of Knowledge*, London: Allen and Unwin.

Murphy, R. (1986) 'Weberian Closure Theory', *British Journal of Sociology*, XXXVII, 1.

Nava, M. (1991) 'Consumerism Reconsidered: Buying and Power', *Cultural Studies* 5, 2: 157–74.

Offe, C. (1974) 'Structural Problems of the Capitalist State', *German Political Studies* 1: 31–57.

——(1985) *Disorganised Capitalism*, Cambridge: Polity Press.

Open University (1972) *School and Society (E282)*, Milton Keynes: Open University Press.

——(1977) *Mass Communication and Society (DE353)*, Milton Keynes: Open University Press.

——(1979) *Schooling and Society (E202)*, Milton Keynes: Open University Press.

——(1981) *Society, Education and the State (E353)*, Milton Keynes: Open University Press.

——(1982) *Popular Culture (U203)*, Milton Keynes: Open University Press.

——(1984) *Popular Culture Supplementary Material*, supplied only to registered students of the course.

——(1988) *Educational Organisations and Professionals (E814)*, Milton Keynes: Open University Press.

O'Shea, M. (1989) 'Television as Culture: Not Just Texts and Readers', *Media Culture and Society* 11, 3: 373–80.

O'Shea, M. and Schwartz, B. (1987) 'Reconsidering Popular Culture', *Screen* 28, 3: 104–9.

Ozga, J. (ed.) (1988) *Schoolwork Approaches to the Labour Process of Teaching*, Milton Keynes: Open University Press.

Ozga, J. and Lawn, M. (1988) 'Schoolwork: Interpreting the Labour Process of Teaching', *British Journal of Sociology of Education* 9, 3: 323–35.

Parkin, F. (1971) *Class, Inequality and Political Order*, London: MacGibbon and Kee Ltd.

Parkin, F. (1979) *Marxism and Class Theory: A Bourgeois Critique*, London: Tavistock.

Philo, G. (1990) *Seeing and Believing: The Influence of Television*, London: Routledge.

Poulantzas, N. (1973) *Political Power and Social Classes*, London: New Left Books.

Ree, J. (1984) 'Metaphor and Metaphysics: The End of Philosophy and Derrida', *Radical Philosophy* 38: 29–33.

Riley, J. (1984) 'The Problem of Drafting Distance Education Materials', *British Journal of Educational Technology* 15, 3: 192–204.

Rojek, C. (1985) *Capitalism and Leisure Theory*, London: Tavistock.

Rojek, C. (ed.) (1989) *Leisure for Leisure*, London: Macmillan.

Rose, G. (1978) *The Melancholy Science: An Introduction to the Thought of Theodor W. Adorno*, London: Macmillan.

Rowbotham, S., Segal, L. and Wainwright, H. (1979) *Beyond the Fragments: Feminism and the Making of Socialism*, London: Merlin Press.

Rustin, M. (1989) 'The Politics of Post-Fordism and the Trouble With "New Times"', *New Left Review* 175: 54–78.

Salter, B. and Tapper, T. (1981) *Education, Politics and the State: The Theory and Practice of Educational Change*, London: Grant McIntyre.

Samuel, R. (1987) 'Class Politics: The Lost World of British Communism, Part 3', *New Left Review* 165: 52–93.

Samuel, R. (ed.) (1981) *People's History and Socialist Theory*, London: Routledge and Kegan Paul.

Sarup, M. (1982) *Education, the State and Crisis: A Marxist Perspective*, London: Routledge and Kegan Paul.

Schlesinger, P. (1989) 'Review Essay – From Production to Propaganda', *Media Culture and Society* 11, 3: 287–306.

Schutz, A. (1971) *Collected Papers I: The Problem of Social Reality*, The Hague: Martinus Nijhoff.

Seiter, E., Borchers, H., Kreutzner, G. and Warth, E-M. (eds) (1989) *Remote Control: Television, Audiences and Cultural Power*, London: Routledge.

Silverstone, R. (1989) 'Let Us Then Return to the Mumming of Everyday Practices . . . A Note on M. deCerteau and Everyday Life', *Theory Culture and Society* 6, 1: 77–94.

Silverstone, R., Hirsch, E. and Morley, D. (1991) 'Listening to a Long Conversation: An Ethnographic Approach to the Study of Information and Communication Technologies in the Home', *Cultural Studies* 5, 2: 204–27.

Sims, S. (1986) 'Lyotard and the Politics of Anti-Foundationalism', *Radical Philosophy* 44: 8–14.

Sivanandan, A. (1990) *Communities of Resistance: Writings on Black Struggles for Socialism*, London: Verso.

Smart, B. (1983) *Foucault, Marxism and Critique*, London: Routledge.

Smith, G. and Hoare, Q. (1971) *Selections from the Prison Notebooks of A. Gramsci*, London: Lawrence and Wishart.

Stacey, J. (1987) 'Desperately Seeking Difference', *Screen* 28, 1: 48–62.

Sylvan, R. (1985) 'A Critique of Deep Ecology', *Radical Philosophy* 40: 2–12.

Taylor, I., Walton, P. and Young, J. (1973) *The New Criminology*, London: Routledge and Kegan Paul.

——(1975) *Critical Criminology*, London: Routledge and Kegan Paul.

Thompson, E. (ed.) (1970) *Warwick University Limited*, London: Penguin.

Thompson, G. and Held, D. (eds) (1982) *Habermas: Critical Debates*, London: Macmillan.

Tomlinson, A. (1989) 'Whose Side Are They On? Leisure Studies and Cultural

Studies in Britain', *Leisure Studies* 8: 97–106.
——(1990) Review of C. Rojek (ed.) Leisure for Leisure, *Sociology* 24, 1: 179–80.
Tomlinson, A. (ed.) (1990) *Consumption, Identity and Style*, London: Comedia and Routledge.
Tucker, K. (1991) 'How New Are the NSMs?' *Theory Culture and Society*, 8, 2: 75–98.
Turner, G. (1991) *British Cultural Studies: An Introduction*, Boston: Unwin Hyman
Urry, J. (1990) *The Tourist Gaze: Leisure and Travel in Contemporary Societies*, London: Sage.
Vallas, S. (1979) 'The Lessons of Mannheim's Historicism', *Sociology* 13: 459–73.
Wagg, S. (1984) *The Football World: A Contemporary Social History*, Brighton: Harvester Press.
Waites, B., Bennett, T. and Martin, G. (eds) (1982) *Popular Culture Past and Present*, London: Croom Helm/Open University Press.
Walker, P. (ed.) (1979) *Between Labour and Capital*, Brighton: Harvester Press.
Walker, S. and Barton, L. (eds) (1983) *Gender, Class and Education*, Barcombe, Falmer Press.
——(1987) *Changing Policies, Changing Teachers?*, Milton Keynes: Open University Press.
Weiner, G. and Arnot, M. (eds) (1987) *Gender Under Scrutiny – New Inquiries in Education*, Milton Keynes: Open University Press.
Westoby, A. (ed.) (1988) *Culture and Power in Educational Organisations*, Milton Keynes: Open University Press.
Whannel, G. (1983) *Blowing the Whistle*, London: Pluto Press.
——(1986) 'The Unholy Alliance: Notes on Television and the Remaking of British Sport 1965–85', *Leisure Studies* 5: 129–45.
White, J. and Young, M. (1975) 'The Sociology of Knowledge', *Education for Teaching* 98: 4–13.
Whitty, G. (1985) *Sociology and School Knowledge*, London: Methuen.
Whitty, G. and Young, M. (eds) (1976) *Explorations in the Politics of School Knowledge*, Driffield: Nafferton.
Williams, R. (1976) 'Notes on British Marxism Since the War', *New Left Review* 100: 81–96.
Willis, P. (1977) *Learning to Labour: How Working Class Kids Get Working Class Jobs*, Farnborough: Saxon House.
——(1978) *Profane Cultures*, London: Routledge and Kegan Paul.
——(1990) *Common Culture*, Milton Keynes: Open University Press.
Wilson, T. (1990) 'TV-AM and the Politics of Caring', *Media Culture and Society* 12: 125–43.
Women's Study Group (1978) *Women Take Issue*, London: Hutchinson.
Young, M. (ed.) (1971) *Knowledge and Control: New Directions for the Sociology of Education*, London: Collier-Macmillan.
Young, M. and Whitty, G. (eds) (1977) *Society, State and Schooling*, Barcombe: Falmer Press.

NAME INDEX

SUBJECT INDEX